D0867390

Beyond Catastrophe

Beyond Catastrophe

German Intellectuals and Cultural Renewal after World War II, 1945–1955

Mark W. Clark

LEXINGTON BOOKS

A division of
ROWMAN & LITTLEFIELD PUBLISHERS, INC.
Lanham • Boulder • New York • Toronto • Oxford

LEXINGTON BOOKS

A division of Rowman & Littlefield Publishers, Inc.
A wholly owned subsidiary of The Rowman & Littlefield Publishing Group, Inc.
4501 Forbes Boulevard, Suite 200
Lanham, MD 20706

PO Box 317
Oxford
OX2 9RU, UK

British Library Cataloguing in Publication Information Available

Library of Congress Cataloging-in-Publication Data

Clark, Mark W., 1965–
  Beyond catastrophe : German intellectuals and cultural renewal after World War II,
1945–1955 / Mark W. Clark.
    p. cm.
  ISBN-13: 978-0-7391-1231-1 (cloth : alk. paper)
  ISBN-10: 0-7391-1231-7 (cloth : alk. paper)
  ISBN-13: 978-0-7391-1506-0 (pbk. : alk. paper)
  ISBN-10: 0-7391-1506-5 (pbk. : alk. paper)
  1. Germany—History—1945–1955. 2. Germany—Intellectual life—20th century. 3.
Literature and history—Germany—20th century. 4. Meinecke, Friedrich, 1862–1954. 5.
Jaspers, Karl, 1883–1969. 6. Mann, Thomas, 1875–1955. 7. Brecht, Bertolt, 1898–
1956. I. Title.
  DD257.2.C53 2006
  943.087'4—dc22   2005037280

Printed in the United States of America

♾™ The paper used in this publication meets the minimum requirements of American
National Standard for Information Sciences—Permanence of Paper for Printed Library
Materials, ANSI/NISO Z39.48–1992.

Contents

Acknowledgements

A book that takes ten years to research and write incurs for its author many debts. It is a great delight to thank the individuals and institutions that assisted me. A grant from the Friedrich Ebert Stiftung made possible my first archival research trip in 1995-6. Earlier assistance, a debt of long standing, was provided by the Department of History at the University of Georgia. During my initial stay in Germany, the following people were of the greatest assistance: Jörn Rüsen, at the time director of the Zentrum für interdisciplinäre Forschung at Bielefeld University, Winfried Pfeifel and Jochen Meyer at the Deutsches Literaturarchiv in Marbach, Germany, Cornelia Bernini at the Thomas Mann Archiv in Zurich, Switzerland, and all of the archivists at the Stiftung Preußischer Kulturbesitz Staatsarchiv in Berlin. I am also grateful for the support offered me by the Neuert family in Bielefeld. My second research trip in 1998 was made possible by the National Endowment for the Humanities and the directors of a summer seminar on Bertolt Brecht in the Berlin years: Siegfried Mews and Marc Silberman. During that stay, and since, Silberman and Meredith Heiser-Duron, with whom I spent many hours in archival research and scholarly discussion, have helped me to clarify my thinking about Bertolt Brecht and East German cultural life. My final research trip in 2001 was made possible by the Academic Enhancement and Faculty Development Committees at the University of Virginia's College at Wise. During that visit, a number of archivists were especially helpful: Rolf Harder at the Bertolt Brecht Archiv, Michael Engel at the Universitätsarchiv, Freie Universität zu Berlin, and Werner Moritz at the Universitätsarchiv Heidelberg.

Others to whom I owe thanks include Jim Schmidt, whose insights helped me refine my understanding of Thomas Mann in particular, and émigré German intellectuals in general, and Jim Tent, who read early versions of the Meinecke and Jaspers chapters and offered gentle, though necessary, corrections to my interpretation of these figures. Over a period of years, I have also learned much from a scholarly exchange with Herbert Lehnert and Georg Iggers, even though our perspectives on many of the issues treated in this book are significantly different. During our work together on a co-authored article assessing reeducation in Heidelberg, Craig Pepin persuaded me to reevaluate my understanding of Jaspers' post-war position. Anson Rabinbach and Eike Wolgast also offered valuable insights on Jaspers and post-war Heidelberg. David Roberts deserves special thanks because of his continued efforts to make my work better, even beyond his formal duties as a graduate advisor. It is to him that I owe my greatest intellectual debt. Kirk Willis went beyond the call of duty, as well, in critiquing several chapters of the book. I would like to emphasize that none of these individuals will agree with every aspect of my argument, and I bear responsibility for any errors of omission or commission.

I am indebted to three editors at Lexington Books for their work on this project: MacDuff Stewart, Audrey Babkirk, and Patricia Stevenson. All were supportive and helpful at different stages—acquisition, review, revision, and production.

Portions of this study have appeared elsewhere in different form. I am grateful to *The Journal of Contemporary History* for permission to use material originally included in my articles "A Prophet Without Honour: Karl Jaspers in post-War Germany, 1945-1948," and "Hero or Villain? Bertolt Brecht and the Crisis Surrounding June 1953."

I would like to thank all of my colleagues in the Department of History and Philosophy for providing an environment that nurtures scholarship, even in a liberal arts college that rightly insists on teaching as its first priority: Tom Costa, Jim Humphreys, Brian McKnight, Dana Sample, Cindy Wilkey, and Brian Wills, Glenn Blackburn, Elizabeth Steele, and David Rouse, also members of the Department, offered important suggestions for the manuscript.

Above all I thank my wife, Leigh, and my children, Aaron and Anna. Their love, faith, and support sustained me these many years and made the completion of this work both possible and worthwhile.

This book is dedicated to my parents, Dale and Eugenia Clark, who taught me the value of historical study and independent thought.

Introduction

Karl Jaspers, Thomas Mann, Bertolt Brecht, and Friedrich Meinecke were all among the leading lights in the German cultural constellation during the first half of the twentieth century. Meinecke was heir to the great historicist tradition initiated by figures such as Leopold von Ranke. Jaspers, along with Martin Heidegger, was a founder of the philosophy of existence. Mann, one of the most important novelists of the half-century, helped establish modernism in Germany. Brecht was not only a prolific playwright, but he also helped initiate a fundamental shift in dramatic theory. Although they were from widely diverse areas of activity, these figures were part of the same social and cultural world, and they played prominent roles especially during the 1920s and 1930s. Historians of the Weimar Republic, such as Peter Gay, Walter Laqueur, and Dagmar Barnouw, have treated them together within the cultural context of interwar Germany. These four prominent intellectuals also played significant roles after World War II. Impelled not by intra-intellectual imperatives but by their sense of broader, public responsibilities, they helped initiate cultural renewal through symbolic, theoretical, and practical efforts. Yet they have never been examined together in the context of post-1945 Germany. This book seeks to show how illuminating it is to do so.

The response of Meinecke, Jaspers, Mann, and Brecht to the immediate post-war crisis points to the scope for intellectual leadership in general and invites an assessment of their effectiveness at meeting the challenges in post-1945 Germany. As they redefined their own roles, they responded both to the immediate challenges facing Germany in 1945 and to broader cultural and political issues that had perplexed Europeans since the turn of the century. But now the attempts to lead came in the wake of cataclysm. There was a sense that not only the German tradition, but also, perhaps, the Western tradition had been indicted in the overall catastrophe. Along the way, these men had to confront a tradition of intellectual leadership in which "responsibility" required a rejection of direct political and social engagement. Informed by philosophical idealism, the German intellectual tradition insisted that the things of higher value, the truths by which humanity operated, were to be found at the level of culture or within the realm of spirit. Intellectuals were thus to seek truth and keep a respectable distance from the corrupting world of special interest or party politics.

The confrontation with this tradition of leadership was especially compelling after 1945 because German high culture had all too easily been coopted by the Nazis. Hence the question of responsibility had unique poignancy. The most notorious individual example was that of the philosopher Martin Heidegger. Heidegger had joined the Nazi Party and accepted a position as rector of Freiburg University in 1933; thus, he seemed to have abandoned the traditional conception of intellectual responsibility. Though he eventually resigned the rectorship, he never left the party or publicly spoke out against the Hitler regime. After the war, the Military Government in the French Zone of Occupation stripped Heidegger of his position as professor at the University of Freiburg: he could neither teach nor publish until 1950. During the immediate post-war period and until his death in 1976, Heidegger was evasive, even dishonest, about his connection to the National Socialists. He never acknowledged any personal moral culpability, claiming only that he had made a mistake in judgment about Hitler and the Nazis, that he had not understood the full implications of political events. Heidegger did not deny that this particular political solution to the cultural crisis had led to disaster. He did deny, however, that a diagnosis could be found on the level of German distinctiveness. The cultural malaise affected the entire West, and any lasting solution had to be based on a reconsideration of the Western philosophical tradition since Plato. Accordingly, Heidegger repaired to his ivory tower—his cabin in the Black Forest—and thought about the "history of being" and the "destiny of the West."

For many German intellectuals at the time, as well as most contemporary historians and cultural critics, Heidegger has represented the archetypal intellectual traitor. He was guilty not only of making poor political choices but also of abandoning his proper role as an intellectual leader. Some have even seen in his philosophy the seeds of fascism. Yet the entire Heidegger controversy points to important questions about the roles that intellectuals have played in post-war Germany *and* the roles that they can ever play at any time. If Heidegger had been woefully inadequate in providing intellectual leadership both during and after the war, then how did other intellectuals who were not tainted with the stain of Nazism measure up? And what are our criteria even in our criticism of Heidegger? Meinecke and Jaspers had remained in Germany and had even voiced camouflaged criticism of the Nazi regime; Mann and Brecht had spent the war in exile fighting against fascism and Nazism. All of these figures possessed both intellectual stature and moral authority and thus appeared to be in an ideal position to initiate cultural renewal.

The Heidegger controversy adds a certain sharpness to the debate about intellectual responsibility, but it is only the most recent example of an ongoing, though sporadic, historical discussion about intellectual leadership, a discussion that gained its greatest currency during the period immediately following the earlier European catastrophe, World War I. Indeed, the cluster of issues that informs this discussion as well as the criteria on which historians commonly judge intellectuals emerged from the questions and responses of the generation to which Mann, Meinecke, Jaspers, and Brecht belonged.[1] It was during the interwar period that intellectuals in Germany, and Europe more broadly, not only discussed the proper role for intellectuals but also sought to offer significant societal leadership. What was to be their relationship to the rest of society? Were they to be a class apart, leading the "masses" while remaining above the political fray, or should they come down from their ivory towers and engage in political activities? Should they articulate a new set of ideas to meet the cultural and political challenges, or must they champion social and economic justice? Should they be public philosophers or Nietzschean self-inventors?

Perhaps the most famous statement by a European intellectual was that of Julien Benda in *Treason of the Intellectuals* (1928). Benda argued that intellectuals or "clercs" generally should not engage directly in politics or pursue material advantage, but rather should stand above the fray, searching for the eternal truths and values through which humanity operated. Traditionally, they had maintained a distinction between what is and what ought to be, and they should continue to do so. Benda did not argue that intellectuals should never engage in public debate. Sometimes it was necessary to do so, but such engagement should always be the result of independent, rather than partisan, thought and should be based on universal principles. Once they had engaged in a public debate, intellectuals should return to their ivory towers, knocking the dust off of their sandals and leaving society to struggle as best it could with truth. Rational and civilized society was possible only when intellectuals performed this function. To do otherwise was to commit intellectual treason—a crime of which most European intellectuals were guilty during and after World War I. They had become political partisans and nationalists and had fanned the flames of irrationalism. As a result they had intensified the racial hatred, class struggle, and nationalism. Only by returning to their proper roles, Benda insisted, could European intellectuals stem the tide of declining civilization.[2]

Often juxtaposed to Benda's vision of intellectuals is that of Antonio Gramsci in *Prison Notebooks*, written in the 1930s but published after World War II. Gramsci claimed that anyone who worked with ideas was an intellectual, but he distinguished between traditional and organic intellectuals. Traditional intellectuals viewed themselves as autonomous from prevailing power relations or hegemony and were similar to Benda's "clercs." Organic intellectuals, on the other hand, were partisans of a particular cause or advocates of an ideological position. They were to elaborate the current hegemony or create a counterhegemony within a democratic capitalist society. Indeed, for substantive change—revolution—to occur, intellectuals had to fulfill this function.[3]

If the categories laid out by Benda and later Gramsci have been crucial to the overall debate about intellectual leadership, the debate in Germany has been especially poignant, because National Socialism came to triumph in Germany with the help of intellectuals. Among the most important historical works on the German intellectual tradition is Fritz Ringer's *Decline of the German Mandarins*. Ringer traces the German tradition back to the late-eighteenth century, but he focuses on the educational philosophy of academic intellectuals in the social sciences and humanities between 1890 and 1933. German professors, he claims, became the arbiters of culture during the nineteenth century. German academic culture was rooted in idealism and German professors, according to Ringer, were men "of pure learning," separated both from the artisanal class and the "relatively uncivilized feudal caste." While they fervently believed that "the word" was "spiritually ennobling," they were contemptuous of the "practical sphere of technique and organization." They insisted on "pure learning" and argued that "the absolutely disinterested contemplation of the good and the true, [was] the principal vocation of man." Because the world had "no purpose and reality itself, no meaning apart from the creative labor of the human mind and spirit," only the person who fully cultivated his own spirit could best serve humanity. In comparison, "everything else—the practical knowledge of everyday life, the details of social organization, and the accidents of worldly rank and station—[was] insignificant."[4]

The mandarins' understanding of learning was thus "the direct antithesis of practical knowledge," and this understanding was expressed in the concepts of *Bildung*, *Wissenschaft*, and *Kultur*. *Bildung*, or self-cultivation, emerged from the German Enlightenment and was usually contrasted to *Erziehung* (education) or *Unterricht* (instruction). More than transmitting information and developing analytical skills, *Bildung* demanded self-directed, self-motivated education. It aimed at the development of an individual's character and critical faculties. According to Ringer, *Bildung* reflected "religious and neohumanist conceptions of 'inner growth' and integral self-development." The classical texts—both ancient and modern—and the moral and aesthetic examples they contained, "affected a person deeply and totally." Ultimately it led to wisdom and virtue, and could "attract, elevate and transform the learner."[5]

Within the university, *Bildung* was promoted through *Wissenschaft* (science, scholarship). Students and professors were encouraged to immerse themselves in the scientific outlook by pursuing individual projects of original research. Such research was supposed to lead to the development of one's critical faculties and moral character, and also objectivity. In this way, professors and students could achieve *Bildung* and thus the moral and spiritual character that would make them better professionals and citizens.[6]

Closely related to *Bildung* was *Kultur*, a concept which originally denoted "personal culture" and referred to "the cultivation of the mind and spirit." Over time, however, it came to mean "all of man's civilized achievements in society." Opposed to culture was "civilization," which German intellectuals associated with "sophisticated social forms," as well as "worldly manners"—qualities usually identified with France. For German intellectuals, "civilization" was little more than an "outward sign of a limited education." It also gradually grew to encompass all results of outward progress in economics, technology, and social organization. *Kultur*, on the other hand, continued to stand for the "inner conditions and achievements of cultivated men." Not until the late nineteenth century was the antithesis fully worked out in the wake of modernization.[7]

Central to the idealist discourse of the German mandarins was the notion that the guardians of culture should not be asked to descend from their ivory towers in order to become directly involved in politics. Some academic intellectuals commented on politics, but even when they did so, their discussions tended to focus on theoretical objectives or ultimate purposes of government. According to Ringer, even "the analysis of political realities was neglected, and relatively little attention was paid to questions of political technique." These "trivial matters"—the details of everyday politics—"were ethically as well as intellectually beneath the notice of cultivated men. In this sense and in this sense only, the German intellectual was and considered himself apolitical: he had an aversion for the practical aspects of the political process."[8] In short, Ringer's mandarins closely resemble Benda's "clercs."

During the second half of the nineteenth century, this aristocracy of spirit became "the functional ruling class of the nation." University professors spoke for the educated middle classes and represented their values. Indeed, before 1890 most educated Germans looked to the professors to define their own views on contemporary cultural and political questions. After 1890, when Germany was transformed into an industrialized society, the mandarins' role as arbiter of cultural values began to collapse. Especially at this moment, German academic intellectuals became conservative defenders of the status quo. Whereas during the early nineteenth century the German academic community had sometimes challenged political elites, now it "[fell] into the role of a vaguely conservative and decidedly official establishment." Thus the German mandarins, despite their claims to apoliciticism, nevertheless usually had active political interests, to which they gave public expression in lectures, newspaper articles, and journal articles. There was, then, a kind of defensiveness on the part of the German mandarins after 1890, and apoliticism in the universities masked political conservatism.[9]

Although there were always exceptions to the rule—Ringer points to modernists such as Max Weber, Jaspers, and Meinecke—the vast majority of German mandarin intellectuals were backward-looking elitists with little understanding or appreciation for the realities of the industrialized age. They overemphasized a sense of cultural crisis, which, from Ringer's perspective, was their defensive response to their waning influence, and they refused to accommodate themselves to the new reality. When World War I came, they jumped into the icy waters of wartime enthusiasm, many of them becoming participants in the "cultural war" that accompanied the military conflict. In books, speeches, and pamphlets, German professors characterized the war as a "cultural war" between German cultural uniqueness and the empty materialism of the Western allies.[10]

After World War I, the mandarins retrenched and were even more determined not to enter into the practical world of politics. According to Ringer, "economic and social questions had to be treated as subordinate, merely practical," and it was "almost immoral to talk about worldly interests." Yet their supposed "apoliticism" masked a conservative, anti-Republican nationalism and the mythical unity of the German people.[11] And it emerged from a defensive attitude; the mandarins were afraid that "the new politics and economics had become emancipated from the cultural sage and his values." They thus rejected the new regime of the SPD (Social Democratic Party) and, generally, were opposed to the Weimar Republic. Even those who did support it, such as Meinecke, were "republicans of reason" with no emotional ties to the Republic.[12]

Unable to adjust themselves to the current reality, "the mandarins were never content to cultivate their own gardens. They thought of themselves as a priestly caste, and they meant to legislate ultimate values to a peasant population."[13] Even the modernists who wanted to "solve the problem of cultural decadence by devising and disseminating a new set of cultural ideals," who sought to reorient men's minds and hearts, faltered.[14] Instead of concentrating on the political and social exigencies, they continued to emphasize only the search for and creation of values, and they insisted on their right to be able to legislate these values.

Ringer concludes that the mandarins ultimately contributed significantly to the triumph of Nazism. Although most did not desire the Third Reich, they shared "ideological affinities and mental habits" with the National Socialists. They discredited "common sense politics, along with the merely practical knowledge of positivist learning." Thus they made it difficult even to raise "an argument against unreason."[15] Furthermore, they helped to destroy the Republic without having chosen its successor. They "willfully cultivated an atmosphere in which any 'national' movement could claim to be the 'spiritual revival.' They fostered chaos, without regard for the consequences." Most dangerously, they "abandoned intellectual responsibility itself," by promoting the "illusion of total escape from interest politics, the yearning to transcend the political mechanism in terms of some idealistic absolute."[16]

Although Ringer focuses on academic intellectuals, there was also an unofficial, unconnected "intelligentsia" in Germany, whose attitudes often mirrored those of the mandarins. In a series of essays, Gordon Craig has examined the role of German "men of letters." Over the long stretch of history, Craig maintains, German writers tended to be neutral in political attitude and they had little influence. However,

> when the desire for engagement arose, as it did periodically, the activists were too intent upon remaining true to themselves to master the facts of politics or the realities of the situations in which they intervened. They sought power on their own terms, confident that they could transform and spiritualize society and create a new race of men. It was perhaps a noble dream, but it did great harm in Germany.[17]

German writers, Craig claims, "always had an ambivalent relationship toward society." Especially after 1871, they, too, came to see "the external world and its works as being of no legitimate concern to the artist." Like their academic counterparts, they saw "aesthetic contemplation and intellectual activity as ends in themselves." At the same time, however, there was an "opposite tendency . . . a desire for engagement, for active participation in political and social reform movements, which was motivated in part by resentment against the indifference of bourgeois society, partly by a guilty sense of unfulfillment and neglect of responsibility, and partly by an unconscious longing for power." This desire to participate in politics was especially prevalent during the nineteenth century, before the creation of the German empire. Indeed, claims Craig, all of the great German writers of the eighteenth and nineteenth centuries—Georg Forster, Heinrich von Kleist, Georg Büchner, Friedrich Hölderlin, and Goethe—gravitated toward politics in one way or another. They sought to be political citizens "either by serving the existing state . . . or by seeking to change or improve it." With the emergence of the Bismarckian Reich, however, most German writers "lost heart and withdrew from the conflict."[18]

Not until World War I and the Weimar Republic did German men of letters have the chance to exercise political influence again. For many literary intellectuals, the Weimar Republic offered the opportunity both to redefine intellectual responsibility and to take a leading role. Heinrich Mann argued that the "*Mann des Geistes* had for a generation betrayed his proper function either by silence or by explicit approbation of the forces of materialism that had debauched Germany." He had made no changes, "eliminated no evil, made no progress along life's way to a better world." According to Mann, "it was time that this came to an end and that the man of letters recognized that it was his duty to be the voice of conscience to his people, instead of a spiritual fellow-traveler, who, by condoning the vices that were destroying the nation, assumed responsibility for them."[19]

Yet according to Craig, German men of letters failed to meet the challenge. They were "singularly ill-equipped" to intervene "in practical affairs" and their forays into politics were "marked by that violence which Gervinus once noted as being characteristic of German intellectuals, as well as by exaggeration, shrillness, abstractness, and utopianism, but rarely by patience or a sense of perspective." For Craig, the engagement that characterized the Weimar Republic was either the "naïve and irrational engagement" of Gottfried Benn or the "bitingly satirical criticism without target of Kurt Tucholsky." This was, in no small part, the reason that the Weimar Republic failed. What Germany needed after the war was "to extricate itself from the desperate condition in which military defeat had left it, a multitude of complicated administrative, financial, and economic problems would have to be resolved, a new state with effective political institutions would have to be created, and time and patience and painstaking labor would be required to achieve even tolerable results." Craig concludes that men of letters were not capable of achieving these results. Indeed, "they were incapable even of sustained interest in the problems affecting the reconstruction of national life." The expressionists, for example, "had no intention of mastering the actualities of German politics and social life; they wanted those things to spiritualize themselves, an attitude indicating that they had not succeeded in overcoming the historical antithesis of *Geist* and *Macht* but were merely re-emphasizing it." None of them became convinced supporters "of the republic or of democratic socialism." Adherents of *Die neue Sachlichkeit* (New Objectivity), including Brecht, Erich Kästner, and Hermann Kesten, were hardly more effective. Made up of "ironists, embittered critics of the ruling society, pure satirists and Voltaireans," they were deeply critical of their time and the Republic, and they focused on "exposing the weaknesses, injustices, and hypocrisies of their time."

The problem, according to Craig, was that Weimar writers "lacked a specific political orientation." Rather than making their criticisms seem more plausible, "they actually left the impression that they and their allies lacked perspective and were politically naïve." Although some remained interested in politics and even turned toward radical alternatives, "the greater number retreated [yet again] to the world of spirit from whence they had come, to the same peripheral social and political position from which they had escaped so enthusiastically in the last years before the outbreak of the war, to the safe neutrality of literature and aesthetic education."[20]

When the worst years of the Weimar Republic hit, most of the literary intellectuals stood back and remained uncommitted. When Hitler came to power, "they not only resigned themselves to this fact but, in distressingly large numbers, acclaimed the new Leader and vied for places in his intellectual establishment." These men were not just naïve, according to Craig. Their reaction was

> the result of other tendencies that had characterized German writers for over a hundred years: hatred of middle-class culture and values and willingness to see them destroyed; a furtive admiration for power and, lacking a realistic appreciation of its uses and limitations, a proneness to idealize it; and a desire to escape isolation, to be absorbed in the community, to play a role commensurate with their own estimation of themselves and thus to satisfy what Arnold Gehlen has called the intellectual's *weltfremder Herrschaftsanspruch*.[21]

Craig is not alone in this assessment. Golo Mann and Peter Gay have both argued that German intellectuals failed because they were not able to present a coherent and cogent answer to the political and social challenges of the Weimar Republic. This fragmented generation offered either elitism and escapism or corrosive criticism and predictions of doom.[22] Although Mann, Craig, Gay, and Ringer have different accents, they thus share the assumption that the proper criteria for judging the successes and failures of twentieth-century intellectuals should be commitment to immediate political, social, and/or economic issues.[23]

Jost Hermand employs similar criteria in his evaluation of West German intellectuals after World War II. In *Kultur im Wiederaufbau*, Hermand notes that even untainted German intellectuals such as Meinecke, Mann, and Jaspers faced unprecedented cultural and political challenges in the wake of Germany's total defeat. Like others who have examined the immediate post-war period, Hermand has seen this particular era as a moment of opportunity, ultimately lost, thanks in large part to the failure of intellectuals to meet the challenge.[24] The proper role for intellectuals in the post-World War II Germany, Hermand maintains, was critical political and economic engagement. Unfortunately, "the majority of intellectuals and artists found no correct relationship to concrete reality during the chaotic years after 1945." To be sure, some in the immediate post-war period offered the "correct" kind of leadership. Leftist-leaning intellectuals such as Alfred Weber were concerned about the immediate task of rebuilding German society on a social democratic basis and they tried to promote their egalitarian message through journals such as *Aufbau* and *Ost und West*. These men were not only in the minority among post-war German intellectuals, claims

Hermand, but they also faced a whole set of detours and roadblocks set up by the Western powers during the Cold War.[25]

Hermand renders an especially harsh judgment on the senior intellectuals who had been the leaders of the old German high culture. Following the argument of Theodor Adorno, he argues that men such as Jaspers, Meinecke, and Mann were little more than backward-looking elitists.[26] They represented the privileged and educated middle classes, the *Bildungsbürgertum*, who did not want their comfortable lives to be disturbed. They saw themselves in opposition to the "fickle mob" that political charlatans and hucksters could easily whip into a frenzy. They stressed their political and moral integrity, and kept themselves above the political fray and away from immediate problems: "the bourgeois intellectual claimed repeatedly in his writings that he could withdraw from history and society without further damage to his own autonomous ego." These intellectuals believed themselves to be the arbiters of cultural value, and they turned away from the masses who lived in the nether world of materialism and popular culture where people possessed no real freedom of decision. When they spoke of liberalism, argues Hermand, they meant less the democratic concept of freedom than the right-leaning liberalism of the Wilhelmine bourgeoisie. If they were politically engaged at all they lobbied for neo-liberal or right-leaning humanistic ideology, "which allowed them a considerable retreat from politics without placing their claim to intellectual leadership in question." Ultimately they failed to win an audience or make a significant difference in the post-war world because they retreated into their private autonomous worlds and withdrew from any form of "real" engagement.[27]

What Germany needed after the war was not a new set of ideas, but rather, according to Hermand, political, economic, and social readjustment. At the one chance to make a significant difference, to change the course of post-war German history, this older generation failed. It could not sacrifice assumptions that prevented an unhampered view of the new realities. To be sure, the emerging cold-war context conspired against them. Yet ultimately they and their generation were tainted, no matter what their individual contributions to an emerging post-war culture, because they were unable to break out of their traditional molds.

Critiques of each individual figure in this study have echoed these findings. The picture of the post-war Meinecke was shaped primarily by the reception of his last significant work, *The German Catastrophe*. The Marxist Immanuel Geiss saw it as the last gasp of tainted bourgeois tradition of historical scholarship, and Meinecke as the symbol of a bankrupt tradition of intellectual leadership.[28] For Robert Pois *The German Catastrophe* represented the final retreat from politics to culture which made "a substantive political investigation of Germany's past impossible."[29]

Jaspers, too, was often deemed irrelevant to post-war German culture, especially after his emigration to Basel, Switzerland. In 1964 Theodor Adorno argued that Jaspers had aided West Germans in their refusal to face up to the past. Because he had employed a "jargon of authenticity," one which was shot through with empty theological overtones and which replaced the language of

National Socialism in the post-1945 period, he helped create an atmosphere in which a meaningful and truthful discussion of the past became impossible.[30] Recently, Steven Remy and Anson Rabinbach have been similarly critical. Remy has charged Jaspers with contributing to the creation of the "Heidelberg myth" that absolved the majority of Heidelberg professors from any connection with Nazism. This myth helped limit denazification and kept college professors from facing up to their complicity in the Nazi regime. Rabinbach has argued that Jaspers reinforced the silent *Vergangenheitsbewältigung* of the immediate post-war years and, through his rigid separation of political and moral responsibility, helped create a skepticism of denazification.[31]

Since the early 1950s critics have also deemed Thomas Mann's contributions to post-1945 German cultural and political history to be inconsequential. Hannah Arendt claimed that Mann always "lived up there on top of his mountain behind the banks of clouds, and he let the world go by. But unfortunately, the clouds would part now and then, and he would emerge and make a pronouncement."[32] Denis Bark and David Gress have argued that after the war Mann explicitly refused to assume the mantle of cultural and moral leadership for Germans.[33] Gordon Craig has claimed that Mann's post-war career was marked by a return to the apolitical stance of his pre-World War I period. Not only did he reject his role as an intellectual leader of Germany, but he also again became deeply skeptical of democracy and sharply critical of Western culture.[34]

Bertolt Brecht, the other figure in this study, has either been considered suspect, because of his role in the workers uprising of 1953, or irrelevant because he effected no long-term change. Few have denied that he attempted to break out of the traditional mold, to become a political intellectual. Especially after 1948, when he returned to East Berlin, he gained both power and influence in his role as a cultural functionary. Yet according to David Pike, Hannah Arendt, Theodor Adorno, and others, it was precisely at this moment that he became an intellectual traitor, a "eulogist for complicity" who "championed" not an "imperfect socialism but a tyranny."[35] Despite having given himself over to an ideology, having sacrificed his "divine gift" for the Stalinist regime of the GDR, he nevertheless effected no long-term cultural change.[36]

These interpretations and the categories they employ are problematic in at least two ways: first, they lose sight of the context, of what was possible under the circumstances, a topic that will be taken up in individual chapters of this book. Second, they are unnecessarily restrictive in that they maintain an artificial dualism between apoliticism and engagement, between the cultural intellectual and the public intellectual. One might plausibly argue that there is scope for intellectuals to play both roles and others besides. For example, T. S. Eliot, in "The Man of Letters and the Future of Europe," asserted that

> The man of letters is not, as a rule, exclusively engaged upon the production of works of art. He has other interests, like anybody else; interests which will, in all probability, exercise some influence upon the content and meaning of works of art which he does produce. He has the same responsibility, and should have the same concern with the fate of his country, and with political and social affairs within it, as any other citizen; and in matters of controversy . . . [but] the

first responsibility of the man of letters is, of course, his responsibility towards his art.[37]

More recently, Richard Rorty has argued that the modern intellectual can have a public and a private persona. She might find "her moral identity—her sense of her relations to most other human beings—in democratic institutions which she inhabits."[38] She can engage in the current political discourse. For example, as Timothy Garton Ash has argued, the intellectual should be a "thinker or writer who engages in public discussion of issues of public policy, in politics in the broadest sense, while deliberately not engaging in the pursuit of political power."[39] But she can also be a Romantic intellectual, a Nietzschean self-inventor, thinking "thoughts which no human being has yet thought, [writing] books unlike any yet written."[40] She can, in other words, create a new set of ideas. One category need not exclude the other. In practice intellectuals can plausibly play many roles within a society.

Edward Said made a similar point in a different way. He argued that all intellectuals speak in their own discourse, their own lingua franca, "which the uninitiated cannot understand," but they also have "a specific public role in society." For Said, the intellectual "is an individual endowed with a faculty for representing, embodying, articulating a message, a view, an attitude, philosophy, or opinion to, as well as for, a public." This vocation is important because "it is publicly recognizable and involves both commitment and risk, boldness and vulnerability." In the modern world, there are no purely private intellectuals because, Said claimed, "the moment you set down words and then publish them you have entered the public world." Nor, however, "is there *only* a public intellectual, someone who exists just as a figurehead or spokesperson or symbol of a cause, movement, or position."[41]

Perhaps most significant is Said's claim that intellectuals are representative figures of a specific time and place who "visibly represent a standpoint of some kind, who make articulate representations to his or her public despite all sorts of barriers."[42] Intellectuals have, as Vaclav Havel has argued, "a broader sense of responsibility for the state of the world and its future." They are "mindful of the ties that link everything in this world together." They should "approach the world with humility, but also with an increased responsibility," and they should "wage a struggle for every good thing."[43] Yet they always speak in specific, individual voices, and they answer questions that are specific to time and place. These may be questions of immediate importance, or they may be challenges that relate to longer-term trends or crises.

Meinecke, Jaspers, Mann, and Brecht went beyond the traditional roles played by German intellectuals, and their post-war careers offer examples of a new type of intellectual leadership, one that transcends the restrictive dualistic categories of apoliticism and engagement. They recognized that some issues could not be resolved by adjustment to immediate political and social exigencies. They understood that the crisis of post-World War II Germany, and Europe more broadly, had to do, at least in part, with cultural foundations, and thus had to be addressed on this level. To be sure, it was not just a matter of thinking completely new ideas, but rather of unearthing the forgotten, making connections that had been denied, plotting alternative trajectories. But there was still a need to answer the broader cultural crisis by reorienting the minds and hearts of the German people. These men recognized, as had Adam Müller a century earlier, that "Even thought at its highest levels does not release us from the more general intellectual obligation of understanding our times. All higher thinking must try to affect the immediate present in its own way, and whoever is truly involved in such thought is also involved in the present."[44]

These four figures were some of the first to think about the nature of the catastrophe and the extent to which it was caused by the German tradition and, more specifically, the old high culture. They also had to grapple, as did other intellectuals of the time, with the extent to which the entire Western intellectual tradition was caught up in the catastrophe. In so doing, they created a space within which such matters could be articulated publicly and debated critically. Some of their books, essays, and speeches got at the heart of the cultural and political crisis. Others were symptomatic of ongoing tensions and uncertainties. But all helped later generations to reformulate, to rearticulate, to renegotiate the meaning of the catastrophe.

There were also other, more immediate levels of the cultural and political crisis, and thus more specific, institutional ways to become engaged. For Jaspers and Meinecke, this meant, among other things, rebuilding the German university system. For Mann, it meant engaging in public debates about the direction of political and cultural events. For Brecht, the challenge was to shape cultural policy in his official capacity as a member of the German Academy of Arts. In responding to their own tradition, and in their practical example, these men challenged conventional notions of "engagement."

This book assesses both the practical leadership efforts of Meinecke, Jaspers, Mann, and Brecht and the ideas of their post-war books, essays, and speeches. It also relates their efforts to a wider constellation of ideas and conflicts about cultural renewal in the post-war period. From a historical perspective, their post-1945 careers reveal the most important cultural, moral, and political issues that faced Germans in the immediate aftermath of the catastrophe. Addressing a common set of problems and concerns, they had different accents and points of emphasis, and thus their ideas were often in tension with each other. This book examines the implicit confrontation of their views and shows how that confrontation helped shape the debate about cultural and political renewal in immediate post-war Germany.

NOTES

1. Here I follow Karl Mannheim's definition of "political generations." Mannheim argues that "political generations" are defined by the experience of especially powerful political events. Karl Mannheim, "The Problem of Generations," in *From Karl Mannheim*, ed. Kurt H. Wolff (New Brunswick: Transaction, 1993), 351-98.

2. Julien Benda, *Treason of the Intellectuals*, trans. Richard Aldington (New York: W.W. Norton, 1969). See also Benda, *La Jeunesse d'un Clerc* (Paris: Gallimard, 1938).

3. Antonio Gramsci, *Selections from the Prison Notebooks*, trans. Quintin Hoare and Geoffrey Nowell Smith (New York: International Publishers, 1971). See also Edward Said's reworking of Benda's and Gramsci's positions in *Representations of the Intellectual* (New York: Vintage Books, 1996). Other recent discussions include Jeremy Jennings and Anthony Kemp-Welch, eds., *Intellectuals in Politics: From the Dreyfus Affair to Salmon Rushdie* (New York: Routledge, 1997).

4. Fritz Ringer, *The Decline of the German Mandarins: The German Academic Community, 1890-1933* (Hanover and London: University Press of New England, 1969), 6.

5. Ibid., 87.

6. For detailed treatment of the concept of *Bildung*, see Reinhart Koselleck, "Enleitung—Zur anthropologischen und semantischen Struktur der Bildung," in *Bildungsbürtum im 19. Jahrhundert. Teil II. Bildungsgüter und Bildungswissen*, ed. Reinhart Koselleck (Stuttgart: Klett-Cotta, 1989), 11-46; Rudolf Vierhaus, "Bildung," in *Geschichtliche Grundbegriffe: historisches Lexikon zur politisch-sozialen Sprache in Deutschland*, vol. 1, ed. Otto Brunner, Werner Conze and Reinhart Koselleck, (Stuttgart: E. Klett, 1972), 508-51.

7. Ringer, *Mandarins*, 20, 86-7, 90.

8. Ibid., 95, 111, 121, 241.

9. Ibid., 30, 124, 126-7; see also Wolfgang Abendroth, "Das Unpolitische als Wesensmerkmal der deutschen Universität," in *Nationalsozialismus und die deutsche Universität* (Berlin: Walter de Gruyter & Co, 1966), 189-208

10. Ibid., 21-60; see also Klaus Schwabe, *Wissenschaft und Kriegsmoral: Die deutschen Hochschullehrer und die politischen Grundfragen des Ersten Weltkrieges* (Göttingen: Musterschmidt-Verlag, 1969).

11. Ringer, *Mandarins*, 241. See also Wolfgang Abendroth, "Die deutschen Professoren und die Weimarer Republik," in *Hochschule und Wissenschaft im Dritten Reich*, ed. Jörg Tröger (Frankfurt am Main: Campus Verlag, 1984), 11-25.

12. Ringer, *Mandarins*, 246; see also Peter Gay, *Weimar Culture: The Insider as Outsider* (New York: Harper & Row, 1968), 23-28.

13. Ringer, *Mandarins*, 258, 268.

14. Ibid., 282, 403.

15. Ibid., 437-8.

16. Ibid., 446.

17. Gordon Craig, "Engagement and Neutrality in Weimar Germany," in *Literature and Politics in the Twentieth Century*, ed. Walter Laqueur and George Mosse (New York: Harper and Row, 1967), 63.

18. Gordon Craig, *Politics of the Unpolitical: German Writers and the Problem of Power, 1770-1871* (New York: Oxford University Press, 1995), xiii-xiv.

19. Heinrich Mann, "Geist und Tat" (1910), in *Essays* (Hamburg: Claasen, 1960), 30, cited in Craig, "Engagement and Neutrality in Weimar Germany," 51.

20. Ibid., 50, 52, 54, 57, 55.

21. Ibid., 60.

22. Gay, *Weimar Culture*; Golo Mann, "The German Intellectuals," in *The Intellectuals*, ed. George B. de Huszar (Glencoe Illinois: The Free Press, 1960), 461ff.

23. Robert Wohl employs similar categories in his treatment of *The Generation of 1914* (Cambridge, Mass: Harvard University Press, 1979); see also David Roberts' criticism of Wohl in *Benedetto Croce and the Uses of Historicism* (Berkeley, California: University of California Press, 1987), 27-30.

24. Craig Pepin, "The Holy Grail of Pure Wissenschaft: University Ideal and the University Reform in Post World War II Germany," PhD diss., Duke University, 2001; Ste-

ven Remy, *The Heidelberg Myth: The Nazification and Denazification of a German University* (Cambridge, Mass: Harvard University Press, 2002); Karl-Ernst Bugenstab, *Umerziehung zur Demokratie! Re-education-Politik im Bildungswesen der U.S.-Zone 1945-1949* (Düsseldorf: Bertelsmann Universitätsverlag, 1970).

25. Jost Hermand, *Kultur im Wiederaufbau, Die Bundesrepublik Deutschland 1945-1965* (Frankfurt, Berlin: Ullstein, 1989).

26. Theodor Adorno, "Auferstehung der Kultur in Deutschland?" *Frankfurter Hefte*, vol. 5, (May 1950), 470ff.

27. Hermand, *Kultur im Wiederaufbau*, 65, 67-68.

28. Immanuel Geiss, "Wie es zur 'deutschen Katastrophe' kam, Die gesammelten Werke Friedrich Meinecke's abgeschlossen," *Frankfurter Rundschau*, 13 January 1971.

29. Robert Pois, *Friedrich Meinecke and German Politics in the Twentieth Century* (Berkeley, California: University of California Press, 1972), 51, 143.

30. Theodor Adorno, *Jargon der Eigentlichkeit: Zur deutschen Ideologie* (Frankfurt am Main: Suhrkamp, 1964).

31. Anson Rabinbach, *In the Shadow of Catastrophe: German Intellectuals between Apocalypse and Enlightenment* (Berkeley: University of California Press, 1997), 164-5, 143-4, 160-1; Remy, *The Heidelberg Myth*, 116-17, 140.

32. Quoted in Craig, *Politics of the Unpolitical*, xi.

33. Denis L. Bark and David R. Gress, *A History of West Germany: From Shadow to Substance*, vol. 1 (Cambridge, Mass: Blackwell, 1993), 162.

34. Gordon Craig, "The Mann Nobody Knew," *New York Review of Books*, 29 February 1996, 34.

35. Theodor Adorno, "Commitment," in *Notes to Literature III*, trans. Shierry Weber Nicholsen (Columbia: Columbia University Press, 1992), 86; Hannah Arendt, *Men in Dark Times* (New York: Harcourt, Brace, and World, 1968), 207-250.

36. David Pike, *The Politics of Culture in Soviet-Occupied Germany* (Stanford: Stanford University Press, 1995).

37. T.S. Eliot, "The Man of Letters and the Future of Europe," in *The Sewanee Review*, Summer 1945, 333.

38. Richard Rorty, "Moral identity and private autonomy: The case of Foucault," in *Essays on Heidegger and Others: Philosophical Papers Volume 2* (Cambridge: Cambridge University Press, 1991), 193.

39. Timothy Garton Ash, "Prague: Intellectuals and Politicians," *New York Review of Books* (hereafter *NYRB*), 12 January 1995, 85.

40. Rorty, "Moral identity and private autonomy," 193.

41. Said, *Representations of the Intellectual*, 10-12.

42. Ibid., 13.

43. Vaclav Havel, "The Responsibility of Intellectuals," *NYRB*, 22 June 1995, 36-7.

44. Adam Müller, *Gesammelte Schriften*, vol. VII (Munich : Bey G. Franz, 1939), 447.

Chapter One

Guardian of the Past: Friedrich Meinecke

In 1945 Friedrich Meinecke was eighty-four years old and almost blind. Heir to the great historicist tradition of the nineteenth century, he was the best-known German historian in the world. He had published three internationally acclaimed historical monographs—*Cosmopolitanism and the National State* (*Weltbürger-tum und Nationalstaat*) (1907), *Machiavellism* (*Die Idee der Staatsraison*) (1924), and *Historism* (*Die Entstehung des Historismus*) (1936)—as well as a host of smaller historical studies and political pieces. Meinecke also possessed a high degree of moral authority among both Germans and the allies after World War II. He had been a vocal, if somewhat ambivalent, supporter of the Weimar Republic and had publicly opposed the Nazis in 1933. Indeed, in 1945 he claimed to have spoken the last word against Hitler before his seizure of power: "I was the last person in the early part of 1933, who, two days before the burn-ing of the Reichstag, warned publicly in the press against Hitler."[1] Not surpris-ingly, Meinecke suffered for his opposition. Although he retired voluntarily in 1932 at the age of 69, the Nazis forced him to resign as chair of the *Historische Reichskommission* in 1934.[2] In 1935, moreover, he had to step down as editor of the *Historische Zeitschrift*. Deprived of active life within the historical profes-sion and influence as a public intellectual, Meinecke went into inner migration.[3]

Having lived in virtual obscurity for thirteen years, Meinecke was neverthe-less in a position to offer leadership to post-war Germany. Indeed, the Allies and the Germans in positions of influence asked him to take up the mantle of leader-ship. Despite his advanced years and frail health, Meinecke considered it his duty as a teacher and scholar to serve post-World War II Germany by helping reestablish its intellectual foundations and by identifying and underscoring its roots in German *and* European history. As Jonathan Knudsen has recently pointed out, he "was a central figure of restoration and continuity in the West German historical profession after 1945."[4] He exercised, as well, practical lead-

ership on a number of levels, most notably in his role as the first rector of the
Free University of Berlin. As a cultural critic, he made public pronouncements
on key political and cultural issues in post-war journals and newspapers, and he
wrote books on issues of immediate historical importance including *The German
Catastrophe* (*Die deutsche Katastrophe*) (1946). In offering leadership to post-
war Germany, Meinecke both responded to and reacted against the tradition of
academic intellectual leadership in Germany—a tradition of which he had been
an integral part.

It is largely as a member of his class and generation of intellectuals that
Meinecke has been judged by historians. Though most have recognized in
Meinecke a man of enormous personal integrity—and some have even argued
that he was one of the most progressive members of his class—commentators
have nevertheless pointed to the blindspots and weaknesses he shared with other
German mandarins. According to Meinecke's critics, it was these weaknesses
that made him a republican of reason rather than a full supporter of the Weimar
Republic; it was these weaknesses that contributed to his limited understanding
of National Socialism before 1933; and it was these weaknesses that ultimately
kept him from grasping the full scope of the German catastrophe. Historians
have been especially critical of Meinecke's post-World War II efforts at intellectual leadership. The picture of the post-war Meinecke has been shaped, to a
large extent, by the reception of his last important work, *The German Catastrophe*. Immanuel Geiss wrote in 1971 that it represented "the intellectual and political bankruptcy of the bourgeois-idealist tradition of history writing in Germany which is only now becoming slowly apparent with the emergence of a
new generation of historians." In this sense it was "full of inner symbolism."[5]
Robert Pois saw *The German Catastrophe* as the final step on Meinecke's
"troubled journey from statism to the cosmopolitanism of his post-World War II
years." The final "separation of *Macht* from *Kultur*—in fact, of politics from
culture—an effort that was meant to preserve the latter from the egotistical and
nihilistic depredations of the former, succeeded only in making a substantive
political investigation of Germany's past impossible."[6] Georg Iggers has been
similarly critical. Meinecke, he claims, "died amidst the spiritual ruins of post-
World War II Germany in the bitter realization that Germany had traveled a
wrong road not only politically, but philosophically and in its historical scholarship. And yet Meinecke . . . remained incapable of freeing himself of many of
the vestiges of a past faith." He "continued to affirm, as essentially beneficial,
the separate way the German spirit had gone since the Enlightenment."[7] Knudsen has taken a more nuanced position, arguing that, although significant in
some ways, Meinecke's work was detrimental to long-term cultural development: "Meinecke's thought even after 1933 remained an odd intellectual blend
of anti-Enlightenment irrationalism, German exceptionalism, and classical political liberalism" which "made it possible for him to serve as a critical mediator
in the years after the war. Yet it also endowed his work with a distinctive and
anachronistic language, epistemology, and approach in the formulation of problems." Specifically, "his writings . . . are permeated with the characteristic un-

ease and even hostility toward mass culture, politics, and society that Fritz Ringer saw as typical for the German academic 'mandarins' as a whole."[8]

While historians have often seen Meinecke as a leading spokesman for a generation of intellectuals that did little to help post-war Germany construct a modern Western political culture, I argue in this chapter that during the immediate aftermath of the war, he used his enormous prestige and moral authority to help rebuild German culture. In essays, books and public speeches, Meinecke articulated a coherent position with regard to post-war cultural reconstruction. Moreover, he provided an important foundation for historical understanding, a new political culture, and a national identity that was based on continuity with the German and broader European past.

As a member of the German professorate, Meinecke shared the social and political attitudes of the *Bildungsbürgertum*. He was by nature and education a conventional conservative. The son of Prussian civil servants from Salzwedel, he lived, as he described in his *Erlebtes*, "in the old and in the natural continuation of the old." The intellectual climate in his home had a "Christian (Pietist) and late romantic air." Meinecke rejected the religious conservatism of his family, but was greatly influenced by late-romantic pantheism and conservative nationalism. He also inclined toward political and social conservatism. Indeed, he claimed that as a young man he was "naively proud of the new empire of Kaiser Wilhelm and Bismarck and satisfied that all world history was merely a sequence of stages leading to it."[9] In the early Bismarckian state, Meinecke saw harmony and unity, and he would look back nostalgically on this period during the early years of the twentieth century.

If Meinecke shared the political and social attitudes of his class, he also accepted the traditional role of the academic intellectual in Germany. Although he did not clearly articulate his own position on the specific societal tasks of intellectuals until the late 1920s, he shared the view that the German mandarins, as the class that had the most direct access to the world of mind and spirit, were to pursue truth and promote *Bildung*. Before the mid-1890s, he also followed the apolitical tradition of the German academic community. According to this tradition, intellectuals best fulfilled their function in society when they remained above politics and the concerns of practical life. By 1895, however, Meinecke began to recognize that he could not remain "merely a man of books," but rather would have to "be a man who actively participated in life."[10]

As politics came to occupy him more during the late-1890s, Meinecke began to question many of the political assumptions that he had earlier accepted uncritically. In 1895, he rejected the conservative party and adopted a position of "political opposition." Though he continued to retain certain conservative attitudes, he was gradually moving toward the social reformism of the liberal politician Friedrich Naumann who, he believed, provided "positive and creative content to a great national party of the middle between the extremes." Naumann also provided the possibility of a creating a "true Volksgemeinschaft (national community" by "winning the workers for the cause of the national state."[11] Although Meinecke continued to modify his political ideas and commitments, it was not until World War I that he made a definitive shift toward the political left.

Initially, Meinecke's historical works conveyed the conventional conservatism that was a part of his education and upbringing. In his first major monograph, Meinecke addressed the rise of nationalism and the development of the national state in Germany. *Cosmopolitanism and the National State* was, essentially, a history of Germany's transformation from a cultural nation to a national state. All nations, Meinecke wrote, were divided into "cultural and political nations, nations that are primarily based on some jointly experienced cultural heritage and nations that are primarily based on the unifying force of a common political history and constitution." Even during the "more vegetative and dormant periods of national life, there are isolated moments when nations open their eyes, when they speak and think through their intellectual leaders, and when they express themselves in great united actions and manifestations of will." Meinecke traced nationalism back through the nineteenth century to Romantic thinkers such as Fichte, Schiller, Hegel, Schlegel and Novalis, because, as he wrote, "the examination of political ideas can never be separated from great personalities, from creative thinkers." These figures worked out their ideas on nationality within a larger universalistic and cosmopolitan matrix. Gradually, intellectuals and even men of politics—who were important for Meinecke primarily in their role as political thinkers—came to recognize that the universal and cosmopolitan ideas could best be expressed in a national state, the German state that was created by Bismarck in 1871. Whereas earlier historians held that "an epoch of cosmopolitan thinking preceded the awakening of the national idea" and that these two modes of thought were mutually exclusive, Meinecke argued that national feeling and cosmopolitanism coexisted—though often uneasily—for most of the first half of the nineteenth century.[12] Only in the second half of the nineteenth century with Leopold von Ranke and later Bismarck did national feeling reach maturity and come to predominate over cosmopolitanism; only then did political thought come into line with political realities; only then could the cultural nation of Germany be turned into the German national state.

For Meinecke, the movement away from cosmopolitanism and toward nationalism was a healthy and progressive development. The "liberation of national thinking and action from universalistic, cosmopolitan motives" he wrote "represented a great achievement of the middle-nineteenth century."[13] So, too, was the creation of the nation state of Germany. Here power (*Macht*) and culture (*Kultur*) could coexist, fused within the state framework; here the power state (*Machtstaat*) and the culture state (*Kulturstaat*) could become one. With *Cosmopolitanism*, as with his politics of the pre-World War I era, Meinecke sought to "to unite in harmony the earth of Goethe and Bismarck, and in so doing to create a new synthesis of spirit and power."[14]

In *Cosmopolitanism*, Meinecke continued to accept many of the conventional attitudes of his day. For him, as for many other German intellectuals, the national state was an object of veneration, a moral or ethical institution. He defended the necessity of military conflict as an extension of politics. Meinecke continued to admire Bismarck, who had done what the liberals of 1848 could not: he had given Germany a constitutional government, one that fused the various elements within German society and secured liberty within a strong and unified state. Furthermore, by creating the German national state he had completed the "marriage between the state and the world of the mind and spirit," a process that had begun during the Prussian reform movement, when the "German spirit descended to the state" and "secured not only its own and the state's threatened existence, but also a whole sum of all inner values, a source of energy and happiness for later generations."[15]

Cosmopolitanism and the National State also challenged some traditional conservative beliefs. In particular, Meinecke recognized that as important as Bismarck's achievement had been, it had not achieved the ideal balance of old and new forces. Instead, Bismarck had opted to preserve the old privileges of the Prussian elite. He understood that eventually the reactionary tendencies of the Prussian nobility, which did not reflect real economic and social conditions, would have to be overcome. But before World War I, he was sanguine; he believed that this clash of opposing forces could be overcome. Meinecke also remained satisfied that the culture state and the power state could continue to exist in a symbiotic relationship.

Meinecke's political ideas were thus, on the eve of World War I, a mixture of traditional conservatism and moderate reformism. According to Fritz Ringer, Meinecke belonged to the modernists among the German mandarins.[16] Politically moderate, he inclined toward Friedrich Naumann's National Liberal party. As Meinecke himself recognized in his *Erlebtes*, by 1895 he began to recognize that the old conservative party was not meeting the needs of the young German state, even if he was still sentimentally attached to it. Indeed, it was tearing Germany apart rather than uniting it. In 1912 he defended the National Liberal Party as the true conservative party in Germany. The old Conservative Party refused to recognize the realities of political life, whereas the National Liberal Party understood and accepted the need for change.[17] In particular, Meinecke, like Naumann, sought to strengthen the state by wedding the masses to it. This did not mean that he wanted full democratization. Like other German academic intellectuals—both orthodox and modernist—he was deeply skeptical of democracy. In particular, he was ambivalent about the uneducated masses and interest group politics, which tended to divide rather than unite the state.[18] What he desired, he wrote in 1912, was a "temporary Dictatorship of trust" which would reform the government. Though it was not possible to move forward without change, reform was preferable to revolution. The best possible solution would be to reform outdated cultural and political institutions so that they continued to preserve "the good and viable parts of the old tradition."[19] Always the dream was, as he later recalled, "to unite in harmony the earth of Goethe and Bismarck, and in so doing to create a new synthesis of spirit and power."[20]

World War I forced Meinecke to reevaluate and further revise his political ideas. Indeed, the war seems to have constituted a turning point for him, as evidenced by the numerous political tracts and his increasing involvement in party politics and public activity during this period. Like other German intellectuals, he initially took a conventionally patriotic line. He gave his intellectual support to the German cause and played a leading role in the so-called "cultural war" (*Kulturkrieg*) that accompanied the military conflict. For many intellectuals, as well as German authorities and publishers, the First World War was also a *Kulturkrieg* because culture was at stake. As Wolfgang Natter has shown, the heart of the culture war was "the mission of German culture to inaugurate a new age in European civilization." Hence, spiritual and intellectual resources, like industrial and agricultural resources, needed to be mobilized. Natter concludes "The First World War was a *Kulturkrieg* not only in the rhetoric of cultural superiority professed by German chauvinists, but also in the sense that the cultural sphere was an essential component that was instrumentalized for the war effort."[21]

For Meinecke, the war also provided the possibility for political and cultural renewal within Germany. The "alliance of culture and politics" that had "never been fully realized" could now be achieved and a "higher historical unity" of the "two Germanies" could emerge.[22] As Meinecke wrote in August 1914, German "culture" had been pressed into "service of the state" but in its wartime efforts the state also served "the highest good of our national culture. . . . The time of alienation between culture and politics, which so many of us perceived in the last century, is past."[23] Meinecke later admitted that even at this time, he had not fully understood the demonic qualities of nationalism and power politics.[24]

Political renewal was especially important at this moment. The solidarity of all classes that emerged at the outbreak of the war convinced Meinecke that political reform could be pushed ahead so that a true *Volksstaat* could be created. By 1917, however, he recognized that instead of uniting Germans, the war was creating more tensions and divisions. In particular, he saw the rift between the political left and right widening in Germany.[25] Meinecke began to argue that the middle class in general and the mandarin intellectuals in particular had to play a leading role in bringing about unity. Its greatest task was to "become the regulator of national life as a whole." It was to unify the elements in German society that were warring against each other. "The ideal aim" he wrote in 1917 "would be to fill all classes of the nation with that specific German middle-class way of thinking" which would "unite freedom of the individual with the order, harmony and strength of the whole and thus realize the political consequence of the ideal of life of our poets and thinkers." But this could only happen when "political dividing walls" were removed. [26] At all costs, the "social democratic workers" had to be won "for the national state" in order to head off revolution and secure Germany's future.[27]

One of the most significant changes in Meinecke's political thinking during the war was his increasing skepticism of nationalism. The hyper-nationalism that he saw expressed in the actions of the pan Germans and the annexationists' war aims struck him as both unrealistic and dangerous. What was worse, the "educated classes" had absorbed much of this "chauvinistic, pan-German mindset" and hence had abdicated their leadership role. In 1915 and again in 1917 he took a stand against the annexationists and publicly defended a war policy of moderation. He also began to advocate a negotiated peace with the Entente. These were views he shared with the chancellor Theobald von Bethmann-

Hollweg, with whom he met frequently during the last two years of the war. Although both Meinecke and Bethmann recognized by 1917 that the monarchy, as it currently existed, would have to go, both were also opposed to "pure parliamentarianism." Meinecke continued to harbor a deep-seated suspicion of the masses, whom he viewed as "politically immature" and unreliable. Meinecke had the ear not only of Bethmann but also of other prominent officials including secretary of state Richard Kühlmann. He was himself apparently even considered for the ministry of culture, though he was ultimately not chosen for the position and, in any case, did not believe himself fit to be a politician.[28]

Meinecke's changing political views were also evident in his second great historical monograph, *Die Idee der Staatsräson*, which he had begun writing during World War I. In an effort to adjust to a new political order, he reexamined the relationship between ethics and power politics. Specifically, he wanted "to understand the transformation in the essence and spirit of power politics since the Renaissance and to pursue the emergence of our modern understanding of history."[29] Meinecke, who had come to recognize during World War I that power and nationalism were, on many levels, deeply troubling, also modified his belief that the state was an ethical entity. He came to doubt, especially after 1918, that the merging of spirit and power was possible. Before the war Meinecke had believed that power was the basis of state life. Since states promoted and protected culture, power, as the basis of the state, also had an ethical quality. World War I had forced Meinecke to reconsider his position. As Georg Iggers has written, Meinecke now believed that the "recurrent problem . . . posed by the tensions between power and spirit" was "never capable of a satisfactory solution. . . . Power and ethics, nature and spirit, now appeared to Meinecke as opposing and constantly struggling forces in perennial conflict. The elemental drive for power as such lacked spiritual content."[30] Yet Meinecke remained hopeful that "reason of state" could provide a "bridge" between spirit and power. He defined reason of state as "the principle of national conduct, the state's law of motion. It tells the statesman what he must do in order to maintain the health and strength of the state." However, "from the being and becoming there emerges through understanding the ought and the must." It was the statesman, according to Meinecke, who had to provide the balance between spirit and power. In order to achieve his goal, the statesman had to "act in accordance with this understanding."[31]

While completing *Die Idee der Staatsraison*, Meinecke also lent his considerable prestige to the foundering Weimar Republic. Despite his public support, however, he was never emotionally tied to the Republic, and the weaknesses of his republicanism have been well-documented.[32] He mourned the loss of the monarchy. He was critical of the Weimar constitution, which he claimed was "not the ideal bond for a *Volksgemeinschaft* (national community)." He continued to distrust the masses and was thus deeply ambivalent about full democratization of the German state. As he wrote in his journal in September 1918, "As unavoidable as democratization was, I also see very clearly its dangers."[33] Among the worst dangers was the political divisiveness that pluralistic democracy entailed. Meinecke hungered, like others of his class, for harmony and unity. Hence, he argued for the necessity of a strong central government that would mitigate the divisive effect of party politics. In particular, he advocated an executive which did not depend on "parliamentary majorities" but was "anchored in the will of the Volk." In this way, the government might be able to head off any military or authoritarian coups from the right.[34] There was also clearly an element of elitism in Meinecke's fear of democracy. Democracy, according to Meinecke, threatened to destroy the "German cultural tradition" and *Bildung*.[35] Western-style democracy, in particular, seemed to him to be a capitulation to mediocrity and shallowness, and a repression of greater spirits.[36]

If Meinecke had his doubts about pure parliamentary democracy, however, he also recognized that a democratic republic was the best possible alternative in the immediate post-war period. His commitment to the Republic as a *Vernunftrepublikaner* was not, as Walther Hofer has pointed out, "from cheap . . . opportunism . . . but because he recognized it as an historical necessity." Bismarck's Germany had been an advancement over the old divided German states. It was "a phenomenal achievement that integrated state and nation, old and new historical forces." However, it remained an authoritarian state and hence "fell short of the last and highest possibility of national coherence. Within it was a hidden fissure that Bismarck himself widened by adopting the wrong tactic in his struggle against social democracy, by driving the masses out of the state." Bismarck had been wrong in his "appraisal and treatment of the mass forces of modern social and economic life, whose development his own creation—the Bismarckian empire—served to foster." Even Bismarck recognized that "the modern war for existence which he foresaw . . . all but automatically pressed toward democracy." It was impossible to fight a long war with the masses unless one included them in politics. According to Meinecke, this was what happened in World War I. "The modern *Volkskrieg* led necessarily to the *Volksstaat*."[37] Perhaps the masses had not yet become fully responsible members of German society, but they nevertheless needed to be wedded to the state through the mediating middle class. Once again, Meinecke exhorted the middle class and its leaders to take up the mantle of leadership.

At a special convention in 1926 in Weimar, sixty-four German university professors signed an appeal to all those of the colleagues who were prepared to work constructively for the common good "within the framework of the existing democratic republican order." The immediate goal, claimed Meinecke, was to engage the critics of the Republic in a discussion and attempt to find common ground. The "higher, ideal goal" was to "bridge the divisions in the nation brought about during World War I and the revolution, and to win the universities, whose spirit can never be indifferent to public life, for the new state." Before the war it was accepted that "scholarship and politics to be separate from each other, that research and teaching are to follow their own laws only, that they serve the life of nation and state only indirectly, through the values they create, and not in an immediate and tendentious way." Academics had believed themselves "in naïve satisfaction to be the representatives of the nation and at the same time the intellectual (*geistige*) leaders of the middle classes." They had, moreover, assumed that the "national interest" and the interests of the middle classes were one and the same. But the war had introduced "all of the disparate elements of national life." Still, Meinecke believed that "behind and underneath all of the fissures and clefts of our national life, lay a powerful, common ground." This was the common ground that the conference sought to find and build on. [38]

The crisis facing Weimar Germany was both political and cultural. Part of the problem, as Meinecke saw it, was that German professors had become too nationalistic and reactionary during World War I. Many had "forgotten all of their rational methods and allowed themselves all of the blunders of emotionalism. They showed that even a highly developed culture and intellectual training could not protect against an unexpected flood of elementary, disorderly thinking." [39] Those who betrayed their calling and fell victim to such irrationality condemned anyone who spoke against aggressive war aims and branded them defeatists. They also refused to consider any kind of political reform. For Meinecke, however, the war had proven that political reform was necessary. It had been an "iron political necessity, not ideology, not doctrinairism that led [Germany] to democracy." [40] Perhaps the Weimar democracy was not ideal, but it was the system that divided least. Hence the Weimar constitution had to "be unconditionally and decisively accepted." He called on his peers to recognize the "immanent ethical value of democracy, the recognition of human worth in each comrade, the joint responsibility of each for the whole." Speaking as much to himself as to his audience, Meinecke said that "we old monarchists were first able to become republicans of reason . . . but whoever has made the first step must now . . . make a second step and wish that the new form of the German state will grow and become firmly rooted." [41] Academic intellectuals had the responsibility of infusing "political democracy" with "intellectual aristocracy" in order to "ennoble" and "protect" it. Politics was still to be separated from scholarship. However, "we are not just scholars but also citizens and as such have the duty to pay what we owe the fatherland with our intellectual capital." [42]

If intellectuals had a public, political function to play, however, their primary role was to attend to culture, which Meinecke now defined as "breakthroughs, manifestations of the spiritual within the natural causal nexus." [43] This was because the current crisis was also, and at its very core, cultural. Of the highest cultural value for Meinecke were "religion in its purest form and art in its highest achievements." "Philosophy and scholarship" ranked just behind religion and art. Although both "contemplative and spiritual life" and "active and productive life" were important, Meinecke suggested that it was in "the spheres of religion, art, philosophy, and scholarship" that humanity could raise itself above mere "nature." Meinecke made use of the familiar mandarin distinction between culture (*Kultur*) and civilization (*Zivilisation*). Culture occurred "where man creates or seeks the good or the beautiful for itself or where he seeks truth for itself." Civilization, on the other hand, had only to do only with "utility" and "profitability" and included such areas "economics," "technology," "pleasure," "wealth," and "power."

It was not enough for intellectuals simply to contemplate and discover values. Although "productive life itself" did not "create the highest cultural values," the "first and most urgent task" was "to create cultural values in it and for it. . . . The contemplative life forms representations of life" which "should and can serve as the guiding stars for productive life in its orbit around cultural values." One of the most significant tasks of the intellectual was thus to "spiritualize and civilize the state in which he lives, even when he knows that it cannot completely succeed . . . because the state forms the most effective and most extensive communities of life and because the person who strives for perfection can only breath freely in a state that strives for perfection." As a historian of political ideas, Meinecke situated himself somewhere between the active life and the contemplative life. In the "sphere of political ideas . . . vita activa and vita contemplativa overflow into one another . . . reality and ideal blend together."[44]

As Germany moved into the 1930s and the Nazis began to make inroads, Meinecke became an open critic of Nazism. In 1930 he saw in National Socialism a variant of febrile nationalism. It had historical precedent in the nationalism that accompanied the declaration of unlimited submarine warfare in 1917. Then, as in 1930, this dangerous nationalism was a response to an "internal and external necessity of the fatherland." The most important cause of National Socialism, claimed Meinecke, was "*the Versailles peace*" and "its imagined and real material consequences."[45] He recognized, as well, that the worldwide economic depression—even without the reparations payments—was bringing the German economy to ruin. He pointed out that the political system was in disarray. Extremism on the left and the right and the "attrition of the parties of the middle" had shaken "pure parliamentarianism," and had allowed the Nazis to gain electoral success. In short, there were important reasons that Germans were now looking to the Nazis. What they wanted was a "faith healer" who promised a "quick fix" to their problems. Finally, he saw in Nazism, as in Communism, the collective desire for "power and security." Meinecke went on to point out that the bourgeoisie would only be able to "save itself and the old European culture from a new cataclysm" if it could take the "useful thoughts of extremism of right and left out of the witches cauldron" and "put them into action on a democratic basis" which meant joining with the social democratic workers in common cause.[46]

In other political writings of the late-Weimar period, Meinecke was sharply critical of the Nazis for their crude and violent tactics, for their demagoguery, and for the divisiveness they created in German society.[47] He understood, on one level, why the Nazi message was appealing to so many in Germany. The National Socialists promised to heal the wounds, to alleviate the suffering of Germans, but ultimately he saw in the Nazis a disruptive force, and hence a threat to national order. Meinecke was, of course, correct to point out that the Nazis were disruptive, but he was at this time unable to appreciate the anti-divisiveness of their political appeal. Nor did he sense the similarities between their message and his ideas. The Nazis, too, demanded a *Volksgemeinschaft* and claimed to cut across class and party lines. But Meinecke certainly understood that they posed a threat to Germany, the threat of a "revolution from above," of a "fascist dictatorship." Such a result could be avoided only if the workers and the middle class worked together in common cause.[48]

Despite Meinecke's hopeful note, he had grown more and more skeptical that a sea change could be brought about. He also doubted that the middle classes and their intellectual leaders, the German professorate, could bring about the harmony and dedication to the Republic that he deemed necessary. Moreover, he began to sense that there was a fundamental cultural crisis that lay at the root of the current political atmosphere. The alienation of power and culture that he had begun to sense in the 1920s now seemed to him almost complete.

After Hitler's assumption of power, Meinecke expected the worst but hoped for the best. As he wrote to Walter Lenel on 7 May 1933, "I try again and again to find the positive in the new order. How often is something new and fruitful born through the most painful labor." Meinecke now recognized, for the first time, "the powerful dynamic strength of the movement" which he had "previously underestimated." The Nazis had been able to achieve a great deal with regard to the "problem of unity, where all previous, weak administrations have struggled in vain." Perhaps the new regime could achieve other things as well that had not been attained during the Weimar Republic. From Meinecke's perspective, "the German people was simply not ready for parliamentary democracy, especially under the weight of the Versailles peace."[49]

In his letters to his own children, however, Meinecke was less sanguine. To his son-in-law Carl Rabl, he admitted his horror at the "lack of intellectual freedom" of the new regime. He could not "believe that a system afflicted with this festering wound can in the long run make the people better and more moral." Like other mandarins, he latched onto the cultural effects of Nazism: "The intellectual classes will be ruined first, and thus the tradition of our great German culture will be threatened." He went on to point out that the roots of the "intellectual/moral breakdown of the nation" were to be found "in the economic-social-technical form of life" that had developed over the previous century, a development that had made "true and great intellectual culture more and more difficult to maintain." He still did not deny that the Nazi regime had achieved some things, but he was particularly troubled by "their methods as a whole."[50] To his daughter Sabine Rabl he noted his "despair" about the decline of Germany's "old great culture and the intrusion of a terrible new and rootless religion," which was "mitigated only by the knowledge that such an unstable system cannot long endure."[51] He and his colleagues, with their "humanistic cultural tradition," felt "in some measure like . . . Boëthius and Symmachus at the end of the classical period."[52]

Meinecke also recognized that he was in no position to offer a legitimate political challenge to the regime. He wrote to Wilhelm Goetz that "we old ones are condemned to resignation, after we have had the good fortune our whole life to have our finger on the pulse of the times."[53] If he felt powerless to effect political change, however, he was willing to challenge the regime on professional issues. Though he had retired in 1932, Meinecke still wielded a great deal of influence in the historical profession. In 1933, he attempted to save the job of his Jewish colleague Gustav Mayer. In 1935, he publicly criticized Walter Frank for his defamatory attack on Hermann Oncken, Frank's former mentor. Frank had published this polemic, "L'Incorruptible, eine Studie über H. Oncken," in *Völkische Beobachter*, the mouthpiece for the Nazi party. Among other criticisms, Frank had claimed that Oncken, along with others of his generation, was nothing more than an epigone of the great nineteenth century historians Ranke and Treitschke. He and his generation had no understanding of the new situation and the new challenges. In "Kämpfende Wissenschaft" Meinecke defended Oncken. "The *Historische Zeitschrift*," wrote Meinecke, had always been "proud to have Oncken's name on its title page." Oncken was a "passionate and uncompromising patriot." Frank had "no idea about the actual intellectual course of events in the prewar period." In particular, he did not understand developments in the historical profession, which he saw only as a "specialized profession of epigones who have lost the living relationship to the fights and struggles of their nation and time." Meinecke recognized that the generation of Oncken—the generation to which Meinecke himself belonged—were in some measure "epigones" when they were measured against Leopold von Ranke and Heinrich von Treitschke. He himself had pointed this out in his study of Droysen. "A certain something" had been lacking in this generation, "namely the symbioses of science and politics that could no longer exist in the political atmosphere after 1871." It was also important to note that all German intellectuals after 1832, when measured against the Goethe and his contemporaries, *were* epigones. Yet the German culture associated with Oncken and his generation was not for all this "poor but rather very rich in unique, creative, and persuasive expressions of the old truth." Furthermore, "one should not believe that that fruitful symbiosis of scholarship, national life, and politics," which was achieved between 1832 and 1871 "was completely extinguished after 1871."[54]

Meinecke's defense of Oncken showed great courage, even if, as Knudsen has pointed out, he found it difficult to differentiate his own ideas from those of Frank.[55] Ultimately, it cost him his position with the *Historische Zeitschrift*. As Meinecke related to his wife, the publisher of the *HZ*, Oldenbourg, who had been trying to replace Meinecke as editor for several years, summoned him to Mittleberg to discuss the matter. The result of Meinecke's defense of Oncken was that he had to "resign immediately."[56] Meinecke had already been forced to step down as head of the *Historische Reichskommission*, which would soon be dissolved in favor of Walter Frank's *Reichsinstitut für Geschichte*. On 30 April 1935 Meinecke received notification that in a meeting of 27 April "members of the *Historische Reichskommission* have decided to dissolve the *Kommission*."[57] Not surprisingly, Meinecke was not asked to play a role in Frank's *Reichsinstitut*.

During the war, Meinecke became, as he wrote to Heinrich von Srbik, "the most private of private individuals." No longer active in the academy, and denied a role within the larger historical profession, he nevertheless went on writing and, occasionally, voicing camouflaged criticism of the Nazi regime. Even as he distanced himself from the Nazis and their domestic policy, however, Meinecke could still applaud some of the foreign policy of the Third Reich. Indeed, according to Iggers, "he faced the policy of expansion with an almost naïve optimism."[58] He celebrated the *Anschluß* with Austria as well as the rapid defeat of France. This suggests that Meinecke shared certain assumptions with the Nazis, and other conservatives in Germany, that made him closer to them than he could either admit or understand.

In 1936, Meinecke published his last major historical work, *Die Entstehung des Historismus*. In this work, he traced the development of historicism from Goethe to the present. Though he continued to be concerned with cultural integration in the state, and the struggle between the ethical and the political, *Die Entstehung* was less clearly political than his other two historical monographs. Like *Die Idee der Staatsräson*, *Die Entstehung* was born of Meinecke's attempt to adjust to changing political and social realities. His emphasis was now on the emergence of historicism within the German tradition and its validity as a way of coming to knowledge. Because he believed that the roots of the current crisis were cultural, and because political action was dangerous even in 1936, Meinecke focused on the cultural foundations and implications of historicism. Yet *Die Entstehung* did argue for the necessity of individual concerns and thus implied an implicit criticism of Nazism.[59]

Meinecke also set to work on his memoirs, which he published in 1942 and 1947. Here he developed the crisis theme in more detail. Rarely had Meinecke attempted to get at the heart of the cultural crisis. As a historian of political ideas, he tended instead to examine the political reflections of that crisis. In the more reflective venue of his memoirs, however, he could address it head on. He traced the cultural crisis to the end of the "bourgeois epoch . . . the epoch, in which the autonomous personality had been able to develop and maintain itself in fruitful tension with all suprapersonal life forces." This epoch, which had been marked by an "ever stronger incorporation of the personality into these life forces," had begun to disappear by the turn of the century and was replaced by an epoch in which "the personality" threatened to become nothing other than "mere function without independent value." In particular, he saw "vast transformations of German humanity," which were perceptible "even in the smallest segments of common life." This did not mean that German culture had not been productive in the first decades of the twentieth century. Indeed, the decade before World War I had been marked by "a heightened interest in the manifestations of spiritual culture."[60] But ultimately, the cultural crisis had continued to run its course and, by 1937, Meinecke felt that "the entire situation appears to me to be ever more hopeless."[61] He seemed to sense that Germany and Europe were headed for catastrophe, though he surely could not have imagined its eventual scope.

At war's end, Meinecke was living near Göttingen, having fled Berlin for fear of the approaching Russians. He had continued to work throughout the war on his memoirs, thinking that he would not survive the war. Meinecke recognized in 1944 that Germany's future looked dim. It was as if "prison doors" were "closing us in forever." The Germans were no longer free to choose their path. "Not free will, but force" would "compel" them to enter the "unholy doors of fate" and "experience the most horrible things that have been reserved for us." That such a fate was just Meinecke did not deny, but he could still hope that "the German spirit, threatened as never before," would be "saved" and would "raise itself again to the good spirit of the West." He believed that the "prison doors" might again "slowly reopen."[62]

After the war, Meinecke was determined to help his fellow Germans take the first steps toward cultural renewal. In offering leadership, Meinecke responded to and reacted against the tradition of mandarin leadership to which he had belonged, and also to his own earlier efforts at leadership. He continued to jettison elements of his thought that began to seem threadbare.

Because of his magnificent reputation, he had the confidence and respect of leading occupation officials and many influential Germans. Meinecke was personally acquainted with Edward Yarnell Hartshorne, the leading American occupation official in Germany and he knew the American historian Koppel Pinson, whom he had met in New York in 1933. It was Pinson who rescued Meinecke from Göttingen and took him back to his home in Berlin during the summer of 1946. Meinecke never forgot his debt, and Pinson, for his part, continued to admire the great German historian and promote his ideas in the United States. He would, as he wrote to Meinecke "always remember 9 July" when "I spared you a winter in Goettingen and gave you so many months more of joyous reunion with your family."[63]

Almost immediately, Meinecke began to receive requests to help former students and acquaintances in their dealings with the allies. These people understood how important it was to have supporters who were politically "uncompromised," and they recognized that a person of Meinecke's stature and moral reputation could help them. One of the most difficult cases was that of Wilhelm Mommsen, grandson of the famous nineteenth-century historian, Theodor Mommsen. Mommsen had been professor of history at the University of Marburg during the National Socialist era. After the war, he had been accused by fellow faculty members of being too closely associated with Nazism and had been dismissed from the university during denazification proceedings in 1945. On 8 October 1945, Mommsen wrote a moving letter to Meinecke asking for his help. He first pointed out to Meinecke that he had entered the party in 1940 "in the interest of my family." He had also, on the misleading advice of his publisher, allowed some lines in his political history of 1934 to be altered. Otherwise, he assured Meinecke, he had not been compromised during the Third Reich. He appealed to Meinecke not only on his own behalf, but also for his family. His wife, he wrote, was in poor health. If he were permanently to lose his position, it would probably be fatal for her, and would destroy not only his "scholarly profession" but also his "spiritual being."[64]

Meinecke apparently did write a letter of support to the American occupation officials, as Hartshorne noted in a letter to his wife on December 10, 1945: "Meinecke has embarrassed me considerably by writing a favorable statement on W. Mommsen whom everybody here, above all his own colleagues, have resolved to eliminate. I must seek to set him right, for I fear he is out of touch."[65] Meinecke would nevertheless continue to work on Mommsen's behalf, even if his letters sometimes indicated that he did not altogether believe Mommsen's account. Eventually, Mommsen did resume his academic career in Tübingen, thanks in no small part to Friedrich Meinecke.

Meinecke also played an important role in the fate of Fritz Fischer, who later wrote the enormously controversial *Griff nach der Weltmacht*. Fischer, who had begun his career as a *Privat Dozent* in History at the University of Berlin in 1939, had spent the remainder of the war in military service. In 1945 he was imprisoned on suspicion of war crimes and he spent the next two years going through denazification and trying to clear his name. As Fischer's letter of 5 August 1947 reveals, Meinecke, along with Edward Spranger, and the rector of Hamburg University, Wolf, had written personal letters of support for him in the summer of 1946. Fischer gained his unconditional release in March 1947 and by the time he wrote to Meinecke was teaching modern and ancient history at Hamburg University. In order to gain a permanent teaching position, however, he needed personal "testimony" from "four uncompromised individuals." He asked Meinecke specifically to confirm that his books on Ludwig Nicholvus (1938) and Bettmann-Hollweg (1939) had "defended the humanistic and Christian tradition and that I have made no concessions to the Third Reich." He also asked Meinecke to write that he had not been politically active in the Third Reich. His political involvement, he told Meinecke, consisted of his entry into the SA in 1933 as a student and his entry into the Nazi Party in 1938, "both without rank and without active participation." Meinecke complied and in 1947 Fischer was cleared to accept a permanent position at Hamburg University, where he served as professor of history until his retirement in 1973.[66] The controversy surrounding his *Griff nach der Weltmacht* helped to destroy the idea that Hitler and the Nazis had no precedent in German history.

American and German officials also asked Meinecke to play a mediating role between leading émigré intellectuals and the German public. For example, Rohwohlt Verlag in Stuttgart asked Meinecke in October 1946 to write a new forward to the book *Entstehung der deutschen Republik 1871 bis 1918* by the late émigré historian Arthur Rosenberg.[67] Meinecke seized this and other opportunities to bring the ideas of historians who had had to emigrate during the Third Reich to a new generation of Germans. In an effort to rebuild the ranks of the German historical profession, Meinecke also tried to convince leading émigré historians, including many of his own former students, to return to Germany. Among those in the United States were Hajo Holborn, Felix Gilbert, Hans Rosenberg, Hans Baron, and Hans Rothfels. In February 1945, Meinecke wrote to his "dear friend [Hajo] Holborn," who was then living and teaching in the United States: "I should like to direct a question to you, completely uninfluenced by any position [I hold] and only on my own initiative: Would you think it possible that emigrants who have already acquired American citizenship, would accept a call to a German academic position today?"[68]

Meinecke's efforts to convince leading émigré historians to return home bore little fruit. Holborn rejected Meinecke's deferential offer as Meinecke himself recognized in a letter of 1 December 1946: "That you will not return to us again in the end, but rather have decided to become an American, I now understand perfectly." In a letter to Gustav Mayer Meinecke wrote: "The emigrants have no desire to leave the U.S.A."[69] Only Hans Rothfels eventually resumed his scholarly career in Germany. Yet Meinecke's students, who became some of the most important historians of Germany in the United States, remained loyal to him and were greatly influenced by his work. Rosenberg reported to Meinecke in January 1947 that he and other former Meinecke students had met at the annual conference of the American Historical Association and remembered fondly their former mentor.[70] Before his return to Germany, Rothfels continued to introduce Meinecke's work in America. It was he who translated and saw to the publication of Meinecke's article "The Year 1848 in German History" in the 1948 edition *The Review of Politics.*[71] Another student of Meinecke's work, Helmut Kuhn, did his best to find an American publisher for *The German Catastrophe*—a task ultimately achieved by Hartshorne.[72] For his part, Meinecke continued to encourage his former students and to try to find ways to involve them in German cultural life. Indeed, he believed that they could still play an important role in the post-war period. He wrote to Holborn, "As a historian of German origin, you have the high mission to build bridges of a new understanding between our two peoples—because you now know both worlds."[73]

As Meinecke hoped, Holborn, along with Gilbert, Rothfels, and Rosenberg, all played important roles in the post-1945 transatlantic exchange and, in this way, influenced West German historians. Konrad Jarausch and Michael Geyer have recently shown that these and other émigré historians "inspired a serious study of central Europe in Anglo-American universities" and thus acted "as an external conscience for German historiography. Through their support of exchange programs for young Germans, their own guest professorships, or their publications illustrating a different intellectual style, they supported innovative dissenters and helped nurture the democratization of the West German historical guild."[74] Perhaps more importantly, they, following Meinecke's lead, inspired a break from the nationalist past.

Meinecke also played an important role in the first years of the occupation by helping to reestablish the *Historische Zeitschrift* and by reestablishing his own historical colloquium at the old University of Berlin. As one of the few German historians to avoid the taint of Nazism, Meinecke was immediately asked to take up his teaching duties again. His colloquia varied widely in their topics and usually mirrored the ideas he was developing in his publications. In the summer colloquium of 1947, for example, Meinecke compared the ideas of Ranke and Burckhardt, while simultaneously working on a theoretical piece about these two men.[75]

But Meinecke's post-war role was not limited to the historical profession. Occupation officials and influential Germans also expected him to play an active role in rebuilding German culture writ large. He began receiving written requests to contribute to the dialogue on German cultural and political reconstruction as early as 1945. Greifenverlag asked him in 1946 to contribute to the journal *Die Waage*, "a critical cultural journal," whose pages would "be stamped by a cultural-political terminology" that would help provide "certain fundamentals and clear ways for the renewal of our cultural life."[76] In 1947, Meinecke received a letter from the German Press Service asking the "Nestor of German historians" to contribute an article reviving a sense of German patriotism. The allies in general, and Lord Pakenham in particular, wanted to "awaken a sense of German patriotism" stripped of its narrow elitist and nationalist trappings and conceived within the more general framework of "European consciousness." In this way, Meinecke could help Germany prepare to rejoin the society of democratic nations. In 1948 Günther Kaufmann of UFER press requested that Meinecke write an article "directed toward the younger generation of Germans" which would help it "summon up courage" and "build a new belief" even in the wake of utter "catastrophe."[77] Specifically, Kaufmann was looking for "the most important living German personalities and Europeans, each of whom . . . because of their maturity and experience have the power and strength to help the wider masses and the disillusioned intelligent youth to their feet again."[78]

Perhaps most importantly on a practical level, Meinecke's greatest role came through his position as the first rector of the Free University of Berlin. In 1948 Meinecke left the old University of Berlin and became the first rector of the Free University of Berlin, which had been founded as an alternative in West Berlin to the old University in the Eastern Zone. The Free University was explicitly linked to the growing tensions between the Soviet Union and the Western Allies. The initiative came primarily from students of the old University who were displeased about the imposition of Leninist-Marxist ideology and the general lack of freedom. A group of students began canvassing the allies in 1948 about the possibility of founding a new free university. As Ernst Reuter wrote to General Herbert of the military government in Berlin "On 19 June 1948 a large group of Berlin professors, students, men and women of public life decided to lay the groundwork for a university in Berlin that is free from Russian influence and oppression." The immediate reasons for this decision were recent events such as "currency reform and the blockade of the city." According to Reuter, there were sufficient resources and teachers to bring such a project about. However, they recognized that "without the approval and cooperation of the three allied military governments, the work we have prepared cannot go any further."[79]

Slowly the supporters of the university gained the support of the allies and influential figures. After initially considering Karl Jaspers for the rectorship, the selection committee decided on Friedrich Meinecke. A small committee consisting of Reuter, Otto Hess and Paul Altenberg called on the aging Meinecke one day in the dark autumn of 1948 during the Blockade to ask if he would become their rector. When they promised that they would do their best to grant him his most needed wish, he asked them in all seriousness for a light bulb and for an allotment of energy to run it. Otherwise, he would be unable to read and to learn. Reuter convinced Meinecke by, among other things, offering to relieve him of day-to-day responsibilities. Edwin Redslob was named deputy rector and he assumed the day-to-day administrative responsibilities for Meinecke.[80]

Meinecke believed that despite his age—perhaps because of it—he was in a position to make a mark on the new Germany, to help usher in a new era. Indeed, in 1948 at the founding of the Free University of Berlin Meinecke spoke from his sickbed:

In the last years I have not begrudged entering into a so-called grandfatherly relationship to many aspiring young students. In the relationship between fathers
and sons, of two immediately successive generations, there is often much
struggle and opposition and mutual misunderstanding. However, grandfather
and grandchild are united through a special secret bond. That which is common
and for the most part unknown becomes more strongly perceptible in the
change of generations; the power and the blessing of the tradition gains life.[81]

In addition to his position as rector, Meinecke held a professorship in history at the new university. As he wrote to Mayor Reuter in October 1948, "I
accept the position of Professor to the Free University of Berlin with heart-felt
thanks. I am prepared to dedicate my remaining working powers to the Free
University."[82] He continued to give seminars and to meet with students on a
regular basis until 1950.[83] Thus he was able to exert a direct influence on a new
generation of German students, and his name is still associated with the Frie-
drich-Meinecke-Institut of the Free University.

Meinecke's support of the Free University was hailed as an act of great
symbolic significance in 1948. Edwin Redslob wrote to Meinecke that "all who
will teach at the university and all who are prepared to work for its aims and
ideals, greet your decision with heartfelt joy, and at the same time with the feeling of duty that such a decision lays upon us."[84] Hans Rosenberg wrote in January 1949: "that you . . . have decided to place your last powers in the service of
the Free University is for your students and admirers in America a moral act."[85]

Meinecke understood that the Free University was founded as a part of the
Cold War. He recognized in his founding speech that "Our attempt to found a
new free university is only a single point of the great battlefield of the world, in
the great battle of the spirits and the real powers." The founders of the Free University were trying to protect the rich tradition of Germany and the "entire West
. . . against deadly dangers: the idea of freedom and closely bound to it the idea
of personality. . . . These ideas of freedom and personality are, seen in a universal historical way, the roots of the idea of Europe and the Christian West."[86] By
accepting the rectorship of the Free University, Meinecke knew he was casting
his lot with the culture of the West. And although he largely eschewed direct
political involvement in the post-war period, he also believed that Germany's
political future lay with the West. In 1946 and again in 1949 he argued that
Germany would have to join with the rest of Europe in forming a "future federation. . . of the central and western European states," a "United States of Europe,
analogous to the United States of North America," which "will naturally accept
the hegemony of the victor powers." In a move which would have been unimag-
inable before World War II, Meinecke argued that such a system could only be
created if member states sacrificed "a part of their sovereignty and put aside all
quarrels that have alienated them from each other."[87]

Living in Berlin, Meinecke saw first hand the strife between the Soviets and
the Western Allies. Although he abhorred the idea of partition, he recognized as
early as 1947 that it was likely to be a reality for the foreseeable future. In 1947
he wrote to his Danish friend Aage Friis that the "uneasy and continually in-

soluble conflict of the great powers. . . . will with 95% certainty not lead to a new war, but because of the Iron Curtain will certainly lead to a continuing division of Germany."[88] As the Cold War escalated, Meinecke remained committed to keeping Germany within the western European tradition. To be sure, he understood that certain elements of the German tradition—including Prussianism and extreme nationalism—would have to be rooted out if Germany were to find its rightful place within the democratic society of nations. However, he continued to believe that Germany could make unique contributions to Western culture.

The most important cultural task for Meinecke was to think through what had happened, to explain the past and thus to purify and intensify Germany's "moral" or "inner existence."[89] In a letter to Holborn, Meinecke wrote that the challenge was to discover "the inner genesis of Nazism and the remaining tasks."[90] Like other German intellectuals, Meinecke was driven by the desire to understand how the greatest cataclysm in human history had emerged from within one of the most civilized cultures in the world, *the* quintessential *Kulturnation*. In *The German Catastrophe*, written in 1945 and published in 1946, as well as in a number of newspaper and journal articles, Meinecke addressed the question of the rise of National Socialism and the overall German catastrophe. He attempted to place the German problem within a broad context, a general European framework. To be sure, Germany had its own unique traditions and institutions that had led it into disaster. Hence it was necessary, as he pointed out in his first post-war article, that Germans "come clean with ourselves."[91] But Germany was also responding to more general trends affecting the entire West including industrialization, modernization, and the rise of mass politics.

In order to get to the heart of the problem, Meinecke looked back to the nineteenth century. The two great trends of nineteenth-century European history were nationalism and socialism. In Germany, as in Italy, the intermingling of these two trends led to "authoritarian, centralized control over state, nation, and individuals free from all checks of a parliamentary nature." This allowed the eclipse of a whole world of liberal and humanitarian ideals and it did away with individuality.[92] In Germany more particularly, these dual movements developed a peculiar character and they reacted upon each other. Nationalism, claimed Meinecke, set in earlier than socialism and this brought about a change in the German character. It bred a materialism that Goethe's generation had not experienced. As a result, a relaxation of the desire for the transcendental, higher, and eternal way of living occurred. This "new realism" took control of spiritual life. "It put an end to the way of living aimed solely at the advancement and enrichment of one's own individuality. . . and. . . directed attention more to corporate living of the masses, to the structure of society and to the nation as a whole."[93]

By the middle of the nineteenth century, the Germans attempted to fuse the heritage of the Goethe period—intellect—and that of the new mass age—force. In addition, the Germans attempted to fuse culture, state and nation. Unfortunately, from the beginning power and nationalism preponderated. With Bismarck's policy of Blood and Iron, argued Meinecke "Machiavellism [triumphed] over the principles of morality and justice in international relations. . . [that]. . . let perish the finer and higher things of culture in a striving after power and pleasure."[94] In a striking reversal of his earlier position, Meinecke now saw clearly the "demonic side of power." He was not yet willing to go to the extreme, as had Burckhardt, and argue that "power in it self" was "evil." But it was a "temptation for evil."[95]

Meinecke traced Germany's path toward militarism as far back as the Prussian kings Friedrich Wilhelm I and II. It was with Bismarck, however, that Meinecke found the recrudescence of Prussian militarism and the burgeoning of what he called "mass Machiavellism." To be sure, Meinecke recognized that mass Machiavellism had affected the entire West and had led to the surge in European imperialism in the late-nineteenth century: "Power political and Machiavellian thinking was not limited to Germany," he wrote in an article for *Der Kurier* in 1946. Although it may have been "preached more often," it was "not exercised more strongly." What was "specifically German" about this development was the way it was "openly" and "frankly" exercised and, more specifically, that it was raised from something "practical" to something "ideological."[96] Furthermore, with Bismarck Prussian militarism and mass Machiavellism came together to put Germany on a unique path—away from the general European course of development.[97] Although Meinecke had long recognized the dangerous side of Prussian militarism and Machiavellism, he had seen both as necessary for the creation of the German nation state.[98] Now he recognized that it was these two forces that had threatened "the primacy of spirit that leads us to the highest level of human existence."[99] More specifically, it was the "hardening of the national idea" that had threatened "the free humane culture that came down from the days of Goethe."[100]

The process of what Meinecke described as national disintegration continued into the era of World War I and the Weimar Republic. Meinecke argued that during the Weimar period "the decisive factor was that a large and important part of the bourgeoisie closed its mind more and more against the democratic idea—against the idea which aimed to close the rift between the bourgeoisie and the working classes and between the national and socialist movements by recognizing equality of rights for both groups and by building up a democratic form of government based on the will of the majority."[101] After this development, the bourgeoisie carried on a secret war against the masses and the Weimar Constitution. The middle classes bore guilt because they lacked mature political judgment and thus lost the gains made by the *Goethezeit* and the reform period.

German historical development in the nineteenth century, Meinecke pointed out, was not altogether unique. Instead, it was part of a larger process in the West. It was the "historical problem of a declining culture," which was Western and not just German. To Meinecke the whole process looked "like the moral degeneration of European society—of the masses as well as of the leading classes."[102] The forces of modernism—capitalism, technology, and industrialism—dissolved the traditions of the past and created the masses. As a result, it loosed the ideological passions. The universalizing aspect of modernity provided the conditions for Germany's decisions, but Meinecke insisted that the Germans *had* made fateful decisions and mistakes. Thus, Meinecke recognized both the broader universalizing tendencies of modernity *and* Germany's unique path toward the final catastrophe.

Many of the positions Meinecke took in *The German Catastrophe* mirrored those he had taken in his interwar works, when he had begun to jettison many of his old assumptions: the criticism of Prussian militarism, the Bismarckian state and the claim that the bourgeoisie had failed to offer viable leadership. Meinecke now explicitly attacked the traditions that he and others believed had helped sustain Hitler and the Third Reich—the same traditions that he had defended in many of his earlier works. The Prusso-German tradition of power politics and militarism was no longer a usable past. Indeed, Meinecke sought to distance post-war Germany from this past, from Bismarck and his hybrid successor Hitler. In later essays, Meinecke would point to the Prussianization of Germany as one of the fateful moments in German history. For example, in his essay "1848, Eine Säkularbetrachtung," he argued that the years 1819 and 1848 were decisive moments in German history. At these crucial junctures Germany might have turned away from the path toward National Socialism. Instead, a formal Prussianism developed and Germany rejected any attempt to establish liberal constitutionalism.

Meinecke saved his most stringent criticisms for Hitler, who represented the ultimate degeneration of the German spirit. The spirit of Hitler and the Nazis was "no true German spirit; it was degeneration of the German spirit based on a lack of freedom, violation and consciousness of the masses, a terrible plague," and they destroyed "everything which stood in their way." Hitler's ideology, "the ideology of *volkish* German culture was at bottom nothing other than the means to power for a fundamentally nihilistic drive, for which any ideology would have been right if it had brought power quickly."[103] But Meinecke also recognized that Hitler was in many ways the culmination of a particular tradition: "German power political thinking, whose history began with Hegel, experienced its most malicious and fateful climax in Hitler."[104]

So powerful were Hitler and the Nazis that, according to Meinecke, the German people could do little or nothing to stop the process. In a letter to Gustav Mayer, Meinecke wrote "we were chained hand and foot." He went on to add "may every foreigner who pronounces the *entire* German people to be guilty, ask himself the question, whether he would have had the courage to bring his family to martyrdom and destruction." Of course, as many critics of the time recognized, Meinecke's claim that Hitler and the Nazis bore the guilt for the German catastrophe, that they had in some ways imposed the catastrophe on the German population, was simply one way of avoiding the question of collective national responsibility. Despite this understandable tendency, however, Meinecke, in his better moments at least, did recognize that individual Germans themselves bore guilt for allowing Hitler to come to power. He wrote to Gustav Mayer: "I am one with you however in this, that a horrible process of degeneration was supported by many classes of the German people, and even unfortunately the social leading classes of the bourgeoisie."[105]

The initial response to Meinecke's book was mixed. Gerd Bucherius, editor of *Die Zeit*, wrote that *The German Catastrophe* was the "most impressive [book] I have read on the history of National Socialism. Especially meaningful for Buceris was Meinecke's argument that "National Socialism attempted to effect the union of nationalism and socialism" that had already begun to develop in the nineteenth century. He did suggest, however, that Meinecke had perhaps not paid enough attention to economic factors, which were uppermost in bringing Hitler to power.[106]

Many critics in the immediate post-war period argued that Meinecke had not gone far enough in his criticisms. For example, the future president of the Federal Republic Theodor Heuss wrote to Meinecke in January 1947, "I have gained much from reading your book, yet I must add that the criticism of the imperialistic course of the entire nineteenth century is not made clear enough for me."[107] Alfred Weber, the Heidelberg sociologist, had similar criticisms. He, too, argued that Meinecke had not been critical enough of previous German history, especially the Prussianization of Germany. In a letter to Meinecke in September 1946, Weber praised Meinecke for his "call for a revision of concepts." Yet, claimed Weber, Meinecke had not gone far enough. Weber's own work, *Von der bischerigen Geschichte*, had been much more radical in this regard. Germans had to see their history fundamentally differently and make a radical break with the past, in particular the Prussian past, "above all because we live in the completely new historical situation in which Hitler's mad acts have placed humanity. Only by rethinking German history in a more fundamental way can we lay a solid foundation." It was necessary, wrote Weber, to "condemn the dominance of the power instinct."[108]

Other critics noted Meinecke's tendency, especially in his later writings, to eschew German responsibility by recurring to concepts such as fate (*Schicksal*). In his last published essay, "Irrwege in unserer Geschichte," Meinecke had begun to move away from the position he seemed to hold in *The German Catastrophe*. He argued again that Germany had taken a number of mistaken paths beginning with the Prussia of Friedrich Wilhelm I. Yet even without Bismarck and his move toward power politics and militarism, Germany would have come to tragedy. Such was Germany's fate.[109] Meinecke received sharp criticism for this position from his former student Holborn and the British historian G.P. Gooch, who argued that he was discarding his previous critical stance in favor of a kind of fatalism unworthy of a historian of his stature. It was necessary to address the guilt question directly and assign responsibility.[110]

Karl Erdmann, who reviewed *The German Catastrophe* for the *Kölner Universitäts-Zeitung*, argued that Meinecke *had* clearly and convincingly addressed the question of German guilt. Indeed, to Erdmann "no indictment could be sharper than the one put forward by Meinecke" which "carries more weight than the loudly proclaimed condemnations because it comes from a balanced and scrutinizing determination to understand and because it ultimately comes out of a benevolent heart whose love for Germany, even in its humiliation, remains constant."[111] Heinz Holldack echoed these sentiments. He also suggested that Meinecke's greatest contribution to the discussion of the German past was his criticism of the *Bildungsbügertum*. It was of central importance that Meinecke spoke "for an the entire educated class, whose political attitude is in the widest sense conservative . . . Meinecke's judgments about the degeneration of the middle class thus have an authentic significance because they are a monologue of the best and most conscious part of this class, a class, which has been destroyed by both world wars and which will never again have the same social status." To be sure, the rise of National Socialism could be understood in other ways as well, but "Meinecke's judgment is valuable because it grows from a cautious consideration into an unconditional repudiation, and his interpretation is instructive because it makes the irrevocable end of a historical epoch understandable from the broadest perspective."[112]

Alexander Abusch, editor-in-chief of *Freies Deutschland* and a leading cultural official in the Soviet Zone of Occupation, also applauded Meinecke's criticism of the German middle classes. He pointed out, as well, that Meinecke's book, despite its weaknesses, had helped "begin a discussion that might invigorate, clarify, and guide the contemporary spiritual situation." After all, the German people, according to Abusch, needed "intellectual illumination and clarity" as much as "bread and apartments." They needed "the courage to think objectively" and the ability to look critically "at the past" because this would allow "inner renewal and make possible an improved relationship to other peoples." Yet Abusch was also sharply critical of Meinecke's book. Perhaps not surprisingly, he was most critical of Meinecke's emphasis on the political and intellectual causes of Nazism. Meinecke had not even begun to discuss the "objective economic causes" that had led to Hitler. From Abusch's point of view, "historical criticism" had to be directed at "the entire previous economic structure of the Wilhelminian-Hitlerian Germany." In order to bring about "a democratization of the German people from the ground up," the Germans would have to address the problems of "monopoly capitalism and agricultural reform" and revolutionize the "form and spirit of the previous educational system in Germany."[113]

Still other critics of the time noted the continuing criticism of popular sovereignty and democratic culture that found its way into *The German Catastrophe*.[114] Along with democracy, Meinecke had noted the "rise of the *terribles simplificateurs*," a longing for the "unattainable happiness of the masses of mankind." Meinecke even pointed to what he termed the "illusions of the Enlightenment and the French Revolution." Meinecke, his critics remarked, had retained some of his old prejudices against the masses and their effect on German society and culture. Perhaps most provocatively, he had written: "Must we not always be shocked at the precipitous fall from the heights of the Goethe era to the swamps of the Hitler period? . . . Only the general picture that leads from the culture of the few to the unculture of the masses can explain it."[115] Thus elements of elitism and even cultural pessimism continued even in Meinecke's post-war writings. It is worth remembering, however, that Meinecke shared his problematic and undifferentiated understanding of the masses and mass society with many other German intellectuals of all different ideological stripes—Theodor Adorno, Hannah Arendt, Karl Jaspers, and Martin Heidegger, to name only a few.

Unlike some of his contemporaries, Meinecke did not throw up his hands. He believed that there was hope for Germany and the West. In 1946 he wrote to Heinrich von Srbik: "May we all—despite everything—still have hope for our beloved fatherland? I gather myself again and again and say: 'Yes, yes!' Only we must free ourselves of everything that was only traditional 'form' of our ideals, and hold therefore to the immortal inner content of these ideals. German spirit, Christianity, the West, in this triad we must live, believe and hope!"[116]

For Meinecke, the answer to the present crisis lay in a return to the ideals of the *Goethezeit* through the development of Goethe societies. Germany could no longer be a great political power, but it could be a cultural force in the world. In a letter to Gustav Mayer, Meinecke wrote "the national state has completely broken down and has left us. . . only the possibility of [being] a purely cultural nation."[117] "The German spirit, we hope and believe, after it has found itself again, has still to fulfill its special and irreplaceable mission within the Western community."[118] Meinecke had begun a turn away from politics and toward culture several decades before 1945 but the turn was complete only at the end of the war. When asked in 1947 what purpose the Goethe societies might serve, Meinecke answered, "I can imagine that from these small circles a special form of social life will develop. It must develop because only then can democracy have a place in Germany." Germany had to rid itself of "all class-snobbery" because "only on the basis of mutual acceptance and respect for all circles of life will the final goal of all democratic development be realized: humanity."[119]

Even in the first years of occupation, many critics recognized that Meinecke's ideas about Goethe societies were at best naive and at worst elitist and escapist. Goethe was a man of an earlier time—a time when there was no Germany, no mass democracy, or popular culture, no German catastrophe. Josef Hofmann, who reviewed *The German Catastrophe* for *Aufbau*, doubted that these societies could ever be established on a large-scale basis and he doubted their efficacy in leading Germany into a new democratic political culture.[120] Alexander Abush argued that Meinecke's "dream of a return to the humanity of Goethe's era" was "no objective precondition for the renewal of the German people" and no plausible answer to the immediate problems of material reconstruction.[121]

To be sure, this was a conservative cultural solution to the current crisis, and the intellectual legacy Meinecke emphasized was an elitist one. Moreover, Meinecke's emphasis on Goethe and Goethe societies illustrated a fundamental lack of understanding of the post-war political challenges. He could not see that Goethe had little to offer Germany in its transition toward Western political culture. Goethe was a man of an earlier time—a time when there was no Germany, no mass democracy or popular culture, no German catastrophe. Despite Meinecke's failure to offer a viable solution to the political challenges, however, the turn toward Goethe was an important and necessary first step toward finding a usable past. As one contemporary reviewer noted, "the most remarkable aspect of the book" was that "the more than 80-year-old teacher . . . does not leave the reader hopeless but rather puts him on the path toward renewal."[122] Meinecke wanted to preserve the best values of the past and he understood that Germany needed to reconnect with some part of its past which was untainted with the stain of Nazism.

Meinecke's turn to Goethe was also a recognition that something deep within the culture had gone wrong, that Nazism's roots went deep and that answers to the current crisis had to be found at the level of cultural foundations. To be sure, economic and political adjustments were important. Yet Meinecke understood that the situation was multi-layered. Germans needed to find some solid cultural ground at bottom when everything seemed to have been devalued by Nazism. That cultural bedrock was Goethe. In Goethe and his era, Meinecke found what he took to be the best and most spiritually pure elements in the German tradition. Here one found a culture that had both "a universal human meaning and content." Post-World War II Germany would do well to emulate Goethe and his age. This would allow Germans to "win back a spiritual contact with the other Occidental countries." Thus, Meinecke was arguing that the answer to the current crisis could be found within the German tradition—before the industrial revolution, the rise of the masses and political unification.[123]

Meinecke's turn toward the culture of the *Goethezeit* in *The German Catastrophe* was mirrored by his post-war preference for the thought of Jacob Burckhardt over that of Leopold von Ranke. Meinecke's early career had been marked by a reverence for Ranke and an emphasis on the necessity of state and power. However in *Ranke und Burckhardt*, published in 1948, Meinecke noted the need for a reappraisal: "What we have experienced in the last fourteen years, presses upon us completely new aspects and problems for our own historical past."[124] Both Ranke and Burckhardt were important for understanding Germany's past. Ranke, the "objective idealist," had been an optimist who had hailed the Bismarckian state as a kind of ideal blend of the old monarchy and the drive for national sovereignty. He had pointed to an "orderly progressive development of world history." Ranke thus reflected, in many ways, the optimism of the nineteenth century, but in the light of the cataclysms of the twentieth century his optimism seemed misplaced. Meinecke surely recognized in Ranke his own earlier optimism about the course of German and world history. Burckhardt, the "subjective idealist," had recognized in his "deeply rooted pessimism" the "frailty of everything earthly." He could thus never believe in the "progressive development of world history." For Meinecke, Burckhardt not only saw "deeper and more sharply into the historical essence of his own time" but also was able to foresee what was to come more precisely and certainly. He therefore stood "nearer to our own time" than did Ranke.[125]

Meinecke also favored Burckhardt for his criticism of power in itself. Whereas Ranke had seen power and the power state as ethical, Burckhardt had recognized the demonic in them. For Ranke, states were "spiritual essences," "original creations of the human spirit," even "creations of God." In "power in itself," moreover, Ranke found "a spiritual essence, an original genius which has its own life." Only through the state was culture even possible. Burckhardt saw "power in itself" as "evil." He was especially wary of the inherent dangers of the Bismarckian power state. Burckhardt's critique, Meinecke argued, could help Germans with the "hardest and most painful task after the collapse of Bismarck's creation—investigating the internal ruptures and dangers that were hidden within it from the very beginning."[126]

Burckhardt was perhaps most important for Meinecke because of his defense of culture over power. As Meinecke pointed out in *The German Catastrophe*, the Bismarckian power state had played no small part in bringing Germany to ruin. Germany's only hope lay in reviving its culture; Burckhardt could thus help with this task. Yet Meinecke was not satisfied with Burckhardt's conception of culture. Burckhardt had defined culture as "the entire sum of those developments of spirit which occur spontaneously and make no claims to universality or absolute validity." Such a definition was too broad for Meinecke. It included not only "art, poetry, philosophy, and scholarship," but also "material works, insofar as they are created spontaneously." According to Meinecke, Burckhardt was conflating culture with civilization. Meinecke insisted on the separation of the two, as he had two decades earlier. Culture was only present where "man creates or seeks the good or the beautiful for itself or where he seeks truth for itself." Meinecke now added that "the holy, or religion in its most profound sense, belongs to highest ideal aims for which humanity strives." All attempts "to realize culture" had to be distinguished from utility and profitability, or civilization.[127]

Meinecke still believed that Burckhardt, because of his emphasis on culture over power—and his sharp differentiation between the two—could be a guide in the rubblefield of post-war Germany. Germans lived "in a rubblefield of state and nation, and everything that concerns our culture is threatened. A new way must be sought and there is much darkness along the way . . . Only one thing remains to us—our German humanity." The task that remained for Germans was to "get to know ourselves again, while we clear up the historical changes in our humanity and the web of guilt and fate in them."[128]

In particular, German historians needed to be clear about "the essence of culture." The answers to this question would be provocative and would raise questions within contemporary German readers which concerned the final and most decisive things in human life:

> Because the fate of Western culture lies in the balance and we desire to be, yea *must* be, clear about what it really concerns. . . not only the man of knowledge but also the man of action desires such clarity about the essence of what we call culture and hold for the highest common good of the West.[129]

Thinking about culture, therefore, was of the utmost importance and German intellectuals were uniquely suited to this task. They had traditionally been more inclined to think about the higher things of culture than other western Europeans and this was a role they could continue to play: "the German spirit with its contemplative inclination to radical depth has undertaken this task (thinking about culture) and is more suited to it than the Western spirit, which, out of practical instincts, prefers the comfortable concept of civilization, which encompasses everything," To be sure, they had abdicated that role during the twentieth century, but they needed to return to it. It is clear, then, that Meinecke did not regard the German intellectual tradition as fully tainted by the catastrophe. Indeed, he continued to argue that there were civilizing, humanizing tendencies within German culture—if it were reconnected with broader Western traditions.[130]

By emphasizing Germany's continuing cultural role in the post-World War II world, and by attempting to play the role of cultural leader himself, Meinecke provided the Germans a sense of hope and mission. He understood that Germans needed to feel that their culture was valuable and that it still had something left to offer the West and the world. Moreover, Meinecke offered intellectual leadership on a number of other levels in the post-war period. None of his attempts at leadership was a clear-cut success. He was not successful in attracting former exiled German scholars to return to Germany. He was too frail to serve as the real rector of the Free University and left the day-to-day work to his deputy director, Art Historian Edwin Redslob. His *The German Catastrophe*, although it was one of the few pieces of genuinely important scholarship in the immediate post-war years and a signpost for postwar Germans who were looking for moral and intellectual leadership, also had its flaws.

Meinecke's confrontation with the German past, though important, was thus not entirely satisfactory. On the one hand, he plausibly located the immediate causes of Nazism in general historical trends within late-nineteenth and early-twentieth Germany and in the decisions of a few powerful men such as Bismarck and Hitler. Moreover, he understood that Germany was responding to wider European trends. The catastrophe was understandable only within a comparative historical perspective. In particular, he rightly denounced the increasingly strident nationalism and militarism that accumulated through the nineteenth century, points many of his students would make as well. But he also convincingly pointed out that modernization and industrialization created moral and political stresses through societies everywhere. After all, fascism was a phenomenon that struck virtually all European states. Even forty percent of the German-speaking Swiss had voted before 1939 for a quasi-fascist movement, hence spawning the avowedly Pro-Helvetica Foundation to promote public awareness of the need for democratic government. There was thus something paradigmatic about the German catastrophe; it was really an intense experience of the more general Western cataclysm. Hence, Germans might serve as a seismograph for other, less sensitive, nations, registering potential dangers hidden from them. If they could draw the appropriate lessons from the German experience, other European nations could head off future problems.

It is also true, however, that Meinecke sometimes emphasized general historical trends in a way that seemed to exculpate Germany. He often also recurred to problematic categories such as fate and destiny. Even the title of *The German Catastrophe* is problematic. It seems to imply that the Nazi Seizure of Power and all the evil that accompanied it was some kind of historical accident. In addition, as his critics recognized, Meinecke tended to eschew the question of individual and national responsibility, especially during the late 1940s. Thus he was unable to provide the Germans with a conceptual framework for dealing with individual and collective guilt.

Finally, there was no place at all in his narrative for the question of the Holocaust—the prism through which all of German history has been viewed since the late 1960s. This failure strikes us with special force today, two generations later. The atrocities against the Jews and other ethnic groups were, from Meinecke's point of view, simply part and parcel of the overall catastrophe. Thus, as Iggers, Pois, Knudsen and others have noted, although Meinecke had begun the process of critically assessing Germany's immediate past, he left much undone. For all its centrality and pivotal significance, however, the Holocaust does not exhaust all the issues that needed (and still need) to be addressed about Nazism. The initial emphasis on the general causes of the catastrophe and the rise of Nazism was not just legitimate; it was crucial. Meinecke saw himself as engaged in an important work of clarification for a war-ravaged Germany. It is as if Meinecke's later critics were asking why the questions of the 1960s and beyond were not those of the 1940s and 1950s. In judging Meinecke's work solely from the perspective of the 1960s and after, these critics underrate his achievements by focusing only on what seems central to historical research now. Yet only through the initial spadework of Meinecke and others was the later, more nuanced, understanding of how the Holocaust emerged from German history possible. The work of later historians built directly on the foundations that Meinecke established.

Even when they disagreed with him or found him to be short-sighted, Germans read his works, often critically, and as a result were able to see more clearly what needed to be done. His last great piece of scholarship, warts and all, helped encourage a new German historical tradition, one which can proudly point to works by Fritz Fischer and Karl Dietrich Bracher, to name only a few. It also paved the way for the next generation of historians to focus on economic and social problems and structures. Historians such as Martin Broszat, Hans Buchheim, Helmut Krausnick, and Hans Mommsen broke with the old German historicist tradition and evaluated, instead, institutions and structures of Nazi rule. This group of historians subsequently gave way to a new emphasis on the Holocaust, one which dominates German historiography today. But Meinecke's attempt, even if it was quickly dated, was important. He addressed questions that could not be answered by focusing only on social and institutional structures or on the Holocaust. Meinecke did not pretend that his reflections, written in the immediate aftermath of the war, could be definitive. After a life dedicated to the historical craft, he knew all too well that historical understanding is never complete or final, but rather finite and provisional.

Meinecke's discussion of cultural foundations was also problematic. He understood that the Germans needed to reconnect with their own cultural traditions, that they needed to have a sense of the positive worth of their culture. Yet while his return to Goethe, and later to Burckhardt, was not insignificant, his ideas about these figures seemed backward-looking and elitist from one point of view. Despite his best efforts to help Germany make a cultural transition, Meinecke argued for a return to the values and standards of the old high culture. But the Germans of 1945 could no more return to an eighteenth-century mindset than Henry Morgenthau could return Germany to the status of a land "largely pastoral and agricultural in nature." The model of the future clearly lay with a mass democracy and a mass consumer society, much like the society that virtually all of the other Europeans were longing for after World War II. Even so, Meinecke was right to direct attention to cultural giants in Germany's past such as Goethe and Burckhardt. To be sure, it was an intellectually elitist legacy, but it formed an important part of Germany's overall intellectual heritage and needed to be emphasized at this moment. Unfortunately, Meinecke was unable to put in perspective whatever cultural icons such as Goethe and Burckhardt might offer to post-war Germany.

It is worth reemphasizing that the Friedrich Meinecke who survived Hitler and the Nazis *was* an old man. He was almost blind in the last ten years of his life. He was frequently sick and was sadly lacking in energy. He lived amidst the ruins on a sparse diet, and he had to cope with a shattered world, a world in which the self-confidence of friends and acquaintances had also been destroyed. Indeed, many of his contemporaries committed suicide in the ruins of Berlin. Yet Meinecke was important to the early period of post-war cultural reconstruction—both as a symbol of a better Germany and as a cultural critic. He helped Germans find a path of recovery by lending his name to the shaky little enterprise that was the Free University of Berlin. Without him, it would have lacked the moral stature it needed, and would surely not have had as significant an impact on West Berliners and Germans in general. His own reflections on the catastrophe helped define and shape the German memory and interpretation of it. If Meinecke was a symbol in 1971 of a tainted tradition, he was seen in 1945 as a symbol of the better Germany. Today he can indeed be seen as among the most progressive of his class, one who began the process of coming to terms with the past.

NOTES

1. Friedrich Meinecke, "Zur Selbstbesinnung," in *Münchener Zeitung*, no. 2, 16 June 1945.

2. Jonathan Knudsen, "*Friedrich Meinecke* (1862-1954)," in *Paths of Continuity: Central European Historiography from the 1930s to the 1950s*, ed. Hartmut Lehmann, and James van Horn Melton (New York: German Historical Institute and Cambridge University Press, 1994), 49.

3. Friedrich Meinecke, *Ausgewählter Briefwechsel,* ed. Ludwig Dehio and Peter Classen, vol. 6, *Werke*, Hans Herzfeld, Carl Hinrichs, Walter Hofer, Ebert Kessel, Georg Kotowski, eds. 9 vols. (Munich, Darmstadt, Stuttgart: Oldenbourg, 1957-1979), 164.

4. Knudsen, "Friedrich Meinecke," 49.

5. Immanuel Geiss, "Wie es zur 'deutschen Katastrophe' kam, Die gesammelten Werke Friedrich Meinecke's abgeschlossen," *Frankfurter Rundschau*, 13 January 1971.

6. Robert Pois, *Friedrich Meinecke and German Politics in the Twentieth Century* (Berkeley, California: University of California Press, 1972), 51, 143.

7. Georg Iggers, *The German Conception of History: The National Tradition of Historical Thought from Herder to the Present*, revised edition (New Hampshire: Wesleyan University Press, 1983, 1988), 195, 226.

8. Knudsen, "Friedrich Meinecke," 51.

9. Friedrich Meinecke, *Erlebtes, Autobiographische Schriften, Werke 8*, ed. Eberhard Kessel (Suttgart: Koehler, 1969), 46, 78, 47.

10. Ibid., 128.

11. Ibid., 124, 213, 215, 125, 212.

12. Friedrich Meinecke, *Cosmopolitanism and the National State*, trans. Robert Kimber, intro. Felix Gilbert (Princeton, New Jersey: Princeton University Press, 1970), 10, 12, 22, 21.

13. Meinecke, *Erlebtes*, 259.

14. Ibid., 318.

15. Friedrich Meinecke, *Das Zeitalter der deutschen Erhebung, 1795-1815* (Bielefeld and Lepizig: Velhagen & Slafing, 1924), 2.

16. Ringer, *Decline of the German Mandarins*, 42.

17. Friedrich Meinecke, "Die nationalliberale Partei," *Straßburger Post*, No. 553, 9 May 1912, in *Politische Schriften und Reden, Werke 2*, ed. George Kotowski (Darmstadt: Siegfried Toeche-Mittler, 1979) 55-60.

18. Friedrich Meinecke, "Sammlungspolitik und Liberalismus," *Breisgauer Zeitung*, 62, 294, in *Politische Schriften und Reden*, 40-41.

19. Friedrich Meinecke, "Der Sinn unseres Wahlkampfes," *Straßburger Post*, 12, 5 January 1912, in *Politische Schriften und Reden.*, 50-51.

20. Meinecke, *Erlebtes*, 318.

21. Wolfgang G. Natter, *Literature at War 1914-1940: Representing the "Time of Greatness" in Germany* (New Haven, Conn. and London, England: Yale University Press, 1999), 123, 205.

22. Meinecke, *Erlebtes*, 262.

23. Meinecke, "Politik und Kultur," in *Politische Schriften und Reden*, 81.

24. Meinecke, *Erlebtes*, 263.

25. Meinecke, "Die Lösung der inner Krisis," in *Politische Schriften und Reden*, 206-212. See also Meinecke, *Erlebtes*, 239.

26. Meinecke, "Das deutsche Bürgertum im Kriege," in *Politische Schriften und Reden*, 248-249.

27. Meinecke, *Erlebtes*, 274.

28. Ibid., 272, 279.

29. Friedrich Meinecke, *Die Idee der Staatsraison in der neueren Geschichte, Werke I*, ed. Walther Hofer (Munich: Oldenbourg, 1963), ix.

30. Iggers, *The German Conception*, 107-8. See also Walther Hofer, *Geschichte zwischen Philosophie und Politik* (Stuttgart: W. Kohlhammer, 1956), 73.

31. Meinecke, *Die Idee der Staatsräson*, 4-5, 1.

32. Richard Sterling, *Ethics in a World of Power: The Political Ideas of Friedrich Meinecke* (Princeton, New Jersey: Princeton University Press, 1958), 174; Waldemar Besson, "Friedrich Meinecke und die Weimarer Republik," in *Vierteljahrshefte für Zeitgeschichte*, 7 Jahrgang, 1 Heft (April 1959); Pois, *Friedrich Meinecke and German Politics*, 86-130; Peter Gay, *Weimar Culture: The Outsider as Insider* (New York: Harper & Row, 1968), 93-97.

33. Meinecke, *Erlebtes*, 308.

34. Meinecke, "Verfassung und Verwaltung der deutschen Republik," in *Politische Schriften und Reden*, 288.

35. Meinecke, "Die Reform des preußischen Wahlrechts," in *Politische Schriften und Reden*, 168.

36. Meinecke, "Der Ansturm der westlichen Demokratie," in *Die deutsche Freiheit*, 96ff.

37. Meinecke, "Das alte und das neue Deutschland," in *Politische Schriften und Reden*, 266-7.

38. Friedrich Meinecke, "Zweites Referat," in *Die Deutschen Universitäten und der heutige Staat: Referate erstattet auf der Weimarer Tagung deutscher Hochschullehrer am 23. und 24. April 1926*, ed. Wilhelm Dahl, Friedrich Meinecke, Gustav Radbruch, (Tübingen: J.C.B. Mohr, 1926), 19.

39. Ibid., 21.

40. Ibid., 24.

41. Ibid., 29.

42. Ibid., 30.

43. Friedrich Meinecke, "Kausalitäten und Werte in der Geschichte," in *Zur Theorie und Philosophie der Geschichte, Werke 4*, ed. Eberhard Kessel (Munich: Oldenbourg, 1959), 68.

44. Ibid., 85-87, 89.

45. Meinecke, "Nationalsozialismus und Bürgertum," *Kölnische Zeitung*, No. 696, 21 December 1930, in *Politische Schriften und Reden*, 441.

46. Meinecke, "Nationalsozialismus und Bürgertum," in *Politische Schriften und Reden*, 444-445.

47. Meinecke, "Von Schleicher zu Hitler," *Berliner Volkszeitung*, vol. 81, no. 89, 22 February 1933, in *Politische Schriften und Reden, 481*.

48. Meinecke, "Von Schleicher zu Hitler," 482.

49. Meinecke to Walter Lenel, 7 May 1933, in *Ausgewählter Briefwechsel*, 138.

50. Meinecke to Carl and Sabine Rabl, 20 December 1933, in *Ausgewählter Briefwechsel*, 142.

51. Meinecke to Sabine Rabl, 30 October 1935, in *Ausgewählter Briefwechsel*, 162.

52. Meinecke to Carl Rabl, 14 June 1936, in *Ausgewählter Briefwechsel*, 167.

53. Meinecke to Wilhelm Goetz, 18 September 1934, in *Ausgewählter Briefwechsel*, 146.

54. Friedrich Meinecke, *Zur Geschichte der Geschichtsschreibung, Werke 7*, ed. Eberhard Kessel (Munich: Oldenbourg, 1968), 448-449.

55. Jonathan B. Knudsen, *"Friedrich Meinecke,"* 53.

56. Meinecke to his wife, 2 July 1935, in *Ausgewählter Briefwechsel*, 156. See also Theodor Schieder "Die deutsche Geschichtswissenschaft im Spiegel der Historischen Zeitschrift," *Historische Zeitschrift*, 189 (1959), 64-7. See also Helmut Heiber, *Walter Frank und sein Reichsinstitut für Geschichte des neuen Deutschlands* (Stuttgart: Institut für Zeitgeschichte, 1966), 227-35, 278-308.

57. From Historical Reichskommission to Meinecke, 30 April 1935, *Geheimnis Preußischer Staatsarchiv Kulturbesitz* (hereafter GsA), Dahlem-Dorf, Berlin, Nachlaß Meinecke (hereafter NM), Rep. 92, No. 15, 397.

58. Iggers, *The German Conception*, 223.

59. Friedrich Meinecke, *Die Entstehung des Historismus, Werke 3*, ed. Carl Hinrichs (Munich: Oldenbourg, 1965).

60. Meinecke, *Erlebtes*, 220.

61. Meinecke to W. Goetz, 4 March 1937, in *Ausgewählter Briefwechsel*, 171.

62. Meinecke, *Erlebtes*, 319.

63. Koppel Pinson to Meinecke, 9 July 1947, NM, GsA, Rep. 92No. 36, 61.

64. Wilhelm Mommsen to Meinecke, 8 October 1945, NM, GsA, Rep. 92, No. 29, 684

65. James F. Tent, ed., *Academic Proconsul: Harvard Sociologist Edward Y. Harts-horne and the Reopening of German Universities, 1945-1946. His Personal Account* (Trier: Wissenschaftlicher Verlag, 1998), 224.

66. Fritz Fischer to Meinecke, 5 August 1947, NM, GsA, Rep. 92, No. 10, 51-52.

67. H.M. Ledig of Rohwohlt Verlag to Meinecke, 18 October 1946, GsA, NM, I Rep 92, No. 233.

68. Meinecke to Hajo Holborn, 19 March 1946, in *Ausgewählter Briefwechsel*, 247.

69. Ibid., 262, 275.

70. Hans Rosenberg to Meinecke, 5 January 1947, NM, GsA, Rep. 92, No. 39, 341.

71. Letter from Hans Rothfels to Meinecke, 24 September 1948, NM, GsA, Rep. 92, No. 40.

72. Helmut Kuhn to Meinecke, 26 October 1946, NM, GsA, Rep. 92, No. 20.

73. Meinecke to Hajo Holborn, 1 December 1946, in *Ausgewählter Briefwechsel*, 262.

74. Konrad H. Jarausch and Michael Geyer, *Shattered Past: Reconstructing German Histories* (Princeton: Princeton University Press, 2003), 46. See also Winfried Schulze, "Refugee Historians and German Academe, 1950-1970," in *An Interrupted Past*, 206-25; Fritz Stern, "The German Past in American Perspective," *Central European History* 19 (1986), 131-63.

75. Meinecke, *Ausgewählter Briefwechsel*, 276, 288.

76. Greifenverlag to Meinecke, 16 August 1946, in GsA, NM, Rep. 92, No. 13 (216).

77. Günther Kaufmann to Meinecke, 11 September 1948, NM, GsA, Rep. 92, No. 18, 61.

78. R. Reyuer to Meinecke, 8 November 1947, NM, GsA, I Rep. 92, No. 8 (117)

79. Ernst Reuter to General Herbert, July 1948, Universitätsarchiv, Freie Universität zu Berlin (hereafter UA, FUB).

80. For a detailed history of the Free University of Berlin see James Tent, *The Free University of Berlin: A Political History* (Indiana University Press: Bloomington, 1988).

81. Meinecke, *Politische Schriften und Reden*, vol. 7, 232.

82. Meinecke to Ernst Reuter, 27 October 1948, in *Ausgewählter Briefwechsel*, 296.

83. Report in *Volksblatt*, 31 October 1949.

84. Edwin Redslob, UA, FUB.

85. Hans Rosenberg to Meinecke, 15 January 1949, NM, GsA, Rep. 92.

86. Meinecke, "Die Stimme des Gewissens," in *Politische Schriften und Reden*, 490.

87. Meinecke, *The German Catastrophe*, 110; Meinecke, "Ein ernstes Wort," *Der Kurier*, 31 December 1949, in *Politische Schriften und Reden, 493*.

88. Meinecke to Aage Friis, 22 July 1947, in *Ausgewählter Briefwechsel*, 283.

89. Meinecke, *The German Catastrophe*, 115.

90. Meinecke to Hajo Holborn, 19 March 1946, in *Ausgewählter Briefwechsel*, 246.

91. Meinecke, "Zur Selbstbesinnung," *Münchener Zeitung*, No. 2, 16 June 1945, in *Politische Schriften und Reden, 485*.

92. Friedrich Meinecke, *The German Catastrophe*, trans. Sidney B. Fay (Harvard University Press: Cambridge, 1950), 6.

93. Ibid., 8-9.

94. Ibid., 13.

95. Meinecke, *Erlebtes*, 259.

96. Friedrich Meinecke, "Bismarcks zwiespältiges Erbe," *Der Kurier*, 2 October 1946, No. 195, 3.

97. Meinecke, *The German Catastrophe*, 11-21.

98. Meinecke, *Erlebtes*, 103
99. Ibid., 319.
100. Meinecke, *The German Catastrophe*, 21-2.
101. Ibid., 31.
102. Ibid., 1-2.
103. Meinecke, "Zusammenarbeit," *Allgemeine Zeitung*, 5 October 1945, in *Politische Schriften und Reden*, 487-488.
104. Friedrich Meinecke, "Bismarcks zwiespältiges Erbe," 3.
105. Meinecke to Gustav Mayer, 25 June 1946, in *Ausgewählter Briefwechsel*, 253.
106. Gerd Bucherius to Meinecke, 28 November 1946, NM, GsA, Rep. 92, No. 5, 466.
107. Meinecke to Theodor Heuss, 6 February 1947, in *Ausgewählter Briefwechesel*, 269.
108. Weber to Meinecke, in NM, GsA, Rep. 92, No. 3.
109. Meinecke, "Irrwege in unserer Geschichte," in *Der Monat*, vol. 1, 3.
110. Hajo Holborn and G.P. Gooch, "Irrwege in unserer Geschichte," in *Der Monat*, vol. 1, 5.
111. Dr. Karl Erdmann, "Die Deutsche Katastrophe," *Kölner Universitäts-Zeitung*, vol. 7 (1946).
112. Heinz Holldack, "Eine Selbstkritik des Bürgertums," *Hochlandredaktion*, December 1946, 176.
113. Alexander Abusch, "Die deutsche Katastrophe," *Kulturpolitische Monatscrhift*, 8 March 1947.
114. Meinecke, *The German Catastrophe*, 16, 78.
115. Ibid., 53.
116. Meinecke to Heinrich von Srbik, 8 May 1946, in *Ausgewählter Briefwechsel*, 249. In a letter of 1948, he wrote "the strong feeling of standing in the struggle for the free German spirit within a great spiritual community gives the remainder of my days a wonderful purpose," in *Ausgewählter Briefwechsel*, 250.
117. Meinecke to Gustav Mayer, 22 March 1946, in *Ausgewählter Briefwechsel*, 248.
118. Meinecke, *The German Catastrophe*, 119.
119. "Parteien und Demokratie: Unterhaltung mit Friedriech Meinecke, dem Altmeister unserer Historiker," *Neue Zeit*, 1 January 1947.
120. Joseph Hofmann, "Bücher zur Zeitgeschichte," *Aufbau*, 23 October 1946.
121. Abusch, "Die deutsche Katastrophe."
122. Dr. K , "Die deutsche Katastrophe: zu Friedrich Meineckes Betrachtungen und Erinnerungen," *Rheinische Post*, vol. 11, Sept. 1946.
123. Meinecke, *The German Catastrophe*, 115ff.
124. Friedrich Meinecke, *Ranke und Burckhardt* (Berlin: Akadamie Verlag, 1948), 4.
125. Ibid., 4, 9.
126. Ibid., 13.
127. Ibid., 15-16, 26.
128. Ibid., 21.
129. Ibid., 23.
130. Ibid., 26.

Chapter Two

A Prophet Without Honor: Karl Jaspers

Of all the intellectuals in Germany clamoring for positions of leadership after World War II—and there were many—Karl Jaspers was perhaps the most favorably situated. A celebrated professor of philosophy in Heidelberg before the war, Jaspers had been an opponent and victim of the Nazis during the twelve-year Third Reich. Unlike other well-known German intellectuals, including his philosophical comrade-in-arms Martin Heidegger, he had refused to compromise with the Nazi regime. Indeed, according to his former student Golo Mann, Jaspers "had not spoken or, so long as he was still allowed, published a single word that might have been interpreted as support for tyranny."[1] Moreover, Jaspers, in contradistinction to exiles such as Thomas Mann, could not be accused of abandoning his country in its hour of need: thus he was one of the few German intellectuals who could hope to use his moral authority to speak to and for Germany. Given this opportunity, Jaspers was prepared to help Germany take the first faltering steps toward cultural and political renewal. To be sure, the Germans would have to work long and hard with little hope of success in the beginning. Yet Jaspers seemed certain in 1945 that Germany would succeed in rebuilding its culture and politics on the basis of the true spirit of Germany—"the great intellectual tradition." As he wrote to his former student Hannah Arendt, "I am optimistic, provided world history does not just roll over us and destroy us. We still have young people eager to learn."[2] For a brief period between 1945 and 1948 Jaspers became the most recognized and the most important intellectual in the Western Zones of Occupation.

Assessing Jaspers' influence in post-war Germany has, however, proven difficult, in large part because of the controversy surrounding his discussion of the guilt question and his emigration to Basel in 1948. Especially after his emigration, many of Jaspers' contemporaries in Germany saw him as irrelevant to developments in the Federal Republic of Germany, even though subsequent discussion would suggest that the categories he pioneered remained appropriate and fruitful. By the 1960s and 1970s he had become the object of condescension, scorn, and neglect in Germany. Although his reputation as an intellectual has recently begun to recover, some critics have continued to find his influence dele-terious to subsequent German cultural and political history. But too often such assessments have lost sight of context, of what could reasonably be expected under the circumstances. This chapter recreates the openness and drama of the immediate post-war situation first and then evaluates Jaspers' effectiveness at meeting the short- and longer-term challenges in post-war Germany.

No one could have predicted that Jaspers would play the role of public, en-gaged intellectual. Before 1945 he had been in many ways a typical German mandarin, as he himself admitted in his autobiography. He had been engaged exclusively in "intellectual tasks," which, he believed, were distinct from and superior to contemporary political affairs. The political world, the sphere of power, was to such a one base and corrupt—at best a pale reflection of the higher world of mind or spirit.

Only gradually and in stages did Jaspers come to change his views about politics. As early as 1914 he learned from Max Weber that though culture and politics were distinct spheres, politics was an important area of human activity. Germany's task in the realm of politics was to defend and propagate "the spirit of radical liberalism, the freedom and manifoldness of personal life, the magni-tude of the Occidental tradition." Through Weber, Jaspers became convinced of the necessity for "politics on a grand scale, i.e., a politics of sure and measured judgment, of self-limitation and of reliable carrying out of pledges, a politics that is oriented toward the totality of human events and which so acts, thinks and speaks that the world turns to it in confidence." He also came to believe during this period that "real politics is possible only if the result is effectuated through the persuasion of others by discourse, pro and con, in which the education of public consciousness takes place by means of a free combat of minds." Thus while adopting Weber's ideas on the importance of politics, Jaspers added and emphasized the necessity of creating an informed and critical citizenry.[3]

Although he had adopted some Weberian political ideas after 1914, Jaspers still did not believe it was his calling to engage in political activity or even to speak or write about politics. Indeed, he accepted Weber's contention that intel-lectuals were ill-suited to provide political leadership.[4] Even as other mandarins were joining in the nationalistic frenzy during the first years of World War I, Jaspers maintained an almost Olympian detachment. During the early years of the Weimar Republic when intellectuals of all different ideological stripes had their say, he resolutely refused to enter into the practical world of politics. As Mann recalled, Jaspers "refused categorically to lower himself to the level of practical politics."[5] Though he had come to recognize that the political sphere was important, the task of the philosopher, he maintained, was to educate, to promote *Bildung* or the cultivation of the individual's character and critical fac-ulties. This meant exercising restraint in political matters. He was also con-vinced, as he told Golo Mann, that politics must not touch the university because it "would destroy the foundation on which the university rests."[6]

Jaspers viewed the university as "the community that wants nothing but the truth, unconditional and limited," and he saw Heidelberg University as the embodiment of this ideal.[7] He outlined his philosophy of education and his views about the role of the university in his first *Die Idee der Universität* (1923).[8] Here Jaspers defended the traditional German university ideal and its two central features: *Bildung* and *Wissenschaft*. As Otto Vossler and Fritz Ringer have shown, the modern understanding of *Bildung* emerged in the late eighteenth century.[9] *Bildung* was understood to be distinct from both *Erziehung* (education) and *Unterricht* (education), and aimed at the cultivation of an individual's character and critical faculties. According to Jaspers, *Bildung* was "more than knowledge" but was "related to the whole empirical existence of the individual." The chief concern of university education, which was to be separated from the concerns of the outside world, was "to form the personality in accordance with an ideal of *Bildung*, with ethical norms... Education is the inclusive, the whole."[10] The pursuit of *Wissenschaft* was also crucial to *Bildung*. By *Wissenschaft*, Jaspers did not mean the knowledge associated only with hard science. Instead, he meant a knowledge that was universal and achieved through active engagement. Passive reception of knowledge, as experienced in elementary and secondary education, led to mere dogmatism, whereas true *Wissenschaft* requires an active understanding of *how* such knowledge is gained. Pursuing *Wissenschaft* and *Bildung*—apart from the concerns of the outside world—was to be the chief aim of both students and professors.[11]

Jaspers' only "political" activity during this period came in his role at the University of Heidelberg. Trained as a psychiatrist, he had won a chair in philosophy because of his reputation as a psychologist (at the time a branch of philosophy). From early in his career he participated in university governance and committee work, and he joined a closed political discussion club at Heidelberg between 1915 and 1923.[12] During this time he had tried to formulate his own political ideas through discussion with other professors. Yet aside from helping Jaspers to refine his own ideas about politics, this academic discussion had amounted to very little in a practical political sense. Closed to all but a very few professors in Heidelberg, the discussion group had never led to any form of political action.

Only in 1931 with *Die geistige Situation der Zeit* did Jaspers discuss political issues in a public forum. In this celebrated work, which was meant to be a popular companion volume to the more important and significantly larger philosophical work, *die Philosophie*, he examined politics as a part of the "total moral-spiritual situation of our age." The greatest political problem of the modern age was whether or not the masses could be democratized and taught to think and act as responsible citizens. Ultimately, however, the political crisis was only one aspect of a larger cultural or spiritual crisis. Like members of the so-called "conservative revolution," such as the Jünger brothers and Oswald Spengler, Jaspers argued that the central problem was that technology and rationalization had overcome European society and had, in turn, created a mass society. This mass society had simply given the "illusion" of equality by encouraging conformity. Thus technology, by creating the masses, had leveled

European society. These characteristics of mass society, according to Jaspers, existed "independently of the particular ideologies or politics of individual modern industrialized nations."[13]

Though Jaspers had believed he was writing on politics, *Die geistige Situation der Zeit* offered neither a practical and understandable analysis of the contemporary political situation nor a prescription for political change. Because for Jaspers the political crisis was only one aspect of the more important cultural crisis, the solution was cultural transformation, not political readjustment. Specifically, the solution was to be found in existence philosophy, "that appealing questioning in which today man is again seeking to come to his true self." Even on this level, however, Jaspers was ambivalent about the possibility for renewal. On the one hand, he saw "possibility of destruction"; on the other, "the possibility for the first time of a truly human life; however, the definitive answer is not yet clear."[14]

Remarkably, Jaspers had seemed almost completely unaware of the disastrous political events occurring all around him in the Germany of the early 1930s. Although published only two years before Hitler came to power, *Die geistige Situation der Zeit* contained only a single short and veiled reference to National Socialism. Jaspers later admitted his political naïveté when he confessed that even after Hitler had come to power, he had dismissed the new Nazi government as an operetta: "In the beginning I deluded myself. I think back on it shamefully. I had not yet even considered the most extreme consequences, but still believed that a quick transformation of the nonsense and a revolution in government was possible. I did not want to accept the worst of it."[15] There is even some evidence that, for a short time, Jaspers saw 1933 as a moment of opportunity for the renewal of the German university system, a system that had succumbed to specialization and fragmentation and had fallen into "dissolution."[16]

All too soon it became clear to Jaspers just how serious the Nazi threat was. In 1933 the Nazis banned him from participation in the administration of the university. On 25 June 1937 he received official notification from the ministry of Culture and Education that he had been prematurely retired. After 1943 he was no longer allowed to publish.[17] Moreover, because he refused to divorce his Jewish wife, Jaspers faced not only professional ruin but also genuine physical danger. He and his wife were on the list to be shipped off to concentration camps in April 1945 and were spared only by the American occupation of Heidelberg in March.

Though Jaspers did not go to great lengths to hide his opposition to National Socialism during the twelve-year Third Reich, he also never publicly criticized the regime, as had Thomas Mann. He certainly did not, as he told American occupation authorities in 1946, fight "against National Socialism in a politically-active manner."[18] Like other German civil servants—including Jewish ones—Jaspers took the oath of loyalty to Hitler in 1934. Only one other time did he state allegiance to Hitler. In 1936, while in Zürich giving guest lectures, he was approached by an editor of the *Zürcher Zeitung* who pressed him to make public statements against Hitler and the National Socialist regime. Recognizing the danger and sensing that the man had little true understanding of his personal position, Jaspers responded "I have taken an oath to Hitler." This was, as he later recalled to Golo Mann, "the only time in my life that I appeared to acknowledge Hitler verbally."[19] With the exception of some veiled criticisms of the Nazis in his Nietzsche book of 1936 he remained silent. He admitted in his *Philosophical Autobiography* that he had "watched powerlessly, for twelve years, thoughtfully careful and cautious, heedful of the Gestapo and the Nazi authorities, determined to commit no act and to utter no word which we could not justify. Fortune was with us. I did not tempt it by any imprudence."[20]

For the remainder of the war, Jaspers, like Meinecke, entered into private retirement. He had considered emigration a number of times during the war, but because he refused to divorce his wife, this line of retreat was unavailable. Thus he retired to his home at Plöck 66, hoping for the "defeat and annihilation of Hitler-Germany: in order that the surviving Germans might be enabled to recreate their existence from their roots, anew and decently." He did not, however, sit idly by, but instead began to sow the seeds of his post-war work. For Jaspers the Third Reich "was a time of reflection."[21] In particular, he began to think about the genesis of the crisis that had led to the German catastrophe and possible avenues for regeneration. He read deeply in the Old Testament and in Indian and Chinese philosophy, and he continued to write because, as he told a young inquirer, "I enjoy writing; what I am thinking, becomes clearer in the process; and finally, in case the overthrow should occur someday, I do not wish to stand there with empty hands."[22]

Already before the end of the war Jaspers had written in his diary: "Whoever survives [the war] must decide upon a task to which he will dedicate the remainder of his life."[23] Jaspers determined to dedicate *his* life to help rebuild intellectual life in Germany. He recognized that the post-war challenges would be daunting and that they would require more than abstract philosophy, disinterested observation, and veiled criticism. If he were to help bring about change, he would have to speak clearly and to as many people as possible. As he wrote to Hannah Arendt: "Philosophy has to become concrete and practical, without forgetting its origins for a minute."[24] Here Jaspers was clearly reacting against his own earlier refusal to become involved in contemporary affairs and against the apolitical bent of the old high culture.[25] Culture, as he now understood it, was distinct from the day-to-day workings of party politics, but it had a public, political role to play.

Jaspers noted in 1945 that the situation looked hopeless: "We have lost almost everything: state, economy, certain conditions of our physical human being and worse even than this: the values and norms which bind us, the moral dignity, the united self-consciousness as a people. Yet Germany has not lost everything: We survivors are still here. We have no possessions but we are here."[26] To be sure, Jaspers understood that the Germans were dependent on the occupying powers and the scope for action that they allowed. Yet hope for a radical new beginning existed because the allies had determined that Germany should not be destroyed, but should be allowed to rebuild itself.

Jaspers recognized, as many of his more giddy contemporaries did not, that 1945 did not mark a zero hour. As he wrote in 1945, "We shall not speak jubilantly of the awakening, shall not fall again into the false belief that all will now be good and noble, and that we will become outstanding people in splendid circumstances."[27] Though renewal was both possible and necessary it could not be based on an absolute break with the past. Nor could it be based on an uncritical restoration of the pre-Nazi past. Jaspers knew that national identity—the Germans' collective sense of themselves—had been shattered and that if they were to act purposively and effectively in the future, they would have to rebuild their collective identity on a redefined relationship to the past. It was thus crucial to initiate an honest critique of the German tradition. This meant examining all elements of German history, even the high culture of which Jaspers had been an important part: that high culture which, Jaspers saw, in its elitism, in its skepticism about democracy, in its inability to withstand the challenge of National Socialism, had been indicted in the overall catastrophe. Yet at the same time it was also necessary to reconnect with the healthier traditions in German history—especially at this moment, when all of German history stood under a cloud.

Jaspers remained convinced that genuine renewal could not be based on a restoration of the old "political Germany" that had ended in disaster and that had never in any case represented "Germany as such." Since the late nineteenth century German national identity had been based on a power-political and militaristic heritage. But that nation-state had been destroyed and the national identity associated with it discredited. What was worth rescuing from the German tradition was its cultural heritage. Germany was properly understood as a cultural and spiritual entity:

> What is German is held together only by the German language and by the spiritual life which manifests itself in it, the religious and moral reality which communicates itself in it . . . What is German lives in the great spiritual realm, spiritually creating and battling. It need not call itself German, has neither German intentions nor German pride, but lives spiritually in the ideas of world-wide communication.[28]

Germany's only chance was "creative work of the mind."[29] Only when Germans understood their predicament intellectually and spiritually would there be "something durable and truly political."[30]

Naturally, there was a practical consideration to this argument. In 1945 Jaspers did not believe that Germany would or should be reconstituted as a political state any time in the foreseeable future. Thus German intellectuals, though they should be engaged in contemporary affairs and not squirreled away in ivory towers, should concentrate on helping Germany toward a moral and cultural transformation.

The new German political order, whenever that came to be, also could not be based solely upon an old set of values and morals: "Germany's political existence can no longer be grounded either morally or spiritually upon restoration tendencies, nor upon the memories of the last century and a half." Instead Jaspers argued that Germany needed to be "recreated anew from its depths in a new situation with a view to the world situation and to her co-responsibility in it."[31] Understanding this new situation included coming to terms with the historical episode that had led into catastrophe. More specifically, the Germans had to admit guilt and responsibility for the Nazi regime, World War II, and what later came to be called the Holocaust.

Although the process would need to begin with individuals, existing cultural institutions could help foster renewal. Among the most important of these institutions were the German universities. Jaspers understood that if Germany were to experience genuine and long-lasting cultural renewal, it would have to rebuild its universities—the training grounds for the best and brightest. "Today," he wrote in 1945, "when we have almost lost ourselves as a people, when in the rubble of state and economy we are not yet a people again, when, for the moment, we must be satisfied with a provisional culture, the university can contribute to the rebuilding of our self-consciousness as a people."[32]

First, however, the universities, like other cultural institutions, had to be cleansed and refurbished. This process included ridding the universities of former Nazis and destroying, root and branch, the vestiges of Nazi ideology. Thus, Jaspers explicitly recognized the right of the allies to denazify the universities. He initially wanted to exclude all professors who "either in their official or unofficial conduct have violated the dignity of their office, who have twisted the objectives, methods, or results of their scholarly discipline to please the party, who have used their influence with the party in order to injure or drive out their colleagues."[33] However, as Klaus von Beyme has recently pointed out, Jaspers could also be tolerant of those tainted with Nazism, if he saw signs of a moral "reversal."[34]

Jaspers later came to criticize the "mechanical" nature of denazification in the American Zone. He knew all too well that the business of survival during the Third Reich involved an infinite number of compromises and denials. Hence, party membership was not a sufficient criterion for determining reliability. He saw first hand that denazification often did not accomplish what it purported to. Often the small fry were punished while the bigger offenders got off. Moreover, official denazification did not allow for rehabilitation. After a few years of denazification, Jaspers, like Germans of all political persuasions, wanted to get it behind and move on to reconstruction.

Jaspers also supported the idea of reeducation, even if he did not necessarily agree with many of the attempts to implement this policy. In particular, he did not see the need for, and actively fought against, a thoroughgoing structural reform of the universities.[35] Jaspers understood that, on the one hand, it was neither possible nor desirable to go back to the system of higher education that had existed in 1933. That system had been all too easily coopted by the Nazis and lost its vaunted "position of honor" in German society.[36] On the other hand, there were many elements worth saving. Germans needed to look back to the origins of the university in the West and refashion their system of higher education based on the "idea" of the university, an idea that was supranational and not simply German. In a speech at the reopening of the medical faculty of Heidelberg University in August 1945, a speech that propelled him onto the national scene, Jaspers suggested that renewal of the university could "only occur through the work of individuals, researchers and students, in the community of their intellectual life. This community must possess the universal idea of the university."[37] Of course, Jaspers recognized that this "idea" was not yet, in 1945, "living" again in German universities. It had been nearly snuffed out during the Third Reich and breathing new life into the universities would take time, courage and enormous effort on the part of faculty members and students. The renewal of the university, he said in 1945, "can only happen through the work of individual researchers and students in the community of their intellectual life. This community must be led by the imperishable idea of the university."[38]

Jaspers fully articulated his views about the idea of the university in a new edition of *Die Idee der Universität* (*The Idea of the University*).[39] Here he drew on the traditional idea of university and his own earlier work. According to Jaspers, the university derived its authority from a supranational eternal idea—academic freedom. It served a dual function: to seek truth for its own sake without limitation and at any price and to train men and women for careers. The most basic of these functions, however, was "to discover what there is to be known and what becomes of us through knowledge." Indeed, society, he argued, had created the university as a refuge for the pursuit of knowledge (*Wissenschaft*), which emerged from the "primary and unconditional thirst for knowledge." Jaspers offered two definitions of science (*Wissenschaft*): In a narrow sense it "addressed the world of concrete, observable phenomena, discoverable by methodical, reproducible analysis." In the wider sense it meant "any clear understanding obtained through rational and conceptual means. Thinking so understood does not provide insights into matters hitherto unfamiliar, but clarifies what it is I really mean, want or believe . . . . [It] is identical with the area of lucid self-knowledge."[40]

Jaspers stressed the importance of the process of scholarly inquiry, in which one acknowledges the limits of *Wissenschaft*, but remains pledged to a "limitless criticism and self-criticism." Universities provided the institutional home for students and scholars to immerse themselves in this process. For Jaspers, this process not only served science, but also molded and formed the character of the researcher: "the scientific outlook stands for more than specific factual knowledge. It involves the transformation of our whole person in accordance with reason." Furthermore, it offers individuals a means of accessing the higher meaning of human existence. This occurs not so much in the results, but rather in the process of pursuing them: "Science (*Wissenschaft*) is not the firm ground on which I can rest. It is the road along which I travel . . ."[41]

Jaspers called for students and professors to immerse themselves in the scholarly outlook by pursuing individual projects of original research. This, the creation of new knowledge instead of the mere reproduction of existing knowledge, was the unique characteristic of universities: "Through participation in science (*Wissenschaft*), [students] will be educated in unconditional truthfulness, and through that, their humanity and their sense of justice will strengthen." Professors and students needed discipline and industry, but also, and most importantly, they needed an intellectual conscience that provided an inner moral compass. Importantly for Jaspers, "no one on the outside can judge whether or not he is proceeding correctly. [The scholar's] intellectual conscience decides for him. No outside advice can lighten the burden of his responsibility."[42]

The professor had the crucial job of awakening this sense of responsibility in his students through the Socratic method. In this process "personal responsibility is carried to its utmost and is nowhere alleviated . . . [The student] is awakened to an awareness of his own capacities, he is not compelled from without. What counts is not the accident of empirical individuality but our true self which emerges in the process of self-realization." Thus the sense of responsibility would grow automatically "through participation in *Wissenschaft*."[43] Students would "be educated in unconditional truthfulness, and through that, their humanity and their sense of justice will strengthen."[44] In essence, Jaspers was reformulating the classic position of *Bildung* through *Wissenschaft* in a way that he believed would lead to "reeducation."

Heidelberg, as the oldest and, in Jaspers' mind, most distinguished of the German universities, would need to set the standard. It would need to reexamine its own recent past and its connection to National Socialism. Jaspers wrote to American occupation officials that German academics first needed to gain a "sharper consciousness of the co-responsibility of the university for its own moral and intellectual decay" since 1933. Only when such a "definite understanding" had been achieved would it be possible to "reestablish its dignity."[45] Among the most poignant signs of what he deemed a "loss of dignity," were: an attitude of "blind trust and obedience," a lack of debate and discussion, a lack of intellectual cooperation, and the tendency to see scholarship as utilitarian rather than an end in itself.[46] More generally, Jaspers noted a lack of academic freedom, which he defined as "the obligation to teach truth in defiance of anyone outside or inside the university who wishes to curtail it."[47]

As a result of his international reputation as a philosopher and his opposition to Nazism, Jaspers had the confidence and respect of the American occupying forces in Heidelberg. He had not only the trust of the CIC (Counter Intelligence Corps) officer Thomas Emmet, but he was also greatly admired by Edward Yarnell Hartshorne, the leading reeducation official in the American Zone of Occupation. On more than one occasion Hartshorne went to Jaspers for advice in dealing with Germans. For example, when he needed a trustworthy German to attend to confidential personnel matters while he was away—one who would be acceptable to the German faculty—he approached Jaspers. When he was subsequently criticized by other German students working for the occupation authorities, Hartshorne again approached Jaspers for help.[48] Moreover, it was Hartshorne who arranged for the translation and publication of Jaspers' address of August 1945 at the opening the medical faculty of Heidelberg University.

Jaspers' unique position thus allowed him to serve as a kind of mediator between the American occupation officials and German academics. He was permitted to serve on, and take an active leadership role in, the thirteen-member "Committee for the Reconstruction of the University." Made up of unincriminated professors, this committee had as its task the "planning of the form of the future university."[49] According to Karl Heinrich Bauer, one of the members and the first post-war rector, the main purpose was to discuss "the foundations of new [university] statutes, the fundamental ideas for a reeducation of the German youth, on problems of denazification yet to come . . . and many other problems which were created by the breakdown of the Third Reich."[50] It quickly became the decision-making body until a new rector could be chosen and a new senate convened. Members of the committee included Professors of Theology Martin Dibelius and Renatus Hupfeld, Professors of Law Gustav Radbruch and Walter Jellinek, Professor of History Fritz Ernst, Professor of Classical Philology Otto Regenbogen, Pyschology *Dozent* Alexander Mitscherlich, from the medical Faculty Professors Karl H. Bauer, Ernst Engelking, and Curt Oehme, and Physics *Dozent* Wolfgang Gentner.

This committee met for the first time on 5 April at Jaspers' apartment, and then in the homes of other members during the next three months. The committee, chaired first by Dibelius and then Professor of Chemistry Karl Freudenberg, helped determine the fate not only of other academics, both in Heidelberg and elsewhere, but also of political figures. For example, Jaspers himself was instrumental in deciding the fate of his former friend, the Freiburg philosopher Martin Heidegger. In his letter to the denazification commission, Jaspers was critical of Heidegger's actions during the Third Reich and recommended that the Freiburg philosopher, although he should be allowed to research and publish, should not be permitted to resume his teaching duties.[51] Jaspers was also instrumental in the fate of Gustav Adolf Scheel, former Gauleiter in Austria whom Jaspers had come to know during Scheel's years as student Führer at Heidelberg.[52]

Among its other duties, the "Committee of Thirteen" also dealt with the basic conception and structure of the University and with writing a new constitution. Jaspers was particularly instrumental in developing the conceptual framework and constitution of the university.[53] After his conceptual work was completed the jurists Walter Jellinek and Gustav Radbruch revised the constitution into legal form. Clearly Jaspers sought to create a constitution that embodied the best aspects of the university ideal, including *Bildung* and *Wissenschaft*, as it had developed in earlier German history. At the same time, he and his coauthors sought to strengthen, as much as possible, independence from the state. As Craig Pepin has shown, full professors dominated all organs of governance, and *Dozenten* (non-tenure track professors) had little representation. Whereas the faculty senate was made up of all the full professors in the faculty, only one "non-ordinary" professor and one *Dozent* could participate.[54] Students were not represented in university governance and, indeed, had almost no ability to participate in political activity of any kind.

Almost all professors, even more traditionally democratic ones such as Gustav Radbruch, a social democrat during Weimar, rejected all student political organization.[55] Jaspers was no exception. He recognized that the university needed to be "devoted to current reality," and that knowledge could never be completely separate from current events: "Today politics, economics, history, justice are of pressing interest for everyone." He also saw that "the building up of political knowledge and thinking is an especially important task of the university." However, the university needed to maintain a "prudent distance" from political controversies. One needed only look at the politicization of the German universities during the Third Reich to understand that political parties had no place in the university. Students and professors could belong to parties, but they were not to form party groups within the university. Even in political discussion, they were always to "listen to their sharpest opponents," and to meet their opponents with objectivity in order to learn, in order to "examine themselves anew."[56]

Also embedded in the new constitution was the notion of an intellectual aristocracy. For Jaspers, it was important that this elite be drawn from all social classes. Indeed, he thought that expanding the scope of the university to include the best and brightest from every class would be one way to help "win back the aristocracy of the spirit or mind."[57] Yet Jaspers also pointed out that those who had come from the educated middle classes, though not necessarily "more talented by nature," had an insuperable advantage over others. They had "a more favorable balance of those educational opportunities which are the condition of achievement." At the same time, it was also wrong to assume "that aptitudes are equally distributed among all social classes, the only differences being those of opportunity."[58] For Jaspers, upper class children who were exposed from an early age to the cultural heritage of the past therefore had an irreversible advantage over those children without such exposure. Jaspers supported this contention by citing a questionable study that purported to show that 83.2 percent of "famous Germans" between 1700 and 1860 had come from the upper classes.[59] Although such an upbringing had to be combined with self-discipline and a sense of obligation, it remained for Jaspers an important part for the traditional determination of candidates best suited for university study.

This elitism was enshrined in the post-1945 constitution: "§ 53a. The basic precondition for academic studies at the university is humanistic preparatory education."[60] An early draft of the new university constitution also put forward in the preamble the notion of an "aristocracy of the spirit" (*geistesaristokratische Ordnung*). In the summer of 1945, Jaspers asked OSS operative Felix Gilbert "what impression the term "aristocracy" would make [on Military Government]. My [Gilbert's] answer was simple and direct: the term 'aristocracy' ought not to be used in the document."[61] Although Jaspers and his coauthors changed the wording, the revised preamble retained the basic idea: "The constitution of the university protects an order of spiritual creativity, ordered according to achievement and personality, and governed in a collegial form."[62] Clearly Jaspers, like many other German academics, was unwilling fundamentally to alter the vaunted German university system. Although understandable, this seemingly intractable stance resulted in some lost opportunities for change.[63] Ratified by the Heidelberg University Senate on 22 September 1945, the constitution was accepted by the president of Baden on 28 November and then by the military government. With the exception of a few minor changes made in 1952, the constitution remained the governing document for Heidelberg University until the 1960s.

Jaspers' post-war role at Heidelberg University was not without controversy. As one of the leading figures at the university, he became embroiled in a controversy that pitted the first post-war rector, Karl Heinrich Bauer, and the faculty senate against the CIC officer Daniel Penham. Penham, a German-Jewish émigré born Siegfried Oppenheimer, arrived in late 1945 and discovered that former Nazis were being retained as both staff and faculty employees at the university. In addition, former officers in the German army were being admitted as students without proper clearance. Part of the problem, as he wrote in his report of 23 February 1946, was that the medical and theological faculties had been opened too rapidly in September 1945 "after a very cursory preliminary screening." Hence, when he took over the task of denazification "a large number of professors who had been screened and accepted in this way were found after a more thorough investigation to be not acceptable." Penham examined not only the official questionnaires (*Fragebogen*) but also books written by the faculty members both before and during the Third Reich, and files of the University. He wrote that "the University officials are either incapable or unwilling to take the responsibility for denazifying the University even partly upon their own shoulders." Hence, he had to undertake his "task against the combined efforts of virtually every member of the University faculty and administrative personnel who out of fear expend their entire efforts in covering up for one another." The opening of the university was, in Penham's opinion, "a tremendous mistake. . . . Hardly had the last echoes of gunfire died away in the distance when with a hurry and flurry completely unjustified by the situation at the time, the doors of the medical school were thrown open last September without consideration for the fact that Heidelberg University . . . had been nazifizied to the core." Penham cited several specific cases in his report, including those of a Sasche Nokk, Gustav Fuhrmann, and Professor Kommerell. He recommended that the university be "temporarily closed" and not reopened until the entire administrative staff was "unconditionally cleared." Moreover, no teacher should be allowed to teach "until he has been finally cleared," and "no student be permitted to attend a lecture until he has received full clearance."[64]

The primary focus of Penham's attention was Bauer. He charged Bauer not only with retaining former Nazis despite knowledge of their brown past, but also of actively working against the aim of denazification. Penham was also deeply suspicious of Bauer because of several publications on racial hygiene, the most notable of which was *Rassenhygiene. Ihre biologischen Grundlagen* (1926). Penham further made a number of specific allegations against Bauer. For example, he accused Bauer of having said after the war that he would not allow Heidelberg University to be turned into a "ghetto for Jewish students." Bauer denied this and other charges. In his own defense, Bauer pointed out that he had rejected all of the central elements of Nazi racist ideology, including the idea that the Nordic race was the master race, the Nazi position on the mixture of races, its categorization of Jews, and its defense of euthanizing deformed children. He reiterated that he had never been a National Socialist, and that he himself had suffered under Nazi rule largely because of his partly Jewish wife.[65] He further addressed each of the individual cases in which he was supposed to have retained former Nazis despite clear knowledge of their past.[66]

The senate defended Bauer and the faculty against Penham's allegations. In its letter to the military government of 26 February 1946 it pointed to a "crisis of confidence in the rule of law, justice and humanity," a crisis that "affects the center of the University, the small circle of professors who, in loyal cooperation with the occupying authority, are willing to give the new University and the new time their spiritual stamp." This crisis had been brought about by Penham who demanded that university officials who had previously been "unconditionally accepted" now be reexamined. More disturbing than the further examination, were the "methods" and "procedures" that Penham employed. He had been given to frequent emotional outbursts and had bullied both students and professors. The senate reported that he had said on more than one occasion that all of the university professors were Nazis. He promised those who had been rejected by the university and the military government "if you will help me, I will help you." Of the rector he was reported to have said: "I have found Bauer's tracks; now I will find the dirt." According to the report, Penham had also more than once criticized and gone around Crum's back. Furthermore, he had made other "serious charges against the University and the members of the senate" without offering proof. For example, Penham had accused the senate of admitting eight Nazi officers into the University, but mentioned only one name and provided no evidence at all. The most dangerous result of Penham's actions, claimed the senators, was that they threatened to discredit the policies of the military government.[67]

Crum, who had allowed the Rector and senators a great deal of latitude in rebuilding the University, ultimately sided with Bauer and the faculty against Penham. Indeed, in an interview with John Elliot of the *New York Herald Tribune*, he publicly supported the Heidelberg professorate claiming that "Heidelberg is not Nazi—neither as regards its faculty nor its student body. . . . Heidelberg is the only university in the American Zone that has never seen a nationalist outbreak nor witnessed a demonstration hostile to the Americans." Furthermore he told Elliot that Penham, "because of his personality is unqualified for his present job. . . . Either Penham will make himself less obnoxious in Heidelberg in the future or we will no longer be troubled by his presence here." Penham's recommendation to close Heidelberg indefinitely was dismissed for a lack of evidence. According to Major John Steiner, chief of the education and religious affairs section at Stuttgart, the military government "found his evidence to be trivial and inconsequential. It seemed to us that it was a tempest in a teapot."[68]

The Bauer-Penham affair and the controversy surrounding the attempt to reclose Heidelberg University has been the subject of much historical debate in the last decade. Some scholars, such as Geoffrey Giles and Renato de Rosa, have been sympathetic to Bauer and the Heidelberg professorate. They have tended to accept the conclusion of the senate that Penham was psychologically unbalanced and that he was unfairly attacking Bauer and the University.[69] Other scholars, such as Anson Rabinbach and Uta Gerhardt, have been more sympathetic to Penham. They have pointed not only to Bauer's writings on racial hygiene between 1926 and 1936, but also clear cases in which he allowed former Nazis to retain their positions. Gerhardt also points out that E. Y. Hartshorne was deeply suspicious of Bauer and kept a close watch on him during his time in Heidelberg.[70]

Steven Remy has been similarly sympathetic toward Penham and critical of Bauer, Jaspers, and others at this particular moment. More generally, he claims that Heidelberg professors, most of whom were deeply complicit with the Nazi regime, fabricated a "Heidelberg myth" in the immediate post-war period which "served to absolve all but a very few of complicity with the Nazis." This myth consisted of three primary elements: first, that "before 1933 the university was a bastion of democracy and tolerance"; second, "in 1933, the new regime smashed its autonomy of self-governance and disposed of academic freedom," and "rid the university of the professors who had been supporters of democracy"; third, the majority of Heidelberg professors, despite the best efforts of the regime, resisted Nazism and "the German Spirit" in scholarship. Ultimately, this myth kept not only Heidelberg, but also German universities in general, from dealing with their brown past. In this way, it contributed to the collective amnesia so prevalent in West Germany after World War II. Jaspers, claims Remy, "reinforce[d] the Heidelberg myth," and thus, by extension, contributed to this collective amnesia.[71]

Although this debate has brought to light many details about the troubling situation in Heidelberg in 1945/6, and Remy's book, in particular, has shown how the Heidelberg professorate often limited denazification through their creation of the "Heidelberg myth," much remains unclear. For example—and most importantly for this chapter—the historical literature and existing primary documents to do little to clarify Jaspers' exact role in the Penham affair. They certainly do not substantiate Remy's claim that Jaspers helped to shape the Heidelberg myth or that he contributed to the collective amnesia of the post-war period. That Jaspers was a present and active participant in at least one confrontation between Penham and Bauer is clear. That he sided with Bauer and the senate against Penham is also clear, though he urged caution in a letter to Bauer on 2 February 1946. He suggested that before Bauer take a "radical step" he consider two possible alternatives: "one could attempt to convince Mr. Penham in a personal conversation that the charges are unfounded and should now cease." But one would have to approach him carefully "without irritation." The other possibility would have entailed going "directly to Major Crum." Jaspers apparently even included a possible letter from the senate to Crum, but he warned that such a step might well "lead to a dead end." The second alternative should be taken only "if the direct way to Mr. Penham should fail."[72]

In the event, Jaspers was one of the signatories of the senate's declaration against Penham. Yet his exact role is still ambiguous. What remains most difficult to explain is *why* Jaspers, who was at this very moment demanding that Germans accept guilt and experience a moral reversal, sided with Bauer, who was clearly allowing former Nazis to retain their positions. Perhaps the answer lies in the curious relationship between these two very different men, as well as in their common agenda in the immediate post-war period. A close reading of the correspondence between Jaspers and Bauer reveals that Jaspers, the sickly, theoretical philosopher, admired in Bauer the robust, practical physician.[73] Moreover, he considered Bauer to be a man of integrity; not once did he criticize Bauer during this crucial period. Jaspers and Bauer also shared a common agenda—the reopening of Heidelberg University. Jaspers, like Bauer, believed that denazification should be left up to the Germans themselves. It was of central importance to Jaspers that Germans assume guilt, lest it be imposed upon them. This was the first step toward radical transformation. From his perspective, Heidelberg had already been purged of the worst Nazis and, under Crum, the university had been allowed to reopen. Penham, it appeared to Jaspers, was trying to rehash what had already been settled—and in the most disagreeable of ways. This did not mean that Jaspers believed a moral reversal had been accomplished, but he did believe, at this time, that Heidelberg had made a good start.

Besides his important work at the University of Heidelberg, Jaspers contributed to the more general debate on cultural renewal in the German press. He had determined to exploit his celebrity and moral authority to reach ever-wider audiences. Whereas before the war he had written almost exclusively for other academics and the highest echelon of the *Bildungsbürgertum*, the changed circumstances of the post-war period required him to "reach the widest possible readership."[74] As he later wrote, philosophy could only "bring about results in the world today if it reaches the majority of individuals."[75] If Jaspers were to play his part in the process of cultural and political renewal, he believed he would need to convince a majority of Germans to undergo a moral transformation.

One way he attempted to reach a wider audience was through his role with the post-war cultural/political journal *Die Wandlung* (*The Transformation*). This journal, which was the brainchild of Dolf Sternberger, was to be modeled on the *Frankfurter Zeitung* of the prewar, pre-Nazi era and was to promote self-evaluation and cultural transformation. Jaspers joined Werner Krauß, Alfred Weber and Sternberger, as coeditor. He wrote early and often for the journal and used it as a forum for his own ideas on subjects such as the importance of biblical religion, the role of the university, and political freedom. Jaspers put his lasting mark on the journal with his introduction to the first edition. In his "*Geleitwort*" he stated that the journal's main task was to stimulate conversation: "We want Germans to speak, to communicate. . . . We also want to hear and make heard the voices of the world." Then, pointing to a theme he would resume in more detail after 1947, Jaspers argued that Germans had to examine "the ground of history," the thousand-year German history, Western history and finally the history of humanity. History was so significant, claimed Jaspers, because "how we remember will be significant for what we become." In short, German identity depended upon a proper understanding of history—especially the recent past.[76]

Crucial to any proper understanding of the recent past was the question of guilt and responsibility for World War II and the destruction of European Jewry. Jaspers argued that pointing to general historical causes was not enough; Germans had to admit that the Nazis could not have accomplished what they did without a willingness in all circles of German society. Though he had spoken about guilt in his August speech in Heidelberg and in his introduction to *Die Wandlung*, he first joined the public debate in October 1945, with his published response to an article by the Norwegian novelist Sigrid Undset. Undset had written an article for *Neue Zeitung* on 25 October 1945, in which he expressed pessimism about the reeducation of the German people. Even more provocative was the suggestion that Germans were collectively guilty for the atrocities committed by the Nazis.[77]

In his reply, Jaspers admitted that Undset's reaction was understandable in light of all that had transpired over the previous twelve years. Yet to condemn all Germans collectively was to think like the Nazis. He pointed out, as well, that "whoever is hopelessly condemned will never be able to respond. Insofar as he still had the will to live, he would be powerless to do anything but obey and suffer. This is not our condition. . . . The victorious powers. . . have said to us: the German people shall not be destroyed. . . . We may rebuild and further develop our own unique, good intellectual life." Granted this freedom, Jaspers continued, the Germans themselves had to undergo a fundamental change of consciousness.[78]

Jaspers sought to promote this moral change in his lectures on the intellectual situation in Germany at Heidelberg University in the winter semester of 1946, parts of which would be published later that same year as *The Question of German Guilt (Die Schuldfrage)*. He reasoned that only after Germans had been purified through "guilt consciousness" would Germany be put on a solid footing for future political and cultural development. Purification was the premise of German political liberty, "for only consciousness of guilt leads to the consciousness of solidarity and co-responsibility without which there can be no liberty." Individuals had to recognize that they were "jointly-liable for the politics of their community."[79]

Jaspers encouraged Germans to admit their responsibility for the catastrophe, to discover the roots of that catastrophe, and thus to try to understand their current situation. Above all, he saw two necessities: first, Germans had to "learn to talk with each other"; second, they had to "understand and accept one another in [their] extraordinary differences." Communication and understanding required not just reiterating opinions. It also required more than pat acceptance of responsibility and ritualistic admissions of guilt. Individuals had to "weigh, visualize and examine . . . reflect connectedly, listen to reasons, remain prepared for new insight."[80]

Jaspers argued that in order to guard against superficiality, Germans had to differentiate between the different levels of complicity. He delineated of four levels of guilt: criminal, political, moral and metaphysical. Criminal guilt was the result of "acts capable of objective proof and [violating] unequivocal laws." Jurisdiction for criminal guilt rested with the court, in particular the international tribunal of the victorious powers. Only relatively few Germans, Jaspers continued, were criminally guilty and faced legal punishment. Even fewer had to atone for "National-Socialist activities." Political guilt involved "the deeds of statesmen and the citizenry of a state" and resulted "in my having to bear the consequences of the deeds of the state whose power governs me and under whose order I live. Everybody is responsible for the way he is governed." Thus, as citizens of the German state, all Germans were politically guilty. Jurisdiction for political guilt rested with "the power and will of the victor." Metaphysical guilt, stated Jaspers, "was the lack of absolute solidarity with humanity as such." And this solidarity was violated by one's "presence at a wrong or a crime." On a metaphysical level, jurisdiction rested "with God alone."[81]

Even more important than these other three categories was the category of moral guilt. Coming to terms with moral guilt entailed admitting that each individual was morally responsible for his or her actions, "including the execution of political and military orders." Because the jurisdiction for moral guilt rested with the individual conscience, "and in communication with my friends and intimates who are lovingly concerned about my soul," each German had to examine his or her own responsibility for the German catastrophe. Everyone shared a measure of moral guilt, except "Hitler and his accomplices, that small minority of tens of thousands," who were "beyond moral guilt" because they were "incapable of repentance and change."[82]

The moral level of guilt was the one level that all Germans could work through themselves. It was on the individual moral level, moreover, that *real* change had to begin. Individuals had to recognize their guilt, come to terms with it and make radical moral change. Individual moral reversal was so crucial for Jaspers because he believed it would lead to collective transformation. As he wrote in his *Philosophical Autobiography* "the future depends upon the responsibility of the decisions and deeds of men and, in the last analysis, of each individual among the billions of men. It depends upon each individual. By his way of life, by his daily small deeds, by his great decisions, the individual testifies to himself as to what is possible. By this, his present actuality, he contributes toward the future."[83] In order for individual change to lead to collective change, however, individuals needed to be accountable to each other and the world; thus he sought to promote public discussion about the Nazi past in the university, in journals and newspapers, in public speeches, and in his books.

If Jaspers' speech at the reopening of the medical faculty had made him a national figure, this series of lectures, and the book that followed, made him the most famous—or perhaps the most notorious—intellectual in Germany. With *The Question of German Guilt*, his first attempt since *Die geistige Situation der Zeit* to reach a mass audience, Jaspers had become the moral voice of the immediate post-war period. It was in this role that he felt an increasing burden during the next few years.

The initial response to Jaspers' theses on guilt was mixed. Dolf Sternberger reported that during his first post-war lecture at Heidelberg University in August 1945, "every corner of the Aula (auditorium) was full, not the smallest disturbance was to be heard, the purity and openness of the speech created incomparable authority."[84] Alexander Mitscherlich wrote privately that Jaspers' first lecture on the spiritual situation in Germany had "so enraptured" him that he had been unable to sleep: "That which I have expected of the University and of you has now begun to be fulfilled."[85] In February 1946, however, Daniel Penham reported that students attending his lectures on the spiritual regeneration of Germany "started laughing and scraping their feet on the floor at the mention of democracy, in connection [with] the spiritual situation of Germany."[86] Jaspers himself lamented to Hannah Arendt that there was a general lack of trust among his audiences and that he was being attacked in private both by the Communists, who called him "a forward guard of National Socialism" and former Nazis who called him "a traitor to my country."[87]

Despite these attacks Jaspers was convinced that his prescription for moral and political renewal was correct. He realized that he had struck a raw nerve in 1945/6, that he had touched on a complex of emotional issues which the Germans preferred not to deal with consciously. But he could still believe, in his better moments, that Germans would eventually respond appropriately to the guilt question. There were some encouraging signs after the publication of *The Question of German Guilt*. For example, a reviewer in the *Badische Zeitung* applauded Jaspers' efforts to provoke private self-examination and public discussion of the guilt question. According to this reviewer, Jaspers "discussed the German question" with "careful consideration of the arguments and counterarguments." He found Jaspers' contention that all Germans were guilty on some level convincing and argued that anyone "who is prepared for self-examination will have to agree with him." Moreover, Jaspers was right to claim say that "consciousness of collective guilt" would lead to the "renewal of humanity." Especially important was Jaspers' rejection of "every kind of loud confession of guilt" which came either of 'self-pity" or "pride."[88] Others reviewers were more critical. Kurt Stavenhagen, for example, acknowledged the importance of moral renewal, but argued that the greatest task was rebuilding the "political and economic apparatus."[89]

Jaspers also received many private letters in response to his book. Many were positive and illustrated that Jaspers' work was resonating with individual Germans. Constance von Gossmann wrote that when she read the book it was "as if our prayer that this confused people receive an important teacher and advisor had been fulfilled."[90] Dr. Fritz Rahn, a secondary school teacher from Würtemberg, wrote that Jaspers had given "clear and liberating expression" to "painful thoughts and feelings." He was certain that Jaspers had "spoken the heart of many Germans, above all those who, with their entire being and soul, feel responsible for what has happened." Rahn went on to challenge several of Jaspers' points, including the claim that the political future of the Germany people depended upon whether or not they recognized and came to terms with their guilt.[91] Martin Dibelius, a theologian and colleague of Jaspers at Heidelberg who was at the time writing his own book on the guilt question, recognized that the "most provocative and important" section in the book was the section that dealt with "moral guilt." It was especially important that Jaspers had rejected the "false excuses" or "evasions" of guilt, because this helped to establish the "integrity" that was so crucial to Jaspers' own philosophy.[92]

A far larger number of private critics, however, attacked Jaspers on specific points or condemned his work altogether. Heinz Finke, who admired Jaspers' book, nevertheless saw a number of weaknesses. In particular, he challenged

Jaspers' theses on moral guilt. "Guilt consciousness" was not an "unchangeable condition, which once achieved or established, could then become both the foundation for a complete understanding and the impetus for transformation." Inner transformation could not be accomplished "simply by admitting and establishing guilt." Dr. Manfred Schmid argued that Jaspers had been overly harsh in condemning Germans. The German catastrophe was not unique. Indeed, the terror of the Bolsheviks was equal to that of the Nazis, and this called into question even the legal foundation of the Nuremberg trials.[93] Franz-Josepf Krautheuser challenged Jaspers' moral condemnation of Germans for not "doing what they knew they could have done" to save their Jewish neighbors and friends. He pointed out that neither Germans nor the allies were doing anything to "stop the atrocities" happening in the Russian Zone of Occupation. Hence, Krautheuser could see "no distinction" between the guilt of Germans and non-Germans.[94]

Though clearly stung by the public and private criticism, Jaspers often left these letters unanswered. At least on one occasion, however, he felt compelled to respond. He explained to Willy Boepple that he was speaking only as an individual German and not as a "spokesman for the German spirit." He was not the head of a state or a church and therefore had no more or less right to speak on such matters than any other German. Moreover, his speeches about guilt were not political acts, but rather a "consideration" aimed at "purifying the German soul" and provoking discussion. Finally, his statement "that we live is our guilt," had not been an "accusation" but "an expression of metaphysical acknowledgment before God."[95]

It was not the acrimony of the first few months, but the apathy with which the majority of Germans responded to the guilt question—especially after 1946—that most disturbed Jaspers. He later wrote to Heidegger that few Germans had read his "little book" and even fewer had been open to its basic premises.[96] Though Jaspers recognized that the indifference was due, at least in part, to the material and psychological circumstances of the immediate post-war period, he was also beginning to sense a fundamental unwillingness among his countrymen to undertake the necessary reexamination. If individual men and women refused to examine their own responsibility for the Nazi regime, Germany would never experience cultural and political regeneration. He sensed long before most others the dangers of refusing to come to terms with the past in an open and honest way. What he probably did not fully understand at this point was that the emerging Cold War was gradually creating an atmosphere in which Germans were not only allowed, but also often encouraged, to repress memories of the brown past.

Despite his disappointment over the German response to *The Question of German Guilt*, Jaspers enjoyed enormous prestige abroad as the representative of the best that German culture had to offer. In 1946 he was invited to become the first German representative to the *Rencontres International*, a gathering of the most important intellectuals in Europe: Albert Camus, Georg Lukacs, Karl Barth, and Julien Benda, among others. The general subject of the conference was to be "The European Mind." As its organizers wrote to Jaspers: "at a time when Europe is uncertain of what her future will be, it appears to us desirable in more than one respect that she should take cognizance—leaving out all political aspects of the problem—of what, in the past, has constituted her spiritual reason of existence, and what, in future, will be her mission in a world which is at present undergoing a complete metamorphosis."[97] For the first time since the end of the war, Jaspers was able to speak about issues that were not solely directed toward the German situation.

Jaspers' theme was Europe's altered role in the world after 1945. In the first half of his speech he defined what he took to be "European," and in the second he considered what he believed had to be done in order to achieve European unity in the wake of the catastrophe. Like Germany, Europe was no longer and would never again be the dominant political power it had once been. Thus, the political world, though it could not be left behind, had to be "transcended." Political life could provide the conditions under which human life could flourish, but in the end it was "subaltern" and had to recognize its limits. Political action, argued Jaspers, was powerless to achieve lasting results: "it is illusory and dangerous without the personal responsibility of everyone."[98]

Jaspers pointed out that Europe, before 1914, had seemed to possess a kind of political and cultural unity and security, especially when compared with to the rubblefield of 1945. However, even the unity and security of pre-World War I had been illusory. Marx, Nietzsche, and Kierkegaard had all illustrated that "European unity was a weak product of the culture of the upper classes." In 1946, after two long and exhausting world wars, Europeans had lost all sense of unity and direction. All that had seemed to hold Europe together was now gone:

> We have no more confidence in humanism but we love it and we wish to do everything to preserve it. We have no more confidence in modern civilization, in science and technique. But we grasp its significance for world history, we do not wish to give it up, but with all our strength to develop it and give it a significant form. We have no more confidence in the society of Germano-Latin nations in their political balance of power. But we wish to save the idea of a unity of independent free European nations. We have no more unconditional confidence in Christian churches. But we hold fast to them as being the most precious vessels of irreplaceable tradition. Humanism, civilization, political balance of power, churches, all these mighty things seem to have become the foreground. They cannot be relied on. They are indispensable to us; but not enough. The culture of humanism is useless as a living power today.[99]

In 1946, the challenge was to "go further back in our historical origins, to where all those now weak powers once drew their strength." Europeans had to leave "behind habits and conventional feelings" and "penetrate the source and goal of our real life." They needed to reconnect to three concepts that had built "the characteristic structure of Europe—freedom, history, science." Of these three, freedom was clearly the most important concept because it was the source of the other two. Freedom, according to Jaspers, was "the conquest of arbitrariness . . . . The claim of freedom means that we act not from arbitrariness, or blind obedience, or outward compulsion, but from our own certainty and insight . . . . Freedom, won by insight, demands that mere opinion be overcome." Moreover, freedom could be "realized only in community. I can only be free to the extent that others are free." Thus "European" was first "the depth of human communication between independent individuals, and second, conscious labor for the freedom of public conditions by means of the forms which shape the will in community."[100]

For Jaspers, however, the answer to the current crisis lay not just in the European tradition, but also in the broader history of humanity. Adumbrating a the position he would take in 1949 in *The Origins and Goal of History*, Jaspers argued that Europeans had to look back to the "Axial Period," the era between 800-200 BC, the first age of fundamental cultural transformation, when the three great civilizations of the world had arisen: India, China, and Europe. During this period, the fundamental questions and concepts which had dominated world history ever since had arisen. It was during the Axial period, for example, that each culture had begun to understand "how brittle man is" and yet simultaneously had created "images and thoughts whereby he keeps on living." Here Europeans, facing a new axial period, would find the cultural bedrock, a useable past on which to build a foundation for the future.[101] Most importantly, Europeans had to recognize their community with the rest of the world.

Jaspers concluded the speech with a section on "world order." He pointed out that the idea of a common humanity had developed in Europe out of Christianity. Although the earlier manifestation of this idea was a desire for expansion and world domination, Jaspers believed that he saw in 1946 a change toward "a desire to understand the other and enter into communication with him in universal openness. This thought makes possible the liberation of the world." Europe, though it was now relatively weak as a world political power, could nevertheless lead the way toward a new world order by championing freedom and the rule of international law.[102]

If Jaspers' attention began to shift sometime in 1946 toward the ancient human past, it was driven by his concern with the overall cultural crisis and his hope for radical renewal. This speech was highly significant because it contained almost all of the ideas and concepts which Jaspers had been evolving in the German context and, in embryonic form, the ideas he would develop more fully in his subsequent post-war works. Europe—and Germany was a key part of Europe—had reached a critical stage in history, a stage that was decisive not only for the West, but also for the world. Thus there was a need for a new world order. First, however, individual men and women had to understand the past and the current situation.

Meanwhile, at home in Germany Jaspers continued to lead by example. He taught philosophy seminars, gave public lectures, and published essays and books on important issues such as political freedom. For example, in an essay of 1946 he argued that Germans had to understand and embrace political freedom. Like Mann, Jaspers argued that Germans had lacked a tradition of political freedom. If Germany were ever to have a political future, it would have to look to the Western notion of political freedom.

In reward for all his service to German intellectual and political life, Jaspers received the Goethe Prize of 1947, a highly prestigious award previously given

in the post-war period to Hermann Hesse and later to Thomas Mann. Mayor
Kolb of Frankfurt wrote to Jaspers on 19 July 1947 that he had "the high honor
to communicate the decision of the Kuratorium that you have been chosen as the
recipient of the Goethe prize for 1947." Jaspers considered the Goethe prize a
"great honor" and saw it as a public recognition of his efforts to rebuilt German
culture.[103]

Jaspers used his acceptance speech as an opportunity to add to the ongoing
discussion about Germany's past. In particular, his speech dealt with Germany's
most important cultural icon: Goethe. Since 1945 hundreds of articles and books
had been written about Goethe and his importance to the contemporary German
situation. Here was one of the few great figures in German history who was untainted with the stain of Nazism and who could therefore be salvaged from the
rubble. This trend intensified in late 1948 as the Germans anticipated the two
hundredth anniversary of his birth. Jaspers, who had already warned against
repressing the recent past, now warned against mythologizing figures in the distant German past. That Goethe helped Germans understand themselves as Germans and as human beings Jaspers did not deny. Yet he also pointed out that it
was difficult to apply Goethe to the present situation. After all, Jaspers cau-
tioned, "Goethe's world is past. . . . We may love him with his world and move
in it only if we do not forget for a moment that it is not our world." The challenge, according to Jaspers, was "to receive Goethe's world by translating his
truth into our world." Though Goethe was an important part of the overall German heritage, he could not guide Germans in "a world which is ours and which
he did not know." Instead, he, like other great intellectual lights of past, could
serve as a "signpost" for Germans.[104]

Jaspers followed his Goethe speech with an essay on the conditions and
possibilities of a new humanism. There had been a great deal of discussion in
Germany and the rest of Europe about the restoration of a humanist culture and
tradition. As we have seen, Meinecke had argued for a new humanism based on
the best aspects of the *Goethezeit*. Mann, too, attempted to outline a new "religious humanism" modeled on the Western tradition. Even Martin Heidegger had
written a "Letter on Humanism," in which he took a decidedly anti-humanist
tack. Indeed, he denied that the term or the project should be maintained.[105] As
Rabinbach has shown, the "Letter" was really both "a philosophical meditation
on the hubris of subjectivity in the blinding light of Being," and "a careful re-
formulation and restructuring of a narrative on the event which Heidegger is
most profoundly concerned: the collapse of Germany, whose chief victim Heidegger considered to be himself."[106]

Jaspers concluded that there was a great deal of confusion about the applica-
tion of humanism to the contemporary German and European situation: "What
we call humanism has widely ramified meanings. It denotes an educational ideal
involving the reception of classical traditions, also the restoration of present man
from the source, and finally the human recognition of human dignity in every
individual." On the one hand, it was evident that any future humanism could
simply model itself on classical humanism. Like the *Goethezeit*, the classical age
of humanism was gone forever. On the other hand, it was neither possible nor

desirable for Europeans—Germans included—to cut themselves off from their history, to make a clean break with the past: "Humanism has a most venerable tradition. Without it, Dante, Michelangelo, Shakespeare, Goethe are unthinkable; its soul produced Hölderlin, Kierkegaard, and Nietzsche; it was spiritually essential to its most radical enemies such as Karl Marx. How could we deny its name." However, in the post-war period

> pro-humanist propaganda is frequently misleading . . . . If we set up Roman humanism, the compound of late Hellenism with strong Roman morality, as a model for humanism in general, it becomes narrow . . . If we regard familiarity with antiquity, knowledge of its languages, and mastery of philological methods as the sole elements of humanism, it becomes arrogant, inhumane, and estimable only for its philological achievements. If humanism is limited to the conservation of culture, if life of the spirit is identified with the traditional *topoi*, many an outrage may become justifiable by instances taken from the humanist tradition.[107]

For Jaspers, the requisites of a future humanism were "the broadest view of human possibilities, penetration of the technological world, a political stand for public freedom of the spirit, a will to preserve tradition, work on the common foundations of knowledge, satisfaction of mass needs, steadfastness in uncertainty." Moreover, the coming humanism would have to be "based on the Western reception of Chinese and Hindu foundations of humanity, and growing in the diversity of its historic phenomena in a common humanism of all men on earth who are their better selves because they know each other."[108]

Although Jaspers was hopeful about Europe's future, and he sometimes even believed he saw a new critical consciousness beginning to emerge in Germany, he was still concerned about the inability or refusal of Germans to confront the past, to accept responsibility for the catastrophe and to undergo a fundamental moral renewal. As he later wrote in his autobiographical work, *Schicksal und Wille,* "The reality was completely different than I had hoped for in 1945. Very soon there was no more talk of an intellectual reconstruction. . . . Politically, the will for a democratic reconstruction resulting from an inner conversion was lost. From 1948 a new state began with new assumptions. The years 1945-1948 were finished."[109]

Coming to an end as well was Jaspers' direct relationship to Germany. By the beginning of 1948, he had decided to leave Germany for what he took to be the more liberal climate of Switzerland. He gave up his chair in philosophy at Heidelberg and accepted a position as professor of philosophy at the University of Basel. Jaspers returned to Heidelberg many times during the 1950s. He was even granted an honorary doctorate in 1953. He also continued to keep up with and comment publicly on the situation in Germany, but the intense period of engagement was over.

The difficult decision to leave Heidelberg was based on both personal and professional reasons. In poor health and feeling personally embattled, Jaspers believed the move to Basel would be a welcome change for him. After the stifling air of Heidelberg, the free spirit of Basel would be exhilarating. It would offer him "quiet and freedom and nothing other than philosophy," though not the disengaged philosophy of his prewar years.[110] He had done what he could, given his age, health and reputation, in Germany. What leadership he had left to offer could be provided as well from Switzerland as from Germany. Indeed, he believed he might better serve Germany as an ambassador to the world. In addition, Jaspers made the move for his wife's sake. She had understandably never felt at home in Germany after the Nazi seizure of power and especially after the full horror of the Holocaust had been revealed. Jaspers wanted to provide her with a peaceful and free atmosphere for her last years.[111]

Jaspers' decision to leave Heidelberg for Basel was, understandably, an unpopular one in Germany. Many of Jaspers' friends pleaded with him to remain in Heidelberg. One of his publishers, Ferdinand Springer, asked rhetorically, "Would Goethe have left Weimar and still been able to complete his life's work"? He went on to suggest that Jaspers could only overcome his difficulties, which were "great and many" if he stayed in Heidelberg, not if he ran away to Switzerland.[112] Others were less kind. Many in the German press accused him of being a "traitor" and, now, a "deserter." He had claimed to represent the "better Germany." Now he was abandoning the misery of the current German situation for the easier life of Switzerland. He had given the German youth a glimpse of what Germany could be; now this *"praeceptor Germaniae"* was leaving them to fend for themselves. Some of the sharpest words came from his friend and colleague Alexander Mitscherlich. Mitscherlich, who had long admired Jaspers and who had served with him on the "Committee of Thirteen," reproached Jaspers not for his decision to leave Germany, but for the official explanation he offered in the *Rhein-Neckar-Zeitung*. Here Jaspers had spoken only of age, poor health and overwhelming duties. He had assured the readers that there was nothing symbolic in his decision to leave Germany. Mitscherlich knew better. He accused Jaspers of being disingenuous and claimed that Heidelbergers deserved better; they deserved to know the "personal reasons" for his emigration. He correctly predicted that Jaspers' emigration would be seen as a "sign of weakness" or an "admission that all is lost for Germany." Not everyone, he pointed out, would be as quick to forgive him as his friends.[113]

As Mitscherlich correctly surmised, Jaspers had personal reasons for leaving Germany that he did not feel ready to divulge publicly at this time. But he had also come to believe by 1948 that the challenge was to address the overall cultural and political crisis accompanying the transition to modernity—a crisis that affected not just Germany but the entire world. To be sure, the German context was important, perhaps even paradigmatic on some level. However, truly to understand the overall crisis, one had to examine more than the immediate German questions. He had already suggested in *The Question of German Guilt* that

> What has happened today has its causes in general human events and conditions, and only secondarily in the special intra-national relations and the decisions of single groups of men. What is taking place is a crisis of mankind. The contributions, fatal or salutary, of single peoples and states can only be seen in the framework of the whole, as can the connections which brought on this war, and its phenomena which manifested in new, horrible fashion what man can be.

. . . At the beginning, therefore, we place a theme which does not even mention German as yet: the generality of the age—how it reveals itself as technical age and in world politics and in the loss or transformation of all faith.[114]

Jaspers now argued in *The Origin and Goal of History* (*Vom Ursprung und Ziel der Geschichte*), as he had in his 1946 speech, that one had to understand first how human culture had become differentiated and then how the West had broken away from the rest of the world. By examining the ancient human past—especially the first age of fundamental cultural transformation or "axial period"—Jaspers believed he could help to illuminate the present situation and open up the possibility of radical regeneration, though he was not yet specific about how this regeneration might take place. In the "Axial Age" was to be found an axis in history that would provide a common historical frame of reference for all cultures. It was "an age of extraordinary beginnings . . . an age of reform." It was during this era that "thinkers speculated . . . how [people] might best live together" and how they might best be administered and governed."[115] Here a basis might be found for a cosmopolitan religious faith, and new human unity, based, as Joanne Cho has shown, on "mutual civilizational grafting."[116] The unity towards which he pointed was "unity through community through communication of the historically manifold origins, which are mutually concerned with one another, without becoming identical in the manifestation of idea and symbol—a unity which leaves the One concealed in manifoldness, the One that can remain true in the will to boundless communication, as an endless task in the interminable testing of human possibilities." Jaspers even pointed toward the possibility of a world state that might eventually replace the various nation states.[117]

In the same year that *The Origin and Goal of History* appeared, 1949, Jaspers' reputation in Germany sank to its nadir because of a public controversy he had with the Bonn classicist Ernst Robert Curtius. The controversy began when Curtius attacked Jaspers for the Goethe speech he had made in 1947. The speech, "Unsere Zukunft und Goethe," was printed in book form during 1949 and then reviewed in *Welt am Sonntag*. Because the book was referred to under the title "Auflehnung gegen Goethe? Eine kritische Untersuchung," Curtius mistakenly believed that this was a new critical work concerning Goethe and that the newspaper was announcing yet a third to come.[118] Curtius, who had called in his own work for a return to the origins of humanism and a study of its major figures—including Goethe—was not about to allow Jaspers to diminish Goethe's greatness. He also saw this as his chance to attack Jaspers for *The Question of German Guilt* and his emigration to Basel. Jaspers, claimed Curtius, had leveled an attack on Germany's most important cultural forefather. Illustrating that he had not, in fact, read *The Question of German Guilt*, Curtius wrote that Jaspers "had proven our collective guilt so clearly that we can now only live with a bad conscience. A Wilhelm von Humboldt of our time, he has given the correct lines for the German universities, until he turned his back on them." Now Jaspers was conducting his "campaign" against Goethe and Germany from abroad (a few miles up the Rhine!). Jaspers had claimed that Goethe's achievements amounted to nothing, that he had been nothing more than the "conclusion of the Western millennia." But Jaspers, according to Curtius, knew nothing of "Goethe's essence," of his great "mystery."[119]

Curtius' invective took Jaspers by surprise. He had known the Bonn classicist for many years and had maintained a cordial relationship with him. It was as if he were hearing "a kind of madness, but it is Ernst Robert Curtius." After all, Jaspers had not been criticizing Goethe so much as he had the "cult of Goethe," which he rightly saw as a kind of escapist mythmaking. The public controversy that followed saw many in Germany siding with Curtius against Jaspers— Gottfried Benn and Kurt Hiller among them. There were, of course, some who defended Jaspers against Curtius' invective, perhaps most famously a group of seven Heidelberg professors including Bauer, Hans von Campenhausen, Karl Geiler, August Grisebach, Gustav Radbruch, Otto Regenbogen and Alfred Weber. No matter what one thought of Jaspers' philosophy and his understanding of Goethe, according to these men "[Curtius] attack was inconceivable, incompatible with the respect which Karl Jaspers is due, and not worthy of a teacher of Curtius' rank."[120] The entire affair simply confirmed Jaspers' belief that the Germans had not come to terms with their immediate past and thus had not even begun to experience a fundamental change. Jaspers began to see his post-war work as ineffective and irrelevant. As he wrote to Dr. Moras, editor of *Merkur*, "I am horrified by the thought that the public German spirit has remained fundamentally unchanged after the Nazi period."[121] This incident confirmed Jaspers in his conviction that he was a prophet without honor, speaking to an audience that was indifferent to his message.[122]

That Jaspers could have been viewed as a traitor for having raised the question of German guilt or for having dared to criticize the cult of Goethe indicates, however, that he had not been irrelevant. Rather, it illustrates just how volatile the German mood was between 1945 and 1948. It also illustrates the difficulty Germans were having in coming to terms with their past. Rather than dealing with it, they tended to suppress it and concentrate first on survival and then, as economic recovery began, on material wealth. This trend continued into the late 1960s and after as Alexander and Margarete Mitscherlich noted in 1967. In *The Inability to Mourn (Unfähigkeit zu trauern)* the Mitscherlichs supported Jaspers' earlier predictions. Using Freudian categories and concepts they argued that the work of mourning had never been accomplished in the wake of the German collapse. The Germans had never come to terms with their guilt and responsibility for the Third Reich and the Holocaust, but had instead repressed memories of the recent past. As a result, old patterns of thinking went unchanged which caused problems for the later Federal Republic.[123] Heinrich Böll dealt with similar problems in his novel *Billiards at Half-Past Nine*. In this novel repressed memories continue to crop up and haunt the novel's main character, Robert Faemel, in all kinds of odd and intrusive ways.

Jaspers himself, writing in 1966, argued that even though the Federal Republic was "a prospering society of producers and consumers," it had still had not performed the political and moral task of founding a new state because it had refused "to be true to the facts of the most recent past. . . . The guilt was not Hitler's; it was that of the Germans who followed him." But the Germans continued to believe in an untruth: "that an incomprehensible fate delivered them into the hands of a wicked criminal. That at bottom, though terror may have beclouded their thinking at times (which is only human), they always remained as decent, peace-loving, and truthful as they had been previously and are today." As a result, "freedom of thought and political will" had not yet been regained. Hence, "Germans as a whole seem unregenerated from the way of thinking that allowed Hitler to rule."[124]

In 1964 Theodor Adorno also noted that fundamental change had not occurred in the Federal Republic. But for Adorno, it was Jaspers, along with other existentialists, who bore a large portion of the blame for this condition because they had created a philosophical "jargon of authenticity." This jargon, which was shot through with empty theological overtones, had its origins in the period before 1933 but became widespread after 1945 when it replaced the language of National Socialism. For Adorno, the "jargon of authenticity" helped create an atmosphere in post-World War II Germany in which a meaningful and truthful discussion of the past became impossible.[125]

Anson Rabinbach has recently sounded this same refrain, but in a different key. He recognizes some of Jaspers' important contributions to post-war culture. He claims, for example, that Jaspers gave "intellectual support to the emergence of a minimum national "consensus" in German political life" concerning the "responsibility of any German postwar state for accepting and dealing with the burdens left behind by Nazism and the Holocaust." Moreover, he writes that "no single intellectual in immediately postwar Germany contributed more to the reorientation of German philosophy toward a reconceptualized Western humanism than Karl Jaspers." Yet Rabinbach agrees with the basic thrust of Adorno's argument. He has focused particularly on Jaspers' division of guilt into the public political/criminal and the private metaphysical/moral levels. He has correctly pointed out how notoriously difficult the concept of metaphysical guilt is. But Rabinbach also criticizes Jaspers' emphasis on moral self-examination, which he argues was no basis for collective renewal. Even more provocatively, he charges Jaspers with having given

> considerable support to the so-called silent *Vergangenheitsbewältigung* of the immediate postwar years. It encouraged the view that politics and morality belonged to separate spheres and that Nazism could be regarded simply as an inevitable consequence of the nation-state idea. The concept of metaphysical solidarity, with its manifest religiosity, was in no small part responsible for so much of the public language of the postwar era, which, as Adorno contemptuously remarked, "grasped at the banal, while elevating it and enshrining it in bronze at the very heights." Jaspers' strict separation of the political and moral responsibility also contributed to skepticism about denazification, and permitted the political culture of the early Federal Republic to substitute financial reparations and public declarations of responsibility for what might have been more effective and less ritualized attempts to reveal the truth of the Nazi past.[126]

In short, Rabinbach suggests that despite Jaspers' best efforts, his influence in the long term was counterproductive.

These are serious charges and, if true, would do much to alter the picture of Jaspers drawn in this chapter. Yet nowhere does Rabinbach adduce specific evidence to support his claim that Jaspers' post-war thinking contributed to a silent mastery of the past or to a "skepticism about denazification." Nor can he support the most damaging claim of all: that Jaspers' discussion of the guilt question validated post-war Germans attempt to "substitute financial reparations and public declarations of responsibility for what might have been more effective and less ritualized attempts to reveal the truth of the Nazi past." What is undeniable is that Jaspers, as he himself recognized, was unable to convince a majority of Germans to come to terms with their guilt. But if he was unable to initiate a continuous deepening of the national self-examination, this did not mean that he had taken the wrong tack. To be sure, there were blindnesses and weakspots in his approach. For example, his concept of metaphysical guilt, with its theological overtones, probably did obscure more than it enlightened. But this criticism does not weaken the central force of Jaspers' insights. He was one of the first to articulate for Germans that there was something unique about *this* war and its attendant atrocities. For many there was no question of guilt or even of discredited traditions. Jaspers not only helped point out the full dimensions of the catastrophe and the German responsibility for it, but he was also one of the few in the immediate post-war period who was courageous enough to demand that the Germans deal with the past in a truthful and thoroughgoing way, even if this meant crying out in the wilderness.

If the Germans did not answer his call, if they refused to face up to their past, there were other, more important, reasons—most notably the developing Cold War context. Because of the growing tensions between the United States and the Soviet Union, the integration of the Federal Republic into the political and economic systems of the Western world became the priority. Dredging up and continuing to wallow in the brown past could serve little useful purpose in this context. As Jeffrey Herf has pointed out, the establishment of what has proven to be a successful democracy was aided by a measure of collective amnesia at first.[127] Caught up as he was in the emerging Cold War context, Jaspers could not have fully understood or done justice to the complexity of the issues. In expecting him to have created a thoroughgoing public discussion of the past in this particular context, we render an ahistorical judgment and risk overlooking what he actually did achieve. Even if Jaspers himself often expected too much of Germans in the immediate post-war period, he recognized, in his better moments, that he was beginning a long and painful process. The process of coming to terms with the past was bound to take generations. As he later wrote in *The Future of Germany* (*Wohin treibt die Bundesrepublik*), "the analysis of any historic event is an endless endeavor, and so is the analysis of what led to 1933. The precedent conditions, a century of history, the special circumstances under which it really happened, the individuals who were temporarily able to push their way into key posts until their turn came to be removed—all this is an inexhaustible subject."[128]

Jaspers saw, long before intellectuals such as Heinrich Böll, Jürgen Habermas, and Günter Grass, that a continual reappraisal of the Nazi legacy would need to be a part of German identity. His initial attempts to deal with the questions of guilt and responsibility, though not convincing on every level, were neither irrelevant, as Jaspers himself came to believe, nor counterproductive, as Adorno, Rabinbach, Remy, and others have claimed. They were a central part of the initial catharsis in Germany. When the next public discussion of the past came in the 1960s many of the categories and issues set out by Jaspers were trotted out again, even if there was rarely any explicit reference to Jaspers' early post-1945 work. Only in the late 1970s did intellectuals such as Jürgen Habermas begin to recognize the importance of Jaspers' post-war works—from *The Question of German Guilt* to *The Idea of the University*—to subsequent critical discussions of the German past. Indeed, Jaspers has served as a source of inspiration for Habermas and others. In so doing, he helped initiate an important shift in German academic intellectual life.[129]

Jaspers also understood that mastering the past required more than a critical dialogue. When all of German history seemed tainted, Germans needed to have confidence in the positive side of their tradition. Thus, he began the process of weaving the thin, sometimes tattered, threads of the German past into the fabric of a new German identity. As a result, he helped Germans understand what it had meant to be German in the past and what, if anything, was worth rescuing from that earlier form of national identity. But he realized that the post-war context necessitated more than looking back to some golden age, more than myth-making. He was sensitive to the need for fundamental cultural and political change. It was of central importance, then, that Jaspers helped reestablish Germany's intellectual foundations and institutions with an eye toward the immediate situation and the future. In this way he helped determine for the first post-war generation of Germans the extent to which it was possible to reconnect with earlier traditions and the extent to which the present is irremediably and irredeemably cut off from the past.

NOTES

1. Golo Mann, *Erinnerungen und Gedanken Eine Jugend in Deutschland* (Frankfurt: Fischer, 1991), 313.

2. *Hannah Arendt/Karl Jaspers Correspondence, 1926-1969*, ed. Lotte Kohler and Hans Saner, trans. Robert and Rita Kimber (San Diego: Harcourt Brace, 1993), 23.

3. Karl Jaspers, *Philosophical Autobiography*, in *The Philosophy of Karl Jaspers*, ed. Paul Arthur Schilp (La Salle Illinois: Open Court Press, 1981), 55-58.

4. Max Weber, "Wissenschaft als Beruf," (1919) in Max Weber, *Gesammelte politische Schriften*, ed. Johannes Winckelmann (Tübingen: J. C. B. Mohr, 1988).

5. Mann, *Erinerungen und Gedanken*, 172.

6. Ibid., 309. Jaspers had also addressed the issue of education and the importance of *Bildung* in his first *Die Idee der Universität* (Berlin: Springer, 1923), 9, 11, 18, 46.

7. Karl Jaspers, "Ein Selbst-Portrait," in *Jaspers Today: Philosophy at the Threshold of the Future*, ed. Edith Ehrlich (Washington, D.C.: University Press of America), 5.

8. A second and substantially rewritten book by the same title was published in 1946.

9. Otto Vossler, *Humboldt und die deutsche Nation, Humboldts Idee der Universität* (Darmstadt: Wissenschaftliche Buchgesellschaft, 1967), 40-43; Ringer, *Mandarins*, 14-90.

10. Karl Jaspers, *Die Idee der Universität* (Berlin: Springer Verlag, 1923), 9, 18.

11. In addition to *Die Idee*, Jaspers wrote "Thesen zur Frage der Hochschulerneuerung," which were responses to Martin Heidegger's 1933 Rector's address. He hoped to be able to influence the university reform being contemplated by the Baden Ministry of Education. Although unpublished in his lifetime, these theses can be found in *Karl Jaspers: Philosopher Among Philosophers/Philosoph unter Philosophen*, ed. Richard Wisser and Leonard H. Erlich (Wurzburg: Königshausen & Neumann, 1993), 293-331.

12. Jaspers, *Philosophical Autobiography*, 58.

13. Karl Jaspers, *Die geistige Situation der* Zeit (Berlin: Walter de Gruyter, 1931), 33.

14. Ibid., 36.

15. Hans Saner, *Karl Jaspers in Selbstzeugnissen und Bilddokumenten* (Reinbek bei Hamburg: Rowohlt, 1970), 44.

16. Karl Jaspers, *Karl Jaspers/Martin Heidegger Briefwechsel, 1920-1963* (Frankfurt am Main and Munich: Klostermann and Piper, 1990), 259-264.

17. Minister des Kultus und Unterrichts to the Rektor of Heidelberg University, 25 June 1937. Universitätsarchiv (herafter UAH), Heidelberg, Germany, PA 460, 1935-1969.

18. Karl Jaspers, *Lebenslauf* (1945), Deutsches Literaturarchiv (hereafter DLA), Nachlaß Jaspers (herafter NJ), Marbach, Germany, Kaste 27.

19. Karl Jaspers to Golo Mann, 30 January 1947, NJ, DLA, 75.8782.

20. Jaspers, *Philosophical Autobiography*, 62

21. Ibid., 63.

22. Ibid., 63.

23. Karl Jaspers, *Tagebuch*, 20 March 1945, cited in Saner, *Karl Jaspers*, 51.

24. Hannah Arendt and Karl Jaspers, *Hannah Arendt/Karl Jaspers Correspondence, 1926-1969*, ed. Lotte Kohler and Hans Saner, trans. Robert and Rita Kimber (San Diego: Harcourt and Brace, 1993), 58.

25. Karl Jaspers, *Philosophie und Welt: Reden und Aufsätze* (Munich: Piper, 1958), 383f.

26. Karl Jaspers, "Geleitwort," *Die Wandlung*, vol. 1, no. 1, 3.

27. Karl Jaspers, "Die Erneuerung der Universität," in Karl Jaspers and Fritz Ernst, *Vom lebendigen Geist der Universität und vom Studieren* (Heidelberg: Lambert Schneider, 1946), 74.

28. Jaspers, *Philosophical Autobiography*, 64.

29. Jaspers, "Rededication of German Scholarship," 180.

30. Jaspers, *Philosophical Autobiography*, 64.

31. Jaspers, "Geleitwort," 5.

32. Karl Jaspers, "Volk und Universität," in *Die Wandlung*, vol. 2, no. 1, 56.

33. Karl Jaspers, NJ, DLA; also quoted in Saner, 51.

34. Klaus von Beyme, "Karl Jaspers—Vom Außenseiter zum *Praeceptor Germaniae*," in *Heidelberg 1945*, ed. Jürgen C. Heß, Hartmut Lehmann, and Volker Sellin (Stuttgart: Franz Steiner Verlag, 1996), 195.

35. Craig Pepin and Mark W. Clark, "Dilemmas of Education for Democracy: American Occupation, University Reform, and German Resistance," in *Educational Policy Borrowing: Historical Perspectives* (Oxford: Symposium, 2004), 167-184; James

Tent, *Mission on the Rhine: Reeducation and Denazification in American-Occupied Germany* (Chicago: University of Chicago Press, 1982), 276-7.

36. Karl Jaspers, "Die sozialen und politischen Verantworlichkeiten der deutschen Hochschulen," NJ, DLA, Kaste 27.

37. Karl Jaspers, "Die Erneuerung der Universität," 21.

38. Ibid., 21.

39. Karl Jaspers, *The Idea of the University*, ed. Karl Deutsch, trans. H.A.T. Reiche and H.F. Vanderschmidt (Boston: Beacon Press, 1959).

40. Ibid., 19-20, 31-33.

41. Karl Jaspers, "Erneuerung der Universität," 23, 39.

42. Jaspers, *Idea*, 63-65.

43. Ibid., 50, 65-70.

44. Jaspers, quoted in Renato de Rosa, "Nachwort," in Karl Jaspers, *Erneuerung der Universität: Reden und Schriften 1945/6* (Heidelberg: Lambert Schneider, 1986)" 373.

45. Karl Jaspers, 17 July 1946, "Jaspers/Nationalsozialisten nach 1945; Heidelberg 1946," NJ, DLA, Kaste 27.

46. Ibid.; Karl Jaspers, "Vom lebendigen Geist der Universität," in Jaspers and Ernst, *Von lebendigen Geist und vom Studieren. Zwei Vorträge von Karl Jaspers und Fritz Ernst* (Heidelberg: Lambert Schneider, 1946), 26

47. Jaspers, *Idea*, 19.

48. Hartshorne to Jaspers, 27 July 1945, NJ, DLA, 75.11682.

49. Alexander Mitscherlich to members of the Dreizehnerausschuss, 5 April 1945, UAH, Rep. 10-2.

50. Bauer, "Report on the activity of Heidelberg University" 7 August 1946, cited in de Rosa, "Nachwort," 368.

51. There is a significant body of literature on Jaspers' role in Heidegger's dismissal and, more generally, on their overall relationship. For the text of Jaspers' letter to Herr Oehlkers, one of the members of the university denazification commission, please see Richard Wolin, *The Heidegger Controversy: A Critical Reader* (Cambridge, Mass.: MIT Press, 1993), 144-151. See also Hugo Ott, *Martin Heidegger: A Political Life*, trans. Allan Blunden, (New York: HarperCollins, 1993), 334-43, and Rabinbach, *In the Shadow of Catastrophe*, 97-99.

52. A record of Jaspers' role in the Scheel prodeedings is located in NJ, DLA, Kaste 20.

53. Minutes of 16 July 1945 meeting of the Committee of Thirteen, UAH, Rep. 10-2.

54. Craig Pepin, "The Holy Grail of Pure Wissenschaft," 155f.

55. Radbruch, like Jaspers, argued that party political organizations and the old student fraternities should be abolished. New student organizations should be allowed only if they had social, sporting, scholarly, artistic, or religious goals. Gustav Radbruch, "Zur Frage politische Vereinigungen an der Universität" reprinted in Manfred Heinemann, ed. *Süddeutsche Hochschulkonferenzen 1945-1949,* (Berlin: Akademie Verlag, 1997), 117-18. See also Christian Jannsen, "Mehr pragmatisch denn liberal. Politische Initiativen und Argumentationsmuster von Walter Jellinek, Gustav Radbruch, und Willy Hellpach im Kontext der Wiedereröffnung der Universität Heidelberg," in Heß et al, *Heidelberg 1945*, 173-196, and Pepin and Clark, "Dilemmas," 14.

56. Karl Jaspers, "Volk und Universität," *Die Wandlung*, vol. 2, no. 1, 59-60.

57. Karl Jaspers, "Hochschulreform? Das Gutachten des Hamburger Studienausschlusses für Hochschulreform," *Die Wandlung*, vol. 4., 340f.

58. Jaspers, *Idea*, 119-120.

59. Ibid., 108. The conclusion he drew from this study was that "German culture was sustained by a few tens of thousands of people as distinct from the remaining millions."

60. The German reads: "Voraussetzung für das akademische Studium ist grundsätzlich die humanistiche Vorbildung." "Entwurf einer neuer Satzung der Universität Heidelberg," 22 August 1945. UAH B-1011/6.

61. Felix Gilbert, *A European Past: Memoirs 1905-1945*, (New York: Norton, 1988), 208.

62. The translation of the draft statutes provided to the military government in 1945 is so vague and confusing that it is virtually incomprehensible: "The University statute appreciates an organization managed as a corporation of spiritual life which is divided as to efficiency and personality." § 5, "Draft of a new constitution for the University of Heidelberg," n.d. (in English) UAH B-1011/6. The German reads "Die Satzung der Universität schützt eine nach Leistung und Persönlichkeit gegliederte Ordnung geistigen Schaffens, die in genossenschaftlichen Formen verwaltet wird."

63. Pepin and Clark, "Dilemmas," 12.

64. Daniel Penham, Memorandum for the Officer in Charge, 307th Counter Intelligence Corps Detachment Headquarters Seventh United States Army, APO 758, 23 February 1946. Smith-Crum Papers, Marshall Research Library, Lexington, VA (hereafter MRL).

65. Karl Heinrich Bauer to the Military Government Office, Heidelberg University, 22 March 1946, Smith-Crum Papers, Box 8, MRL.

66. Karl Heinrich Bauer to the Military Government Office, Heidelberg University, 20 March 1946, Smith-Crum Papers, Box 8, MRL.

67. Senate of Heidelberg University to the Military Government, 26 February 1946, Smith-Crum Papers, Box 8, MRL.

68. John Elliot, "CIC Man Causes Furor at Heidelberg: AMG Acts to Curb Agent's Interference in Work of Ancient University," *New York Herald Tribune*, 17 March 1946.

69. Geoffrey Giles, "Reeducation at Heidelberg University," *Paedagogica Historica*, vol. 33, 1, 1997. Special issue: Mutual Influences on Education: Germany and the United States in the Twentieth Century, 201-219; Renato de Rosa, *Politische Akzente im Leben eines Philosophen. Karl Jaspers in Heidelberg, 1901-1946*; de Rosa, "Nachwort," 301-423. For a thorough recent account of the CIC role in the process of denazification, see Ralph Brown, "Removing 'Nasty Nazi Habits': The CIC and the Denazification of Heidelberg University, 1945-1946," *The Journal of Intelligence History*, vol. 4 (Summer 2004), 25-56.

70. Uta Gerhardt, "Die Amerikanischen Militäroffiziere und der Konflickt um die Wiedereröffnung der Universität Heidelberg, 1945-1946," in Heß et al., 30-54; Anson Rabinbach, *In the Shadow of Catastrophe: German Intellectuals between Apocalypse and Enlightenment* (Berkeley: University of California Press, 1997), 134-135.

71. Steven Remy, *The Heidelberg Myth: the Nazification and denazification of a German University* (Cambridge, Massachusetts, and London, England: Harvard University Press, 2002), esp. 116-17, 140.

72. Karl Jaspers/Karl Heinrich Bauer, *Briefwechsel 1945-1968*, ed. Renato de Rosa (New York and Berlin: Springer, 1983), 37.

73. Ibid., 44. See also Eike Wolgast, "Karl Heinrich Bauer—der erste Heidelberger Nachkriegsrektor. Welbild und Handeln, 1945-1946" in Heß et al., *Heidelberg 1945*, 107.

74. Jaspers to Klaus Piper, 27 November 1945, in NJ, DLA, 75.13609.

75. Karl Jaspers, "The Task of Philosophy in Our Day," in *This is My Philosophy*, ed. Whit Burnett (New York: Harper, 1957).

76. Jaspers, "Geleitwort," 3.

77. Sigrid Undset, "Die Umerziehung der Deutschen," *Neue Zeitung*, 25 October 1945.

78. Karl Jaspers, "Antwort an Sigrid Undset," *Neue Zeitung*, 4 November 1945.

79. Karl Jaspers, *The Question of German Guilt*, trans. E.B. Ashton (New York: Dial Press, 1947), 28.

80. Ibid., 11, 16.

81. Ibid., 28-9, 52-3, 60-1, 71.

82. Ibid., 62

83. Jaspers, *Philosophical Autobiography*, 69.

84. Cited in Karl Jaspers and Klaus Piper, *Karl Jaspers Werk und Wirkung* (Munich: Piper, 1963), 134.

85. Alexander Mitscherlich to Jaspers, 7 January 1946, NJ, DLA, 75.13118.

86. Daniel Penham, "Report to 307th Counter Intelligence Corps Detachment Headquarters Seventh United States Army," 23 February 1946, 7, Box 8, MRL.

87. *Hannah Arendt/Karl Jaspers Correspondence, 1926-1969*, 121.

88. Dr. R.G., "In Hintergrund der Gespräche: Ein Beitrag von Karl Jaspers zur Schuldfrage," *Badische Zeitung*, 26 July 1946.

89. Kurt Stavenhagen, "Das neue Buch," paper unknown, NJ, DLA, Kaste 20.

90. Constance von Gossmann to Jaspers, 1 September 1946, NJ, DLA, Kaste 20.

91. Dr. Fritz Rahn, Studienrat, 22 September 1946, NJ, DLA, Kaste 20.

92. Martin Dibelius to Jaspers, 17 August 1946, NJ, DLA, 75:10803.

93. Heinz Finke to Jaspers, 2 December 1946; Dr. Manfred Schmid to Jaspers, 23 August 1946, NJ, DLA, Kaste 20.

94. Franz-Josepf Krautheuser to Jaspers, 18 Septebmer, 1946, NJ, DLA, Kaste 20.

95. Jaspers to Willy Boepple, 11 June 1946, NJ, DLA, Kaste 20.

96. Jaspers to Heidegger, *Karl Jaspers/Martin Heidegger Briefwechsel*, 199.

97. Rencontres International to Jaspers, 11 December 1945, NJ, DLA, Kaste 32.

98. Karl Jaspers, *The European Spirit*, trans. and intro. Ronald Gregor Smith (London: SCM Press, Ltd, 1948), 9.

99. Ibid., 29-30.

100. Ibid., 36, 38.

101. Ibid., 33, 30, 9.

102. Ibid., 52.

103. Oberbürgermeister Kolb to Jaspers, 19 July 1947, Jaspers to Kolb, 4 August 1947, NJ, DLA, Kaste 96.

104. Karl Jaspers, "Our Future and Goethe," in *Existentialism and Humanism* (New York: R. F. Moore Co., 1952), 40-41, 57.

105. Martin Heidegger, "Letter on Humanism," in *Martin Heidegger: Basic Writings* (New York: HarperCollins, 1977), 190-242.

106. Rabinbach, *In the Shadow*, 104.

107. Karl Jaspers, "Premises and Possibilities of a New Humanism," in *Existentialism and Humanism*, trans. E.B. Ashton (New York: R.F. Moore Co., 1962), 65, 85-87.

108. Ibid., 85, 88.

109. Karl Jaspers, "Warum ich Deutschland verlassen habe," in *Schicksal und Wille* (Munich: Piper, 1967), 52.

110. Ibid., 143.

111. Saner, *Karl Jaspers*, 56.

112. Ferdinand Springer to Jaspers, 20 January 1948, NJ, DLA, 75.9522.

113. Alexander Mitscherlich to Jaspers, 31 March 1948, NJ, DLA, 75:13118.

114. Karl Jaspers, *The Question of German Guilt*, 24-5.

115. Karl Jaspers, *Way to Wisdom* (New Haven: Yale University Press, 1951), 101.

116. JoAnne Cho, "A Cosmopolitan Faith in Karl Jaspers: Decoupling Commitment and Narrowness," *Journal of Ecumenical Studies*, vol. 37, nr. 1 (2000), 57.

117. Karl Jaspers, *Origin and Goal of History* (New Haven: Yale University Press, 1953), 234, 264.

118. Saner, *Karl Jaspers*, 58.

119. Ernst Robert Curtius, "Goethe oder Jaspers"? *Die Zeit*, 28 April 1949. For a contemporary account of the entire controversy, see Hans Heinrich Schaeder, "Karl Jaspers und sein Kritiker," *Die Zeit*, 12 May 1949.

120. In *Rhein-Neckar-Zeitung*, 7 May 1949.

121. Karl Jaspers to Dr. Moras, 14 October 1949, NJ, DLA, 75:13017.

122. Karl Jaspers, Letter from Jaspers (addressee not provided) 14 October 1949, cited in Saner, *Karl Jaspers*, 59.

123. Alexander and Margarete Mitscherlich, *Die Unfähigkeit zu trauern* (Munich: Piper, 1967).

124. Karl Jaspers, *The Future of Germany*, trans. and ed. E.B. Ashton (Chicago and London: University of Chicago Press, 1967), 57, 60, 89-90. This book also provoked a public controversy. However, it is outside the purview of this book.

125. Theodor Adorno, *Jargon der Eigentlichkeit: Zur deutschen Ideologie* (Frankfurt am Main: Suhrkamp Verlag, 1964).

126. Rabinbach, *In the Shadow*, 164-5, 143-4, 160-1.

127. Jeffrey Herf, *Divided Memory: The Nazi Past in the Two Germanys* (Cambridge, Massachusetts and London: Harvard University Press, 1997).

128. Jaspers, *The Future of Germany*, 18.

129. See especially Jürgen Habermas, *Stichworte zur geistigen Situation der Zeit* (Frankfurt am Main: Suhrkamp, 1979); Habermas, *The New Conservatism: Cultural Criticism and the Historians" Debate*, ed. and trans. Shierry Weber Nicholsen (Cambridge, Massachusetts: MIT Press, 1989).

Chapter Three

The Insider as Outsider: Thomas Mann

When Thomas Mann left Germany in 1933 for a European lecture tour, he hardly suspected that he would spend the next sixteen years in political exile. At war's end Mann was living in Pacific Palisades, California, finishing his most important literary statement about the German catastrophe: *Doctor Faustus: The Life of the Composer Adrian Leverkühn as told by a Friend.* Despite his long absence from his homeland, Mann appeared to be in an ideal position to offer intellectual leadership to a war-ravaged and defeated Germany. Like Meinecke, he had a great deal of moral authority during the post-war period, having been a vocal supporter of the Weimar Republic, an open critic of Hitler and the Nazis, and a political émigré. While in exile, Mann had defended freedom and democracy and he had fought against National Socialism in speeches, essays, and, most notably, his fifty-five BBC broadcasts to German listeners. Mann's actions and political stances before and during the war had endeared him to the Allies and to many opponents of the regime in Germany. However Mann, unlike Meinecke, had a tortured relationship with the German cultural elite and educated middle classes that dated back to the 1920s and that would play a major role in his post-war reception in Germany.

Despite his troubled history with the educated classes of Germany, however, Mann seemed in one sense a popular figure in the very different circumstances of 1945. Mann's son Golo, an occupation official in post-war Germany, reported to Katia Mann in April 1945 that as far as the "good people" in Germany were concerned "[Thomas Mann's] prestige and influence are astonishing."[1] Many wrote personally to ask Mann's help in all kinds of sensitive matters. Hans Friedrich Blunck, president of Hitler's writers' organization, the *Reichsschriftumskammer*, asked for his help in resolving legal issues.[2] Leading German intellectuals of the "inner emigration," even requested that Mann return to Germany and take his rightful position as the preceptor of German culture.

They had forgiven and forgotten. Now, he needed only forgive and forget and return to Germany like a good physician.

Mann, however, was unwilling either to forgive or to forget. Such requests from the very people who had made their peace with the Nazis and who had attacked him in the 1920s and 1930s sounded all wrong to him. The Germans, Mann believed, were not yet ready to be granted freedom to make their own future. Moreover, he doubted that they were really prepared to accept direct leadership from him. Mann refused to go back to Germany in the immediate aftermath of the war. Indeed, he never returned to live and made only occasional visits between 1949 and 1955, the year of his death. He chose to remain on the outside, unaccommodated, and resistant. Mann's refusal to return to Germany combined with his often harsh judgments of "the Germans" widened the already existing rift between Mann and his homeland and made him appear "a deserter from Germany's destiny," a permanent exile, even if he continued to consider himself a true German.[3] Connected inextricably with his post-war reception was his work *Doctor Faustus*, a novel that seemed, on a superficial reading, to demonize the entire German people.

Some critics, such as Denis Bark and David Gress, have argued that in refusing to return to Germany Mann "rejected the role of a cultural and moral leader of a people he felt he no longer knew (or wanted to know)."[4] For Jost Hermand, the post-World War II Mann belonged to a group of backward-looking, neo-humanist intellectuals who retreated from the political/economic exigencies of the post-World War II period into their ivory towers.[5] Hence he was irrelevant, because apolitical, to developments in either post-war German state. Gordon Craig also argues that Mann's post-war career was marked by a return to the apolitical.[6]

Scholars have recently begun to reappraise Mann's broader role both before and after World War II. The historian Joachim Fest argued that although Thomas Mann never liked politics, he nevertheless transformed himself from an apolitical *Dichter* into a thoughtful, though always ambivalent, supporter of democracy in Germany and the world.[7] More recently still, three biographies have pointed to Mann's role as a public intellectual: Klaus Harpprecht, *Thomas Mann: Eine Biographie*, Donald Prater, *Thomas Mann: A Life*, and Ronald Hayman, *Thomas Mann*.[8] Prater, who presents the most convincing case for Mann as a committed public intellectual, admits that Mann always felt his public political life took him away from his real task: literature. Yet Mann learned to make public pronouncements and to take difficult political positions. Prater, like Fest and others, sees the Weimar Republic as a decisive moment in Mann's transformation from apolitical *Dichter* to public intellectual, but he also argues that Mann also played a public, political role in the West even in the post-World War II period.[9]

Herbert Lehnert and Eva Wessel have proposed a subtler argument. To be sure, Mann was, like other German intellectuals, suspicious of "politics," which was always inferior to "culture,"(*Kultur*) and which he equated with ideology and partisanship. Yet, according to Lehnert and Wessel, he was interested in the

"political" as early as 1908, and he wrote about politics, even if often in a conservative tone. There was, therefore, no fundamental turn (*Wandlung*) during the
Weimar Republic; Mann did not suddenly become political. Nor did he experience a sudden conversion to democracy. Rather, he slowly came to believe that
culture required a democratic political framework, and this meant that the Weimar Republic and its institutions, even if they were not ideal, had to be safe-
guarded. It also meant that he, as an intellectual leader of his people, had to lend
his public support to the Republic. Mann thus did become more politically
committed and outspoken during the 1920s—and this commitment transformed
him into an ardent critic of fascism and a defender of Western democracy.[10]

Although emphasizing Mann's importance as a public intellectual, the new
literature on Mann's political commitments has given only scant treatment to the
role he played in Germany after 1945, and it does almost nothing to place him
within the broader context of post-World War II cultural renewal. Even
Hermann Kurzke, whose biography focuses significant attention on *Doctor
Faustus* and its reception, has missed the central force of Mann's post-WWII
position.[11] Although he refused to return to Germany, he felt a responsibility as
the most recognized German writer in the world to write about and speak on
issues relating to the reconstruction of German culture and politics. It was precisely in his role as "outsider," or permanent exile, that his work had force in the
post-war world. In speeches, essays, interviews, and in *Doctor Faustus*, Mann
addressed the themes of guilt and responsibility, the history of the German catastrophe and the German character. He helped initiate, along with Meinecke,
Jaspers, and others, the quest for a usable past, by trying to discover in the German cultural tradition a basis for political and intellectual freedom. Mann also
attempted to reconnect Germany with the West both politically and culturally.

Mann established his literary reputation with his first major work, *Buddenbrooks* (1901), which became an instant sensation among the educated German
middle class. Other important pre-1914 works include *Royal Highness* and
Death in Venice. Despite the renown he gained with his fiction, however, Mann
was not much of a public intellectual before World War I. He was committed to
his art and even to considering politics on an abstract plane, but not to making
public political statements. Nor did Mann intend for his fiction to be explicitly
political. To be sure, even in his early literary works one of his central themes
concerned the function of art and the artist in society at large. But artists appear
as ironists and outcasts, removed from society and isolated from life. It is precisely in their ironic distance from life—especially politics—that Mann's artists
fulfill their proper role in society.[12] In this sense, Mann shared the basic sentiments of most German intellectuals. University professors and artists, including
especially *Dichter*, believed it was their responsibility to promote and protect
culture, to educate and guide the educated middle classes. Although they were
interested in political issues, they tended not to become involved in party politics, which they considered low-grade. The true *Bildungsbürger* considered matters, including politics, from a "higher" standpoint.

Despite his aversion to party politics, Mann gradually became more embroiled in public and often explicitly political debates. He understood that as a
cultural leader, a *Dichter*, a certain amount of political leadership was expected
of him, and he came to feel a responsibility to make political statements. His
first significant public political statements came during World War I, when he
took a conventionally patriotic line by defending the war and the German cultural tradition. As he told Richard Dehmel, he wanted to take part in the "extremely important work" of "spelling out, ennobling, and giving meaning to
events."[13] Like many other German intellectuals he believed the war might
cleanse, purify and liberate Germany and Europe from its peacetime "civilization."[14] In trying to provide an intellectual basis for the war, he, like Meinecke,
became a leading participant in the "cultural war."[15]

By 1915, Mann was at work on his full-length statement on the War, politics, and German culture: *Reflections of a Nonpolitical Man* (*Betrachtungen
eines Unpolitischen*). This essay was to be about the conflict of "culture" and
"civilization," Germany and the West. Mann wanted a new Europe, reorganized
around German culture. The idea of "world liberation" and progress through
Western ideas was mere "superstition." Instead, "progress, revolution, modernity, youth, and originality are with Germany." Mann inveighed against "democratic doctrinaires and tyrannical schoolmasters of revolution" within Germany itself, especially "the literati, the 'intellectuals' par excellence, who claim
'the spirit,' while it is really only the literary spirit of the bourgeois revolution
that they mean and know." They were, as Mann wrote to Paul Amann, nothing
other than traitors who had a fanatical hatred of the "German essence."[16]

In the section called "Politics," Mann argued that Germany was by nature
unpolitical. For Mann, politics was coterminous with democracy and ideology.
A "nonrelationship" existed between the German citizen and political democracy. German high culture, in particular, "thoroughly resists being politicized.
Indeed, the political element is lacking in the German concept of culture." Mann
derided politics for making one "rough, vulgar, and stupid. Envy, imprudence,
covetousness, is all it teaches." It brought chaos, destroyed traditional values,
and threatened "complete leveling, of a journalistic-rhetorical stultification and
vulgarization. . . . Away, then, with the alien and repulsive slogan, 'democratic!'
Never will the mechanical-democratic state of the West be naturalized with us."
Mann went on to defend "monarchy . . . because it alone guarantees political
freedom, both in the intellectual and in the economic spheres." He wanted nothing to do with "the parliamentary and party economic system that causes the
pollution of all national life with politics. . . . I do not want politics. I want objectivity, order, and decency. If this is philistine, then I want to be philistine. If it
is German, then in God's name I want to be called a German."[17]

Mann published *Reflections* in October 1918. Both an autobiographical
statement and a genuine attempt to preserve traditional culture in the face of a
foreign threat, this "nonpolitical" book by an "unpolitical" man became a force-
ful political statement, and it drew Mann ever deeper into the world of politics
he so detested. It also made him the quintessential "insider" in certain German

circles. Especially among conservative *Bildungsbürger*, Mann found a supportive and enthusiastic readership for the *Reflections*. Although initially flattered
by the attention, he soon became uncomfortable with their support and began to
distance himself from his own earlier chauvinistic conservatism.

Like most Germans of every political stripe, Mann was bitterly disappointed
with the outcome of the war. He could not accept that Germany's "entire national existence" was "to be condemned as guilty and erroneous." Neither would
he believe that "the great tradition of Germanism from Luther to Bismarck and
Nietzsche should be refuted and discredited." Yet as early as 1919 he could "re-
signedly" accept "that the victory of England and America seals and completes
the civilizing, rationalizing, pragmatizing of the West which is the fate of every
aging culture."[18] Mann also began to recognize that conservative nationalists had
misunderstood his purpose in writing the *Reflections*. He had defended German
culture not strictly on chauvinistic lines—and not from an ideological position—
but also because he believed that Germany had a unique role to play in bringing
about a more unified Europe and world.

Between 1919 and 1925, Mann gradually moved to support the Weimar
Republic and the Social Democrats. But the transition was slow and painful.[19]
During World War I, he had believed that German culture had been maligned
and mistreated, both from within and without. As a result, he had given his support to the fatherland, the monarchy, and the conservative tradition. Even after
the war he had continued to think along conservative lines; he even shared certain affinities with the so-called "conservative revolution." But by 1925 he had
come to believe that culture needed a democratic political framework for protection, and that the Bismarckian compromise between the middle classes and the
aristocracy had not sufficed. Democracy was the form of the body politic suitable for the contemporary German nation and for the future of humanity.

Yet Mann saw that the Republic had not gained wide acceptance. By the
mid-1920s, he feared that right-wing ideologues were endangering the Republic.
If he were to play the role of spiritual and moral guide, he would have to help
educate the German people and win them over for democracy. Like Goethe before him, Mann saw himself as the preceptor of the German people. In several
essays during this period, Mann explicitly linked himself with Goethe and thus
attempted to legitimize his own role as preceptor. "Goethe," he wrote, "was an
educator par excellence." The proof was to be found in "the two great monu-
ments of his life: *Faust* and *Wilhelm Meister*." Here the role of the writer was
seen as an "educational mission," which was defined by a "readiness to confess
inner problems; it is a calling to transform unusual experiences into representative ones that are capable of such symbolism: it only has to express itself in order to give voice to a general concern. . . . The writer can be defined as the educator who himself is educated in the most unusual way." He wrestles "with the
larger self, the nation," and thus "corrects and transcends the personal sphere
and establishes solidarity with his social environment, with the people."[20]

It was in *his* role as a guide and educator that Mann gradually moved to defend the Republic and, by the 1930s, the Social Democrats as the best safeguard for culture. The democracy Mann embraced, both at this time and later, was a beneficial authoritarian system run by intelligent people for the benefit of the whole. As late as 1943 he wrote:

> I understand democracy not so much as a demand for equality from *below*, but as goodness, justice and empathy from *above*. I do not consider it democratic when Mr. Smith or Little Mr. Johnson taps Beethoven on his shoulder and cries out: "How are you, old man!" That is not democracy but tactlessness and a lack of sense for distance. But when Beethoven sings: "Be embraced, millions, this kiss is for the whole world!," *that* is democracy. For he could have said, "I am a great genius and something special, while people are mob; I am much too delicate to embrace them." Instead, he calls them all his brothers and the children of a father in the heavens whose son he is as well. That is democracy in its highest form.[21]

Mann first clearly formulated his public support for the Republic in "The German Republic," a speech that was supposed to celebrate Gerhard Hauptmann's sixtieth birthday, but that was written in response to the assassination of Walter Rathenau by reactionaries. It was especially important "to infuse something like an idea, a soul, a vital spirit into this grievous state without citizens." The Republic, after all, represented the unity of state and culture. Mann argued, moreover, that the speech did not represent a "disavowal" of his position in *Reflections*. It was, instead, a "direct continuation of the essential line of the *Betrachtungen*, I assure you! In the name of German humanitarianism I took up arms against the revolution when it was starting. Today, out of the same impulse, I take up arms against the reactionary wave which is sweeping over Europe"[22]

Mann recognized correctly that he would be branded a traitor after the speech: "You would shout at me: 'And what about your book? What about your antipolitical, antidemocratic meditations of the year 1918? Renegade, turncoat! You are eating your own words, you are riding for a fall! Come down from the platform, and stop having the effrontery to think that the words of an unprincipled apostate can win us over.'" In answer to such objections, Mann admitted that he was still, in many ways, a conservative, that he wanted "to preserve not to destroy." What he wanted to preserve, however, was

> the explicit, legal form of. . . humanity. . . the mean between aesthetic isolation and undignified leveling of the individual to the general; between mysticism and ethics; between inwardness and the state; between a death-bound negation of ethical and civic values and a purely ethical philistine rationalism; it is truly the German mean, the Beautiful and Human, of which our finest spirits have dreamed.[23]

"The German Republic" marked a public turning point for Mann. The conservatives among the *Bildungsbürgertum* never forgave him for what they saw as political and intellectual treason. He had reversed his "correct" national-conservative position in favor of a Western, democratic one. The rift between Mann and the conservatives would continue to grow, and he would also gradually lose the support of most of the educated middle classes that had long made up his admiring audience. Opposed by the right, he nevertheless came to represent the German republic inside and outside Germany.

Mann continued to have private doubts about the Weimar Republic. Occasionally, as in 1926, he expressed these doubts publicly: "[democracy] is in a way rather a hindrance. . . . What Europe needs today is an enlightened dictatorship."[24] Nevertheless, he defended the Republic against attacks from all sides. In October of 1930, Mann made his most important post-*Reflections* statement: "German Address: A Call to Reason." Here Mann appealed directly to the German bourgeoisie that, until this point, had been his primary audience. He leveled an attack on National Socialism which, he claimed, had an "orgiastic, radically antihumane, frenziedly dynamic character." It was antithetical to everything that was innately German. It was hatred "not of the foreigner but of all Germans who do not believe in its methods, and whom it promises to destroy root and branch." Mann concluded by calling for conservatives *and* social democrats to stand against the danger of National Socialism and support the Republic.[25]

The most decisive moment for Mann came in February 1933. On 10 February in Munich, he gave a speech entitled, "The Sufferings and Greatness of Richard Wagner." ("Leiden und Grösse Richard Wagners") Speaking to a relatively small audience in the Auditorium Maximum of the University of Munich, Mann had pointed both to Wagner's unparalleled greatness as a synthesizer of musical styles and genres and to his limitations as an original musical creator.[26] Although critical, the speech was full of admiration for Wagner, and it received a cordial welcome at the time Mann gave it. Two months later, however, a signed letter appeared in the *Neueste Nachrichten*: "Protest der Richard-Wagner-Stadt-München." This was not a National Socialist initiative but rather a conservative nationalistic one. Spearheaded by the conductor Knappertbusch and the Wagnerian establishment, its forty-five signatories included many of the most important names in Munich's cultural life such as Minister of Culture Hans Schemm and the composer Richard Strauss.[27] These cultural figures latched on to some critical terms, especially to the expression "dilettantism," which in Mann's text is qualified by "monumentalized" and "driven to the level of genius."[28] They were also dismayed that he related Wagner to psychoanalysis and Freud, which the conservative *Bildungsbürger* considered not only a Jewish affair but also indecent. The signatories protested Mann's "calumny" against Wagner and Germany. Moreover, they criticized him for giving it in Amsterdam, Brussels and Paris as if he were somehow the "representative of German culture and opinion."[29]

Mann, already abroad in Switzerland, wrote an immediate reply. The "Protest" had been based on "a complete ignorance of the role which Wagner's gigantic work has always played in my life and my own work could have led them to take part in this iniquitous action against a German writer. I sincerely beg the silent friends of my work in Germany not to be led astray into doubting my devotion to German culture and tradition, and to them."[30] This "betrayal" by the Munich cultural elite was the beginning of Mann's "national excommunication," and it played a key role in establishing the problematic and highly complex relationship between Mann and the German cultural elite. The incident was more than just a public row. Mann felt personally betrayed. To be sure, he hated Hitler and the Nazis. In his diaries he wrote that he despised the political and moral condition to which his country had sunk. Germany had been "rebarbarized." The national socialist "revolution" was the "most hateful and murderous" in history. He had nothing but "disgust and loathing" for the regime's "inferior, pathologically murderous assault on the intellect." Its "whole being" was "nothing but hatred, resentment, revenge, meanness."[31] He came to despise "the Germans" as well, by which he meant the intellectual elite and bourgeoisie, because they did not resist but more or less tolerated, and eventually even accepted, Hitler and Nazi ideology.

After his response to the "Protest," Mann was undecided about the proper course of action. He resolved not to return to Germany at least until things had settled down. Yet he had not fully come to terms with his break from Germany. He would never compromise with the "outlaw" regime, but he apparently sometimes considered returning to Germany. It still might be possible to live in Germany in isolation without kowtowing to the Nazi regime. As he wrote to Hermann Hesse on 31 July 1933 "There are moments when I ask myself: Why really [do I keep up the struggle?] It might be possible to live differently in Germany, like Hauptmann, Huch, Carossa." Yet "the temptation passes quickly." Mann saw that he would surely "suffocate" in the stifling air of Nazi Germany.[32] Still he refrained from entering into further public disputes with the regime, though he did take some political stances.

Mann's relative silence between 1933 and 1936 was deafening, especially to other exiles who felt that the most recognizable German writer in the world should use his influence to speak out more forcefully. Even his own children, Klaus and Erika, were bitterly disappointed about their father's refusal to take a clear political stand.[33] But Mann was determined to steer a careful course so as to be able to exert some real moral influence when the time came. The definitive moment arrived in January 1936 when Eduard Korrodi, an editor for the *Neue Zürcher Zeitung*, published an article equating German émigré writing with Jewish writing and claiming that it was not representative of Germany. Korrodi had gone so far as to claim that no great German writers were to be found in the emigration, though he seemed to make an exception for Thomas Mann.[34] Mann found it impossible to remain silent in the face of such claims. He thus responded with an open letter of his own in which he attacked Korrodi and, more importantly, the Nazi regime in Germany. The Nazi regime, he claimed, was not simply against Jews. It was also

directed against Europe and against that loftier Germanism itself; it is directed
. . . against the Christian and classical foundations of Western morality. It is the
attempt (symbolized by the withdrawal from the League of Nations) to shake
off the ties of civilization. That attempt threatens to bring about a terrible alienation, fraught with evil potentialities, between the land of Goethe and the rest
of the world.

Because he was convinced that "nothing good can possibly come of the present German regime," he was forced to "shun the country in whose spiritual
traditions I am more deeply rooted than the present rulers who for three years
have vacillated, not quite daring to deny me my Germanism before the eyes of
the world."[35] Following closely on the heels of this letter, Mann lost the remainder of his
German assets and, in December of the same year, his German citizenship. But
this open letter turned out to be an important step for him and the exiles. It reaffirmed the decision of many to fight Hitler and the Nazis from abroad. Moreover, it established Mann as the most recognizable leader of the emigration. This
would be vitally important even after World War II, when many Germans took
Mann's opinions to be those of the entire emigration.

Mann resided in Switzerland until 1938, when he emigrated to the United
States. He lived first in Princeton, New Jersey, where he held a position in German literature at Princeton University. In 1941, he moved to Pacific Palisades,
California. While in the United States Mann became a vocal opponent of appeasement and isolationism. He continued to speak out against Hitler and the
Nazis through speeches, essays and, most notably, BBC radio addresses to Germany. Moreover, he continued to work out his ideas about the relationship between culture and politics, particularly as it regarded Germany. Most importantly, he began working on his novel *Doctor Faustus* in 1943. Notable among
his political pieces during exile were "The Coming Victory of Democracy,"
"The Tragedy of Germany," and "Germany and the Germans."

Yet Mann eschewed other forms of direct political involvement, most famously in 1943 when a number of émigrés asked him to become the honorary
president of a "German-American Council for Liberation from Nazism," a "Free
Germany" committee of exiled politicians who desired to resume power in a
future Germany.[36] Mann refused even to sign an appeal to the German people.
Ernst Reuter, who would become the mayor of Berlin after WWII, asked Mann
to participate. But Mann had long ago given up trying to convince Germans "to
shake off the Nazi yoke before it is too late." The Germans, after all, were not
ready to make such a move and, in any case, were not now physically able to do
so. Moreover, as he wrote in a very revealing passage, the émigrés had no authority to speak:

With what authority are we to speak to the German people? Surely only on the
most personal grounds, for we have nothing behind us. We cannot speak in
agreement with the governments of the countries in which we live, we have no

guarantee as to their intentions, and we even at times feel evil presentiments as to their intentions. . . . I cannot in fact see either the practical or even the idealistic purpose of coming forward in this way, or the justification for it.[37]

After World War II, it was not clear exactly what kind of role Mann would play in Germany. He had no intention of returning to Germany, though the Germans themselves were unaware of this until late 1945. Nor was it clear how the Germans would receive him, given his previous troubled relationship with the intellectual elite and the educated middle classes, his exile, and his well-known anti-Nazi stance during the war. All many Germans knew about Thomas Mann was what the Nazis had told them, or what they had heard of Mann's BBC broadcasts. Mann had often been extremely harsh in his condemnation of the Germans. For example, in one of his last broadcasts Mann declared that

> The terrible torture chamber, into which Hitlerism has made Germany, is broken up, and our disgrace lies open before the world. . . . Because all Germans, all who speak German, write German, have lived in Germany, are affected by this dishonorable compromise. It was not a small number of criminals; there were hundreds of thousands of a so-called German elite, men, boys and women, who, under the influence of insane teachings have committed these misdeeds with sick desire. . . . Humanity shudders before Germany! . . . Even the German who escaped in time from the realm of human leadership by the National Socialists, who not like you lived in the neighborhood of these places of atrocities, [who not] like you conducted his businesses in seeming honor and tried to know nothing, even though the stench of burned human flesh blew into his nose from there, even such a person is ashamed in his deepest soul by what had become possible in the land of his forefathers even though that [disgrace] was possible only through the regime of Hitler, [also he] is shaken from a human degradation which could happen only by the Nazi-Regime in a people which is good by nature, loving justice and morality.[38]

The point of this message that the Germans fundamentally misunderstood was that Mann included himself. He intended to resume the role of German mentor rather than become simply the accuser from abroad. Yet it was the harshness of Mann's pronouncements which most Germans heard. Even critics and victims of the National Socialist regime came to believe that he was condemning all Germans to the devil. Karl Jaspers, for example, admitted to Golo Mann after the war that Mann's criticisms from abroad had been "painful" to him. He knew all too well the barbarity of the National Socialist regime, and that Mann had been justified in his criticisms of "the Germans," but he "suffered" nevertheless from Mann's speeches.[39] For those who had been even more tainted than Jaspers with the stain of National Socialism, the feeling of resentment toward Mann ran much deeper, and it would only intensify after the publication of his speech "Germany and the Germans," his novel *Doctor Faustus*, and the interviews he gave in 1947 and 1949.

In the immediate aftermath of the war, however, Mann seemed to some an ideal person to help lead Germany toward recovery. Many in the German press, which was controlled by the military government and which therefore allowed only anti-Nazi statements, praised Mann as the spiritual leader of his country. In July 1945 Friedrich Rasche wrote an article for the *Neuer Hannoverscher Kurier* in which he claimed that despite the ban on Mann's works during the war, he had "in no way" been forgotten. He praised Mann for being "one of the few German writers of rank" to use "the entire dialectical trenchancy of his words against National Socialism." Mann, claimed Rasche, had "raised his voice for a better Germany . . . warning, admonishing, exhorting, bitterly accusing, and prophesying the end that has now engulfed us. In the depths of our need we still rest our hopes in him."[40] Herbert Burgmüller, a German literary historian and critic, wrote that Mann was first among "bearers of the German spirit in foreign lands." He had been the keeper of classical Weimar humanism while in exile, and he was listened to everywhere, except in Germany. "We should recognize him because recognition of him is recognition of ourselves, recognition of the German spirit."[41]

The most public entreaties for Mann's return came from the Communist and Christian Democratic party newspapers and from the "inner emigrant" Walter von Molo. On 1 September 1945 the Communist and Christian Democratic party newspaper in the Soviet Zone had published a resolution requesting Mann to return: "You are one of the greatest and ablest sons of the German people. We believe you now have a historic work to accomplish in Germany. We need your help."[42] Von Molo, a former president of the Prussian Academy of the Arts, had initially championed Nazism, swept away like other members of the *Bildungsbürgertum* by the feeling of unity that the Nazi "revolution" promoted. But he had then gone into "inner emigration" during the war, and came to believe that he, like Mann, had always internally resisted the Nazis. On 4 August 1945 he sent an open letter to Mann that was published first in the *Hessische Post* and then in the *Münchner Zeitung*. In this letter, von Molo begged Mann to return to help Germany rebuild.

> Please, come soon, see the faces of sorrow, see the unutterable sorrow in the eyes of many who have not participated in the glorification of our dark side, who were not able to abandon the homeland, because it was a matter of too many millions of people, for whom no other place on earth would have been home. Please come back soon and give the crushed hearts the sincere hope that there is justice, the assurance that one may not tear humanity asunder, as it happened here so horribly. . . . Please come soon and show that man has the duty to believe in common humanity . . . Your people, which has hungered and suffered for a third of a century now, has in its true essence nothing in common with the misdeeds and crimes, the terrible canker, which has taken so much of their health and perfection. . . . Come soon like a good doctor who sees not only the symptoms, but rather seeks the cause of the sickness and endeavors to heal it. . . . Let us again seek together the truth as we did before 1933.[43]

Mann was not prepared to return to Germany and forgive all. He told the United Press that he had "no intention of returning to Germany to live, although he might "visit there when travel conditions permit."[44] In addition to the atrocities perpetrated by the Nazis against humanity, the Germans had revoked *his* citizenship, confiscated *his* books, taken *his* money and property. Although Mann recognized that German suffering was genuine, he was not sympathetic because the Germans had brought the disaster on themselves. In light of all of the suffering they had inflicted on others, it was repulsive to read their self-pitying letters.[45] Where was "the renunciation and condemnation of the *deeds* of nationalism, the declaration of a desire to return to truth, to justice, to humanity?"[46]

In his public reply to von Molo, which was subsequently published in German newspapers and broadcast over allied radio, he stated:

> Now it has to please me that Germany wants to have me back. . . . However this appeal has for me something unsettling, something saddening, and something illogical, even unjust about it. Well-prepared entreaties do not appeal to me. You know only too well, dear Herr Molo, how costly advice and action are today in Germany, considering the almost unholy position into which our unhappy people has been brought. And it appears doubtful to me that a man who is already old . . . can still contribute much . . . to the raising up of a people which you describe as so humbled.[47]

Von Molo did not understand all he had suffered in exile. It had been hard enough to leave his home and country, his books, his thoughts. And he would never forget the

> illiterate and murderous radio and press campaigning against my Wagner speech. . . . What followed then was hard enough: the wandering from country to country. . . . All of you who swore allegiance to the "charismatic leader" and operated under Goebbels' culture, have not had to go through this. I do not forget that later you have gone through much evil, which I avoided. But you can never know the heart arrhythmia of exile, the uprooting, the nervous horror of homelessness. . . . Today I am an American citizen and have explained both publicly and privately long before Germany's terrible defeat that I had no intention of leaving America. My children, of whom two sons serve today in the American service, are rooted in this country. English-speaking grandchildren grow up around me. I myself am rooted in this ground. . . . I would like to end my life's work here, taking part in an atmosphere of power, reason, abundance and peace. . . . I do not see why I should have to give up the few advantages I have. . . . namely because I do not see the service which I could give the German people—and which I could not give them from California. . . . Germany has become foreign to me in all of these years. . . . It is, you must confess, a frightening country. I confess that I am afraid of German ruins—not only the rubble but also the people.

Mann would "never stop feeling [himself] a German writer," but neither would he return to Germany. If there was a definitive moment when Mann went from being an insider to an outsider in the eyes of post-war Germans, it came with his public response to von Molo.[48]

Most Germans focused on Mann's harsh condemnation of Germany and his refusal to return home. Many readers, such as Max Barth, who was himself living in American exile at the time, saw in Mann's refusal to go back and live in the ruins a "wide chasm between word and deed, between moral imperative and action." How could "the most prominent representative of the other Germany," refuse out of fear to return to a land that was already "on the way to denazification," that was "protected by foreign bayonets," when so many "tens of thousands of Germans during the years of the Republic and in the period of the Nazi dictatorship died because of their anti-nazi position?" Such a shameful refusal was a sign of cowardice.[49]

The sharpest attack came from the writer Frank Thieß. Thieß, who had embraced the regime in the beginning, had later written a novel on the Byzantine empire that was read as a clandestine attack on tyranny and the abuse of power. He wrote an open letter to Mann only eight days after von Molo's. Writing on behalf of the "inner emigration," Thieß had pleaded with Mann to return and help his "misled and suffering people." Thieß argued against Mann's wartime pronouncement that the only unambiguous opposition to the Nazis had come from those in exile. He maintained that the inner immigrants had in fact found an "inner space" from which to oppose Hitler and the Nazis. Indeed, he went so far as to say that he was "richer in knowledge and experience than if I had viewed the German tragedy from the ground of a foreign continent."[50]

After reading Mann's reply to von Molo, Thieß composed a second letter in which he was even more critical. Thieß wrote acerbically that no one wanted to take Mann from his "life in Florida [sic!]" to have him come and live in the rubble and misery. This would mean that he would have to make a real sacrifice. According to Thieß, Mann had already sacrificed "his membership in German literature." A writer could not live for decades in the air of a different country and still be German. Mann would have to decide whether he belonged to Germany and Europe or to the United States. Then the whole German people, not just the critics and writers, would determine if Mann was German or foreign. What mattered, claimed Thieß, was not that Mann still wrote and thought in German but whether or not he could still open his heart to the German people. For his part, Thieß believed that there was "not just an ocean between him and us but an abyss." Germans would continue to read his books, but "what will lead us out of our need and remorse, our anxiety and our uncertainty into a new hope and a new certainty of indestructible inner worth, cannot be achieved by a society of German-writing 'American World Citizens,' but can only be the fruit of the bloody seeds of German and European sorrow."[51]

The controversy between Mann and the "inner emigration" was played out before the German public in post-war newspapers and on the radio during late 1945 and early 1946. It provoked further attacks on Mann, though some rose to his defense. Many of the older generation who had remained in Germany already saw Mann as a traitor. His refusal to return to Germany combined with his condemnation of Germany during the war only confirmed their view. A whole

generation of younger Germans knew almost nothing about Mann or his literature. For young men such as Klaus Harpprecht, the first experience with Mann
came during the post-war period and, for some, through this public controversy.[52] Here was a German *Dichter* who had abandoned Germany in its hour of
need and who was now, it appeared, condemning all things German. The criticisms thus took on an ever-harsher tone. In October 1945 August Enderle of the
Weserkurier claimed one such as Mann who had "lived in Germany on the highest intellectual level" and "enjoyed all of the advantages of this position" had a
"moral duty to live and work with and among this people." It was both "sad and
shameful" for a person of Mann's stature to refuse to return out of "self-
interest." He should have remained silent because "whoever refuses to live with
a people has nothing to say to them!" No longer a true German writer, Mann
was simply a "satisfied American citizen."[53] Herbert Lestiboudois wrote that
Germans could "be reconciled with the entire world, but not with Thomas Mann.
. . . He hates us and besmirches us because he senses from a distance that
through suffering we are becoming and have already become more deeply, more
essentially, human than he. . . . What does he know about Germany, even though
he is a German? Nothing! There is nothing that links him to us."[54]

Mann was not without friends and supporters in Germany. Johannes R. Becher, although disappointed with Mann's intractable attitude, privately reproached Thieß because he had intended to have Mann return and become the
first president of the *Kulturbund*. As he wrote on 26 January 1946, "Your first
open letter to Thomas Mann is inappropriate in its timing, its content, and its
tone. You would have been better advised to consult beforehand with Germans
who more fully understand the attitude abroad toward Germany and who could
have clearly explained to you the attitude toward emigration and in particular
Thomas Mann's emigration within it."[55] Others in Germany supported Mann's
decision not to return to Germany, and defended his right to speak on German
matters from afar. Dolf Sternberger, co-editor of *Die Wandlung*, reaffirmed
Mann's position in German literature and history. He had produced great German literature both from within and from outside Germany. He had created new
worlds and had explored the "one really important world—the human world."
Moreover, he could still experience from outside what his countrymen experienced from inside.[56] Nicholaus Benkiser, book critic for the *Badische Zeitung*,
argued that despite the "politics of some who say that Mann rejected Germany
and has no understanding of the intellectual and spiritual course of events which
led Germany toward disaster," Mann really did understand Germany's fate.[57]
For Erich Kästner, Mann was "the most important and most famous among living German writers," and he could offer more to Europe and to Germany from
America than "if he were in his former homeland."[58]

Yet the public controversy sparked by Mann's exchange with the "inner
emigrants" illustrates that Mann was not in a position to play the same kind of
role in post-war Germany as Meinecke, Jaspers, and Brecht. Mann himself often
recognized that Thieß and others had been justified in saying that, as an émigré,
he had not experienced the German catastrophe directly and therefore could not

always speak authoritatively about many issues concerning Germans. Sometimes he also recognized that he probably had little to say to German youth: "I
do not believe that my work is advantageous for the German youth. The young .
. . are full of mistrust, they are skeptical, even nihilistic. Thus the parody of my
books is not good for them."[59]

Mann was also keenly aware that many Germans considered him and other
emigrants *personae non grata*. In his introduction to the journal *Schriftsteller*, a
direct response to von Molo and the controversy his letter to Germany caused,
Mann claimed he understood that "those who suffered (during the Third Reich)
have a strong dislike for those who would speak with them and for them even
though they were not there. . . . I have no illusions about the reputation of us
emigrants in Germany." Yet he believed that as a German writer and as one who
had made a personal moral stand he could and should speak.[60] A surgically clean
separation from his homeland was impossible, and his role as an exile, an outsider, provided him with an avenue to speak truth. At least some in Germany
were willing to listen, and Mann continued to speak on German political and
cultural issues in speeches, interviews, essays and novels.

Mann recognized that as a world-famous German writer and public figure
he had to do more than speak about artistic and cultural issues. In a stance strikingly different from his position in the *Reflections*, Mann wrote in 1947 that
artists—German artists in particular—had to come down from the ivory tower to
speak and act. It was no longer enough to be involved in a fictional soliloquy
about the role and function of intellectuals. "We artists," he wrote, "are concerned with the beautiful. However, that is not to say that we can be aesthetes;
that is no longer possible today. . . . The world has come out of an aesthetic epoch (the bourgeois) into a moral and social one." With Nietzsche artists had to
recognize that "there are no fixed points outside of life, from which we can look
out over human being and reflect. . . . I believe that the task of the writer today is
none other than it was from the beginning, namely to be a judge and a caretaker
of life. In a time which would like to be seduced into despair, into giving up,
into apathy, he gives, through intellectual work, an example of vigor, of an unwillingness to bend, of inner freedom, of courage to act. This may be especially
the obligation of the German writer."[61]

As a German artist, Mann considered it his duty to speak about broader political and intellectual issues affecting the entire West: "What is necessary is the
intellectual type, who represents the European tradition as a whole. Europe is
powerless today; however as one who lives outside (of Europe) I feel very well
the respect which the world continues to have for the most experienced continent, and its intellectual leadership may nevertheless continue." And Mann recognized that his task included not only helping to bring about revolutionary
change, but also had a reconstructive and restorative element.[62] Nothing had
come or ever would come from a German Europe. However, Germany needed to
become Europeanized again, and Mann believed it was his responsibility as a
German artist to help accomplish this task.[63]

Mann was guardedly hopeful in the immediate aftermath of the war. In spite of all that had happened, he said on 10 May 1945, "Germany's return to humanity is a great moment." It was "cruel and sad that Germany was not able to accomplish this on its own." The German name had been "terribly dishonored" and "German power" had been forfeited. But for Mann, as for Jaspers and Meinecke in the post-war period, "power is not everything, nor even the main thing, and Germany's standing was never a mere question of power." Just as it had once been "Germany's fortune to secure respect and admiration by its human contribution and by the free range of the spirit," so it might be again.[64]

As a first step, Germans had to come to terms with the German catastrophe and the part they played in bringing it about. Mann's first attempt to talk specifically about the catastrophe was his speech "Germany and the Germans," which he wrote before the end of the war and presented originally on 29 May 1945 at the Library of Congress in Washington D.C.[65] Mann had been asked to offer his reflections about what had happened to Germany, the home of so many great and beautiful things. He recognized that this was a "risky business," especially given the "violent emotions that it raises today," and yet he also understood that as a native German he had to deal with the German catastrophe. This was not an attempt "to arouse sympathy, to defend and to excuse Germany." Mann was also not prepared to play the part of judge, "to curse and damn his own people in compliant agreement with the incalculable hatred that they have kindled."[66]

Once, claimed Mann, universalism and cosmopolitanism had marked the German spirit, but it had always been a "philistine universalism, cosmopolitanism," with "something scurrilously spooky, something hiddenly uncanny about it, a quality of secret demonism." Indeed, there was "a secret union of the German spirit with the Demonic, a thesis which is, indeed, part of my inner experience, but not easily defensible."[67] Mann pointed to the hero of Goethe's *Faust* as the prime example of this union. Here, he said, was a character that stood "at the dividing line between the Middle Ages and Humanism, a man of God who, out of a presumptuous urge for knowledge, surrenders to magic, to the devil." Even the devil himself, according to Mann, was "a very German figure," and the pact with him "to win all treasures and power on earth for a time at the cost of the soul's salvation" was "exceedingly typical of German nature."[68]

Moreover, argued Mann, Germans were "musical" in nature. What Mann intended by the "musicality of the German soul," was simply its "inwardness, its subjectivity, the divorce of the speculative from the socio-political element of human energy, and the complete predominance of the former over the latter." Martin Luther, one of the greatest incarnations of "the German spirit," was "exceptionally musical." He was "unalloyed Germanism—Separatist, Anti-Roman, Anti-European" in "the guise of evangelical freedom and spiritual emancipation." He was a "conservative revolutionary. . . . a liberating hero, but in the German style, for he knew nothing of liberty. . . . I am speaking. . . of political liberty, the liberty of the citizen—this liberty not only left him cold, but its impulses and demands were deeply repugnant to him."[69] Whereas Mann had identified himself in the *Reflections* with Luther, North German Protestantism, and "inwardness," he now claimed that Luther and his legacy were largely responsible for the wayward path that Germany took.

The other key German cultural figure to whom Mann referred was Goethe. Like Meinecke, Mann found something exceptional about Goethe: "He represents well-mannered, civilized strength and popular robustness, urbane Demonism, spirit and blood at once, namely art. . . With him Germany made a tremendous stride in human culture." Unfortunately, the Germans were "always closer to Luther than to Goethe." They had gotten their sense of political freedom from Luther, not Goethe. Luther's "anti-political servility, the product of musical-German inwardness and unworldliness," was responsible "for the centuries-old, obsequious attitude of the Germans toward their princes and toward the power of the state." In addition, it was "chiefly typical" of "the purely German sundering of the national impulse and the ideal of political liberty."[70]

The German concept of political liberty, claimed Mann, "was always directed outward; it meant the right to be German, only German and nothing beyond that. It was a concept of protest, of self-centered defense against everything that tended to limit and restrict national egotism, to tame it and to direct it toward service to the world community." Both racial and anti-European, this concept of liberty "behaved internally with an astonishing degree of lack of freedom, of immaturity, of dull servility." The German concept of liberty was tantamount to inner enslavement because Germany never experienced a revolution and "never learned to combine the concept of the nation with the concept of liberty."[71]

Goethe had a much broader understanding of liberty and was much more European than Luther. He "approved everything of a broad and generous nature, the supernational, world Germanism, world literature—his painful loneliness in the patriotically, 'liberally' excited Germany of his day cannot be overemphasized." But Goethe, Mann wrote, had to disavow the "political Protestantism," the turning of liberty against Europe, which had served "as a deepening of the Lutheran dualism of spiritual and political liberty throughout the nation and particularly among the intellectual leaders so that they were prevented from accepting the political element in their concept of culture." Indeed, Mann wrote in a passage strikingly similar to the phrasing he used in his *Reflections*: "This much is certain, that the German relation to politics is a negative one, a lack of qualification."[72] Now, however, Mann saw this "negative relation" to politics *not* as Germany's greatest strength, but rather its most serious weakness.

Unlike peoples who were "born and qualified for politics," who "instinctively know how to guard the unity of conscience and action, of spirit and power, at least subjectively," the Germans were "not born to get along with life." Germans saw politics "as nothing but falsehood, murder, deceit, and violence, as something completely and one-sidedly filthy." If they were forced to engage in politics they did so "in the light of [their] philosophy."[73] This was both an unhealthy and an unrealistic position because, as Mann wrote to Hesse, "nothing alive escapes politics. Refusal is politics, too; it is a political act on the

side of evil." Even "mind" if it is "the power which desires the good; if it is a
sensitive alertness toward the changing aspects of truth, in a word, a 'divine so-
licitude' which seeks to approach what is right and requisite at a given time . . .
is political."[74]

Germany was also the "true home" of Romanticism. Indeed, Mann maintained that "the Germans are the people of the romantic counterrevolution
against the philosophical intellectualism and rationalism of enlightenment." It
was "not feeble sentimentalism" but rather "depth, conscious of its own strength
and fullness. It is pessimism of sincerity that stands on the side of everything
existing, real, historical against both criticism and meliorism, in short, on the
side of power against the spirit." It had contributed "deep and vitalizing impulses to European thought," but its "life and death pride" had denied Germany
"any correcting instruction from Europe, from the spirit of European religion of
humanity, from European democracy." Like Meinecke, Mann claimed that
German Romanticism was wedded to Realism and Machiavellianism "in the
person of Bismarck" and this resulted in "the German victory over France, over
civilization, and the erection of the German power empire." Finally, with Hitler,
"German Romanticism broke out into hysterical barbarism, into a . . . paroxysm
of arrogance and crime, which now finds its horrible end in a national catastrophe, a physical and psychic collapse without parallel."[75]

This "melancholy" story of German "inwardness," argued Mann, should
convince of one thing: "that there are *not* two Germanies, a good one and a bad
one, but only one, whose best turned into evil through devilish cunning. Wicked
Germany is merely good Germany gone astray, good Germany in misfortune, in
guilt and ruin." Mann did not want to claim that he was "the good, the noble, the
just Germany in the white robe." Rather, "it is all within me, I have been
through it all." Far from being an absolute condemnation of all things German,
this speech was thus "a piece of German self-criticism."[76]

Mann ended the essay on a positive note. A "great good" existed in Germany. However, it could not come to fruition "in the traditional form of the national state." Mann desired "a world condition in which the national individualism of the nineteenth century will dissolve and finally vanish, and which will
afford happier opportunities for the development of the 'good' in the German
character and the untenable old conditions." He wanted "world economy, the
minimizing of political boundaries, a certain depoliticization of states in general,
the awakening of mankind to a realization of their practical unity, their first
thoughts about a world state. . . social humanitarianism."[77]

With "Germany and the Germans" Mann had only a restricted space in
which to speak about themes that really required much more detailed and sophisticated treatment. Moreover, the speech was at first only printed in excerpts
in Germany. Yet many in Germany received the speech positively. Mann received encouraging letters from Germany: "[My] interpretation of the German
tragedy . . . in the old homeland [won] back many hearts totally alienated from
me."[78] Still some critics in Germany recognized that this short speech was problematic as an explanation of the German catastrophe. The German art critic A.

E. Brinckmann wrote that Mann's history of liberty in Germany leading from Luther directly to the Nazis far too facile a historical explanation. Brinckmann also criticized Mann for identifying Germany as the "people of the romantic counter-revolution." After all, there had always been important defenders of enlightenment and humanism: Lessing, Humboldt, and Max Planck, to name only a few.[79] Surely others in Germany read the speech as did the reviewer from *Time* who wrote that Mann could "do what neither Edmund Burke nor Nürnberg's Robert H. Jackson dared—indict a whole people."[80]

Mann himself recognized that this speech to an American audience was perhaps not the best venue for him to talk about the German catastrophe. What he wanted to show was that Nazism was deeply rooted in the German tradition. At bottom, National Socialism had to do with cultural foundations as they emerged through German history. Much more important and promising for him was thus the treatment he gave this theme in *Doctor Faustus* (1947). Here Mann offered a fictional account of the German catastrophe and touched on a vast number of related themes including the question of general German guilt, the responsibility of artists and intellectuals for the fate of Germany, the broader character of the European bourgeois epoch, and the great temptation of fascism. Moreover, he was able to address the sensitive and controversial question of the German character without the limitations that the historian Meinecke or the philosopher Jaspers faced. None of Mann's works so captivated the German nation as *Doctor Faustus*, but over time none gave him so much trouble.

Although *Doctor Faustus* was surely Mann's most important and enduring attempt to deal with the German problem, it did not represent his clearest statement. Indeed, like all modern novels, it is ironic and its message is, in many ways, ambiguous. Mann used different figures—especially Serenus Zeitblom and Adrian Leverkühn—to represent many of his own often ambivalent views. Zeitblom, he wrote to Paul Amann, was "a parody of myself." Indeed, much of what Mann had already said in "Germany and the Germans," was relativized and parodied in the words of Zeitblom. There was also much of "Leverkühn's *Lebensstimmung*," in Mann himself.[81] As he told Leonard Frank, Adrian was "really my ideal, and never have I loved an imagination as much, neither Goethe, nor Castorp, nor Thomas Buddenbrook, nor Joseph or Aschenbach."[82]

For Mann, *Faustus* was above all a treatment of the cultural crisis. As he wrote his friend Bruno Walter, "Music, as well as the other arts—and not only the arts—is in a crisis which sometimes seems to threaten its very life. . . . What the novel treats of is paralysis stemming from cleverness, from intellectual experience of the crisis." Of course, there was also "a pact with the devil springing from the craving for an inspired breakthrough."[83] It was this aspect of the novel that allowed Mann to explore the connection between the cultural crisis and Germany's descent into Nazism. Indeed, the central idea of the book was "the flight from the difficulties of the cultural crisis into the pact with the devil, the craving of a proud mind, threatened by sterility, from an unblocking of inhibitions at any cost, and the parallel between pernicious euphoria ending in collapse with the nationalistic frenzy of Fascism."[84] Thus *Faustus* was, in part, a discussion of German peculiarity. As Mann recognized in his journal, "National Socialism was an enthusiastic and scintillating revolution, a German people's movement."[85] Yet *Faustus* was not, as Steven Aschheim has suggested, simply an attempt to "relate barbarism to the particular cultural modalities of a *German Sonderweg*."[86] Indeed, it was closer in its treatment of the cultural crisis and European fascism to Horkheimer's and Adorno's *Dialectic of Enlightenment* than most have recognized. Mann not only read *Philosophy of Modern Music* and an early draft of the *Philosophische Fragmente* while he was writing *Faustus*, but he also had frequent and detailed discussions with Adorno about both music and the cultural crisis, as his diaries of the period clearly illustrate.

Just as Horkheimer and Adorno were examining the extent to which Enlightenment itself was caught up in the catastrophe, *Faustus* examined the more general cultural crisis and problem of European fascism. Nazism was one response to a general cultural and political crisis—a crisis to which Germany was particularly vulnerable. As Mann wrote in *Story of a Novel*, he knew that he had to "attempt, as much as possible, to fuse [the crisis themes] to the universalities of the era and of Europe."[87] In this sense, as Mann wrote to Charles Jackson, "Adrian Leverkühn is much more a representative of our time than an allegory for Germany. He is simply a man who bears the sufferings of the epoch."[88]

Faustus also contained much of Mann's own life experience and was more or less a self-criticism: "How much *Faustus* contains of the atmosphere of my life! A radical confession, at bottom. From the beginning that has been the shattering thing about the book."[89] Because Mann himself had been an apolitical artist, had argued that Germany was unpolitical, and had been an enthusiastic nationalist during World War I, the novel was a recognition of the part he himself had played in the German catastrophe. It was, moreover, "a penance for having been away," as he wrote in 1947.[90] Both socio-political and intensely personal elements are present and join to make the spectacular richness of *Doctor Faustus*.

More generally, the novel was a criticism of the German intellectual elite and its political irresponsibility—seen both through Adrian and through other characters that inhabit the Kridwiß circle of intellectuals—an elite that attributed the highest social value to artistic endeavors and thereby missed its mission of social leadership. Especially at this moment, it was crucial to understand the role that German intellectuals, and the culture they created, played in bringing about the catastrophe. As he asked Hans Polack: "Does it not disparage and diminish the realm of the intellect to acquit it of all responsibility for its consequences, its real manifestations? That Hegel, Schopenhauer, and Nietzsche contributed to shaping the German mind is as undeniable as the fact that Martin Luther had something to do with the Thirty Years' War, whose horrors he explicitly took 'upon his neck' in advance." To deny the guilt of intellectual leaders would belittle "them, and we Germans today have every reason to be concerned with the ambiguous role of German thought and the German great man, and to ponder it."[91] *Faustus* was also a criticism of the German middle class and its subservience to the cultural elite, and it was an indictment of the German people who were apolitical, nationalistic, inclined toward mythology, and duped by Hitler. Finally, the book was a defense of liberal democracy and humanism.

As the title suggests, the novel is a story of the composer Adrian Leverkühn as told by his friend Serenus Zeitblom. Zeitblom was the representative of the bourgeois tradition, "the values of culture, enlightenment, humanity, in short such dreams as the uplifting of the people through scientific civilization."[92] He also bore all of the prejudices of his class, including cultural elitism. "People of my sort," claims Zeitblom, "have doubts whether everyman's thoughts are the right ones." He had a fear of and an aversion to the masses, which represented for him the possibility of revolution: "As a moderate man and a son of culture I have indeed a natural horror of radical revolution and the dictatorship of the lower classes, which I find it hard, owing to my tradition, to envisage otherwise than in the image of anarchy and mob rule—in short of the destruction of culture."[93]

Zeitblom, like the class he represented—and like his creator—had also been a conservative nationalist, especially during World War I. He joined in sword-waving and defended German national interests, all the while retaining his loyalty to and admiration for his friend the artist, who kept himself above the fray. For all his faults, however, Zeitblom becomes the voice of reason in the novel. Mann used Zeitblom despite, or perhaps because of, his earlier nationalist conservatism, his elitism and his political short-sightedness, to defend Western democratic humanism and to condemn the rise of the Nazis.

This representative of the German educated middle class tells the story of the "life of art and artist."[94] Zeitblom follows Adrian's life and career so closely of his "out of the imperative to hear what he heard, know what he learned, to 'keep track' of him." Yet he feels no need to change Adrian:

> I was clear in my own mind that this was a life which one might indeed watch over, but not change, not influence; and my urge to keep a constant eye on my friend, not to stir from his side, had something like a premonition of the fact that it would one day be my task to set down an account of the impressions that molded his early life.[95]

Mann thus used Zeitblom's own statements as a means to criticize the educated middle classes in Germany for their subservience to the artistic elite. Just as Zeitblom uncritically follows the career and life of Leverkühn, so the German *Bildungsbürgertum* allowed itself to be led by the German cultural elite—an elite that was itself all too easily coopted by the Nazis.[96]

Adrian Leverkühn has a penchant for the metaphysical, the religious, and the musical, and he has a mind that requires order. He feels compelled to find relations between everything, to come up with a grand scheme, a grand order for culture. "To look at the relations between things," claims Adrian, "must be the best thing, after all. Order is everything."[97] Adrian's particular areas of interest are music and theology. In theology, according to Adrian, there is "love of wisdom" which lifted

> itself to contemplation of the highest essence, the source of being, the study of God and the things of God, and the noblest sphere of knowledge, the apex of all thinking; to the inspired intellect its most exalted goal is here set. . . in the words of the Scriptures, it is "higher than all reason" and the human spirit thereby enters into a more pious, trusting bond than that which any other of the learned professions lays upon him.[98]

In music there is something of "the elemental, the primitive, the primeval beginning. . . as well as the richly complicated and finely developed and marvelous structure she had developed into in the course of the centuries—had never got rid of a religious attitude toward her own beginnings."[99]

As in "Germany and the Germans," music in *Faustus* is intimately related to theology. Mann has Adrian say in arcane language:

> in theology and music (are) neighboring spheres and close of kin; and besides, music has always seemed to me personally a magic marriage between theology and the so diverting mathematic. Item, she has much of the laboratory and the insistent activity of the alchemists and nigromancers of yore, which also stood in the sigh of theology, but at the same time in that of emancipation and apostasy; it was apostasy, not from the feith that was never possible, but *in* the feith; for apostasy is an act of feith and everything is and happens in God, most of all the falling from Him.[100]

As Mann pointed out in *Story of a Novel*, music represented something larger: "music was only foreground and representation, only a paradigm for something more general, only a means to express the situation of art in general, of culture, even of man and the intellect itself in our so critical era."[101] Music also, as in "Germany and the Germans," is a symbol for the "inwardness," the aestheticism of modern Germany, in particular the German cultural elite. Zeitblom, who is both a member and a critic of this element of German society, tells the story of Adrian and his circle of friends in their inwardness.

Adrian, as an artist, is very much removed from society. Immersed in his art and trying to break through the cultural crisis, he keeps himself "at a distance" from the world, remaining on unfamiliar terms with it.[102] He tells Zeitblom at one point that art is the highest calling:

> But do not say that it is speaking only of aesthetics, do not say *only!* One does wrong to see in aesthetics a separate and narrow field of the humane. It is much more than that, it is at bottom everything, it attracts or repels, the poet attaches to the word "grace" the very widest possible meaning. Aesthetic release or the lack of it is a matter of one's fate, dealing out happiness or unhappiness, companionship or hopeless if proud isolation on earth.[103]

In aesthetic isolation, Adrian makes a pact with the devil in return for greatness and in pursuit of a lofty ideal: a new musical system to help break through
artistic sterility. He comes to believe that new order and lawfulness must be imposed on music, which was falling into subjectivity and arbitrariness. Eventually, Adrian creates twelve-tone music to reimpose order, a musical system that
aims at objectivity and strict composition. Yet Adrian discovers that the new
order he has created is stifling and that it, like he, is completely divorced from
the rest of the world. Especially after the composition of the *Apocalypsis cum
figuris*, his masterpiece of twelve-tone music, Adrian becomes increasingly
aware that he needs some connection, a "bridge," to the rest of society.[104] Furthermore, Adrian wants his art to move out of aesthetic isolation into a relationship with the people.[105] Nevertheless, he remains always separated from life,
from the "real" world. Feeling himself to be above the rest of society, and yet,
like Mann himself, needing the approval of society, he finally rejects every opportunity to join the world. Indeed, because of his pact with the devil, he is denied any intimate relationship with the outside world.[106]

Zeitblom, the good and faithful bourgeois servant, defends again and again
the right of the artist in general, and Adrian in particular, to lead society, always
moving ahead of the general populace: "I am an old-fashioned man who has
stuck by certain romantic notions dear to me, one of which is the highly subjec-
tivizing contrast I feel between the nature of the artist and that of the ordinary
man."[107] Moreover, Zeitblom defends the hermeticism of art, though he also
recognizes the inherent dangers of aestheticism which, he claims is "the herald
of barbarism." There is "a pre-cultural, a barbaric condition of cult-art. . . . Can
it be denied that this was pre-cultural, a barbaric condition of cult-art; and is it
comprehensible or not that the late and cultural revival of the cult in art, which
aims by atomization to arrive at collectivism, seizes upon means that belong to a
stage of civilization not only priestly but primitive?"[108]

The aestheticism, the inwardness to which Germany was so prone, appeared
to have been broken immediately following World War I. The war ushered in
the Weimar Republic, an epoch in which Germany seemed to be joining Western democratic ideas. Yet despite this "courageous friendliness to the outer
world and the cause of freedom," there were still "the nationalistic-Wagnerian-
romantic forces of reaction" which eventually won Germany over.

An old-new world of revolutionary reaction, in which the values bound up with
the idea of the individual—shall we say truth, freedom, law, reason?—were entirely rejected and shorn of power, or else had taken on a meaning quite different from that given them for centuries. Wrenched away from the washed-out
theoretic, based on the relative and pumped full of fresh blood, they were referred to the far higher court of violent authority, the dictatorship of belief—
not, let me say, in a reactionary, anachronistic way as of yesterday or the day
before, but so that it was like the most novel setting back of humanity into
theocratic conditions and situations.[109]

The members of the Kridwiß circle, Adrian's closest artistic colleagues, simply stood by as "disinterested observers." They "fixed their eyes on the general readiness . . . to drop out of hand our so-called cultural conquests for the sake of simplification." They pretended not to be caught up in it all: "It is interesting, it is even good, simply by virtue of being what is inevitably going to be. . . . It is not our affair to go on to do anything against it. Thus these learned gentlemen, in private." Yet, claims Zeitblom, "they sympathized with what they recognized; without this sympathy they could not have recognized it."[110]

Mann echoed these sentiments in private letters of the period. He wrote to Hans Blunck, president of the *Reichsschriftungskammer* between 1933-1934:

> Only the German writer did not know. He had no problem; he could be a pure-hearted simpleton and cultivate a placid temper, without moral indignation, without any capacity for detestation, for anger, for horror at the altogether infamous *Teufelsdreck* which National Socialism was to every decent soul from the first day on. . . . Nothing can ever dispel my grief and shame at the horrible heartless and brainless failure of the German intelligentsia to meet the test with which it was confronted in 1933.[111]

As the novel draws to its conclusion, Adrian himself becomes ever more separated from world events. While his physical and mental health worsens, he works out new forms of musical composition. Yet his fate is bound up with Germany's. Indeed, argues Zeitblom, there were "symbolic parallels between [Germany and Adrian]."[112] Just as Adrian descends into syphilis-induced madness, so the National Socialist illness destroys Germany from the inside.

Mann used Zeitblom's words to show the decline and ultimate fall of Germany. As a German intellectual who had been caught up in the intellectual currents of the time, who had been himself an enthusiastic nationalist during World War I, Zeitblom, as one representation of his creator, is a credible witness to Germany's downfall with the Nazis:

> Our prison, so wide and yet so narrow, so suffocatingly full of foul air, will some day open. I mean when the war now raging will have found, one way or the other, its end—and how I shudder at this "one way or the other," both for myself and for the awful impasse into which fate has crowded the German soul! For I have in mind only one of the two alternatives: only with this one do I reckon, counting upon it against my conscience as a German citizen. The never-ending public instruction has impressed on us in all its horrors the crushing consequences of a German defeat; we cannot help fearing it more than anything else in the world. And yet there is something else—some of us fear it at moments which seem to us criminal, but others quite frankly and steadily—something we fear more than German defeat, and that is German victory. . . . But my mental state is only a variant of that which, aside from cases of ordinary self-interest or extraordinary stupidity, has become the destiny of a whole people: and this destiny I am inclined to consider in the light of a unique and peculiar tragedy. . . .But considering the decency of the German character, its confidingness, its need for loyalty and devotion, I would fain believe that in our

case the dilemma will come to a unique conclusion as well; and I cannot but cherish a deep and strong resentment against the men who have reduced so good a people to a state of mind which I believe bears far harder on it than it would on any other, estranging it beyond healing from itself.[113]

While Germany plunges headlong into the barbarism of National Socialism, Leverkühn finishes his final masterpiece, the *Lamentation of Doctor Faustus*, after which he confesses his pact with the devil and then lapses into madness. He breaks down over the piano with outstretched arms, as if crucified, but, at the same time he falls down as if pushed by the devil. The *Lamentation*, claims Zeitblom, is without "consolation, appeasement, transfiguration . . . one group of instruments after another retires, and what remains, as the work fades on the air, is the high G of a cello, the last word, the last fainting sound, slowly dying in a pianissimo-fermata. Then nothing more: silence, and night."[114] In a letter to Emil Preetorius Mann wrote that the *Lamentation* was "an ode to sorrow, since Adrian's destiny obviously does not include the Ninth Symphony's 'Joy,' whose heralding must therefore be cancelled."[115] Similarly, Zeitblom laments the German fate in an almost hopeless tone:

We are lost. In other words, the war is lost; but that means more than a lost campaign, it means in very truth that *we* are lost: our character, our cause, our hope, our history. It is all up with Germany. . . . She is marked down for . . . economic, political, moral, spiritual, in short all-embracing, unparalleled, final collapse. . . . Our "thousand-year" history, refuted, reduced *Ad absurdum*, weighed in the balance and found unblest, turns out to be a road leading nowhere, or rather into despair . . . a *decensus Averno* lighted by the dance of roaring flames.[116]

Just as Adrian confesses his pact with the devil, so Zeitblom expresses the guilt and utter condemnation that the Germans—all Germans—bear for their actions: "Everything German, even the German mind and spirit, German thought and the German Word, is involved in this scandalous exposure and made suspect." The National Socialists, those "liars and lickspittles mixed us a poison draught and took away our senses. We drank—for we Germans perennially yearn for intoxication—and under its spell, through the years of deluded high living, we committed a superfluity of shameful deeds, which must now be paid for." Zeitblom makes clear that the entire path toward collapse, "at every single one of its turns. . . was everywhere wrong and fatal."[117]

Though all seems hopeless, there is an element of grace in Adrian's *Lamentation*, in Zeitblom's words and, finally, in Mann's own view of the German and the Western future. In the *Lamentation*, the last tone, a high G, "vibrates in the silence, is no longer there, to which only the spirit hearkens, and which was the voice of mourning, is so no more. It changes its meaning; it abides as a light in the night."[118] In a sense, this lamentation is both an end and a new beginning. Grace and condemnation retain equal validity, a sign of the unresolved inner division within Mann himself. As Mann noted in a letter to Praetorius, "man's first and truest expression is a lament, and as soon as music freed itself for expression, at the beginning of its modern history, it became *lamento* and '*Lasciatemi mori.*'"[119]

Similarly, there may yet be hope for Germany. Zeitblom says in the end of the novel:

> Today, clung round by demons, a hand over one eye, with the other staring into horrors, down she flings from despair to despair. When will she reach the bottom of the abyss? When, out of the uttermost hopelessness—a miracle beyond the power of belief—will the light of hope dawn? A lonely man folds his hands and speaks: "God be merciful to thy poor soul, my friend, my Fatherland!"[120]

Zeitblom believes that politically the only hope for Germany is in joining with the Western democracies. The racist totalizing solution of Nazism to the political crisis has ended in disaster. Only in democracy can renewal occur. Democracies "in all the anachronistic state of their institutions through the passage of time, all the rigidity of their conceptions of freedom in resisting the new and inevitable, is after all essentially the line of human progress, of goodwill to the improvement of society and its renewal."[121] Culturally what Zeitblom desires for Germany, as for the world, is a new "religious humanism":

> Piety, reverence, intellectual decency, religious feeling, are only possible about men and through men, and by limitation to the earthly and human. Their fruit should, can, and will be a religiously-tinged humanism, conditioned by feeling for the transcendental mystery of man, by the proud consciousness that he is no mere biological being, but with a decisive part of him belongs to an intellectual and spiritual world, that to him the Absolute is given, the ideas of truth, of freedom, of justice; that upon him the duty is laid to approach the consummate.[122]

Both of these themes would recur in Mann's non-fictional writings of the late 1940s and early 1950s.

Mann published *Doctor Faustus* in 1947, first in the United States and Switzerland, and then Germany. Between 1945, when "Germany and the Germans" was first printed in Germany, and 1947 he gave a number of interviews and several speeches which developed further his ideas from "Germany and the Germans" and *Doctor Faustus*. These interviews and speeches, along with the fact that *Doctor Faustus* was virtually unavailable in Germany until 1949, made Mann's reception in Germany even more problematic. As Johannes R. Becher recognized in a private letter to Mann, many in Germany were writing critiques of a book that had not yet even appeared. So desperate was Becher to make the novel available, and thus to create an informed discussion of it, that he suggested a "joint production" between the East German Aufbau press with Bermann-Fischer and Suhrkamp.[123]

In many of his speeches, essays, and interviews Mann hammered away at the theme of collective German responsibility for Nazism and its crimes against humanity. If there was a "general culpability" in the West for the catastrophe, Mann insisted that "the Germans have played a special, terribly authentic role in the drama."[124] He wrote in 1945 that "it is impossible to demand of the abused nations of Europe, of the world, that they shall draw a neat dividing line between 'Nazism' and the German people. If there is such a thing as a people, if there is such a thing as a Germany as an historical entity, then there is also such a thing as responsibility, quite independent of the precarious concept of 'guilt.'"[125]

Because Mann believed all Germans bore some responsibility for Nazism, he expected contrition. Germans needed to accept responsibility for the catastrophe. When they did not, he responded angrily.[126] In an interview with *Die Welt* in 1947 he said that the Germans

> lack the insight, that all the sorrows and misery are the final and necessary consequences of a collapse, like the world has never before seen, that they themselves are responsible for their own misery and not some democracy and the occupation troops. They must therefore accept the consequences: that they led themselves into the darkness and that they served this regime for twelve years. They have squandered their national power, the German intelligence, their spirit of inventiveness, courage and efficiency in the service of a mad regime.[127]

These kinds of comments, which were printed in newspapers throughout Germany, left a bitter taste, especially when taken in conjunction with Mann's speeches and *Doctor Faustus*. As one interviewer said in 1947, it was easy to see why Mann had so many enemies in Germany: "Mann has not yet forgiven and forgotten, and has, at the same time, rejected the position of intellectual leader of a leaderless people. Instead, he has criticized—perhaps a bit too long— in the old tone." Thus he had "become the chief of enemies in a land where the national socialistic resentment continues apace, almost unconsciously."[128]

Complicating matters still further was Mann's return to Europe in 1947 and his continued refusal even to visit Germany. He still was not ready to see the ruins of his former homeland and Germany was not yet ready for his visit. He asked his brother Viktor,

> What should I, what can I say to the Germans, sensitive plants that they are today, sore, thin-skinned, overwrought? At bottom the Germans don't want any slurs cast at their Third Reich. So we must speak only of the future! But that lies completely in the darkness, and we have no idea what we ought to wish for, hope for, recommend. [. . .] Saying anything would be empty posturing, evasion, lying, comforting wishy-washiness—and even at that it would be impossible to avoid giving offense.[129]

In an interview with *Die Welt*, he recognized that it might be wiser to "put aside" his visit to Germany. He had the "feeling, that such a visit, which could certainly never be completely private, but rather would have to be connected with a public expression of opinion" would "be more fruitful and happy, when the minds there have been more reassured and clear." Germany, he believed, "shared this feeling" because he had thus far received "no official invitation."[130]

It is very difficult, then, to distinguish between the German response to Mann's *Faustus* in 1947 and the more general question of Mann's standing with the German public as a result of his earlier public pronouncements. Complicating matters further is the fact that virtually no copies of *Faustus* were available in Germany in 1947. Because of copyright restrictions for American authors, the German-language edition of the novel was originally distributed in Switzerland. Hans Mayer, a literary historian who reviewed the book for *Neue Zeitung*, wrote that the book "simply is not obtainable here (in Germany)."[131] Yet the Germans were certainly interested in the book. Peter Suhrkamp wrote to Mann that "The general public is obsessed with *Doctor Faustus*. Not only are extensive critiques appearing in newspapers and journals, but the book is also the subject of lecture and discussion groups."[132]

Many of the German reviewers of *Faustus* saw it only as a criticism and a misreading of German history and culture. Hans Paeschke, the publisher of *Merkur*, wrote in his review that the novel showed clearly that Mann hated all things German—past, present and future. Moreover, claimed Paeschke, "it is hardly to be expected that a spirit like Thomas Mann," this "mere *Schriftsteller . . .* could have written the sort of work that Germany needs."[133] In a similar vein, Hans-Egon Holthusen attacked Mann for his treatment of the German catastrophe. He argued that Mann now understood neither German history nor the German character. Mann equated German character with music, which was "the opposite of Enlightenment, civilization, and democracy," and saw Faust as "the symbol of the German soul." According to Holthusen, Mann had "demonized" German history and the best German traditions and had reduced German history "to a scandalous affair."[134] Walter Boehlich, in his review of the book for *Merkur*, also attacked Mann for using Faust to demonize Germans. He fastened on Mann's exile as a reason for the novel's failure. Mann had lost "the very soil"—the German soil—to which he owed everything. Having lived in the Untied States, "a country without a great literature," a country where "symbols cannot flourish," he could no longer understand Germany and thus could not possibly understand Faust, the chief "symbol of Germany." Moreover, because he had not personally experienced the events of 1933-1945, he could not accurately describe them.[135]

Other reviewers, such as Werner Oehlmann of *Der Tagespiegel*, were much more positive. For Oehlmann, a music critic, *Faustus* was "perhaps the greatest literary work of the epoch."[136] Nikolaus Sombart argued that Mann was "the greatest and most important teacher in German literature." He was especially important as a guide for the young intellectual elite.[137] Martin Beheim-Schwarzbach, a writer from Hamburg, praised *Faustus* in his review for *Die Welt* and wrote to Mann that he was "more thankful for this colossal achievement of German literature than I can say."[138] Privately Caroline Newton wrote that Faustus was "a sacred book, a book blessed by God. So long as the word Germany lives, this book will live and be essential reading for those who seek to understand Germany."[139] The composer Hanns Eisler also privately celebrated not only Mann's understanding of musical composition, but also the "political formulations . . . and the insight into the historical weaknesses of the Germans, which one finds elsewhere only in Marx."[140]

More incisive were reviews by Walter Viktor, Viktor Sell, and Iring Fetscher. They recognized that Mann was not attempting to distance himself from the Germans, either in *Faustus* or in his speeches. Mann recognized that he, too, was implicated in the German catastrophe and he wanted to help rebuild German culture. Viktor, writer and cultural critic for the East German *Aufbau*, argued that *Faustus* was a story about the German catastrophe, but not a judgment from an objective person. It was also Mann's own "life story" and came "from his own breast."[141] In his review for *Die Wandlung*, Sell, a literary historian, wrote that Mann, "even though he now lives in California, is still in touch with the German experience. . . . *Doctor Faustus* tackles the problem, which the wider masses of Germans took up only after total defeat: the question of how it was possible that a people with a highly-developed culture could let "evil have its way."[142] Fetscher, of the *Studentische Blätter* in Tübingen, wrote that Germans greatly misunderstood Thomas Mann: "The careful reader of *Faustus* will see the apparent love Mann has for Germany." To be sure, his consciousness "is stamped by the old bourgeois spirit—naive-realistic, as it appears in *Betrachtungen*." But if he spoke of the German culture and the German essence he was speaking of his own experiences and he was beginning to come to terms with its breakdown.[143]

As Fetscher, Sell and Viktor all pointed out, Mann was writing about the decline of an epoch, a culture, and a nation. In so doing, he joined with Meinecke and others in criticizing the German traditions that had led to disaster and in trying to come to terms with Germany's troubled past. He also recognized that Germany had been part of the wider cultural malaise that affected the entire West. Since at least the time of Nietzsche's moral critique, Mann claimed in 1948, the Occident had "lost the moral and intellectual authority which bound everything together at all times. . . which supported everything and gave everything an assured belief." Now the West longed "for a new belief, a religious bond, which . . . grants support to the life of the individual against nihilism." This cultural crisis had been one of the reasons for the rise of fascism and Nazism, and it was still very much a part of Western culture. Yet the West, unlike Germany, had avoided the worst aspects of this crisis by clinging to the notion of individual freedom within the general framework of democracy.[144]

Mann believed that Germany, too, had a promising future if it would turn toward humanism and democracy. Between 1945 and 1947, he repeatedly stated his belief that, if the Germans would come to terms with their responsibility for the Nazi regime and turn toward the West, Germany could and would rejoin the democratic society of nations. At times, he believed he saw the kind of contrition he expected. For example, he wrote in 1947 that even the German youth, who had been indoctrinated from birth by the Nazis, were recognizing that they had been misled by Hitler and his henchmen. Mann also had doubts about Germany's future. Privately he had "a deep mistrust of the political development in Germany." As he noted in his journal, there existed "no good will for cooperation with the Allies."[145] For the most part, however, Mann argued that Germany had a future, no matter how hopeless things looked at the time. After all, the Germans also possessed the humane and democratic spirit to which he had pointed in "Germany and the Germans" and "Schicksal und Aufgabe." Germany had the ability to change to a new form of life. It could drive out hatred and darkness, and it remained a land full of "value which can count on the ability of its people and the help of the world." [146] Mann hoped, and sometimes believed, that Germany, like Switzerland, would eventually have a "democratic-federalistic constitution."[147] Moreover, he believed that Germany would become "member of the European federation and further the world federation, which—I hope—will one day be achieved without a war." [148]

If Germany were to renew itself culturally and politically, however, it would have to resurrect from its own history the spirit of democracy and humanity. Mann recognized better than many of his contemporaries that Germany could not begin with a tabula rasa. It had to build from the traditions and institutions it already possessed. Germans had to "announce the new *and* inherit the old," to "bring out the new from the tradition." Out of "historical tumult" had to come first a moment of "restoration."[149] In this way, Mann attempted to resurrect and, in some ways, reinvent two key cultural icons, Nietzsche and Goethe, while leaving behind two others, Luther and Bismarck. Luther had "shattered the unity of Christendom." He had despised the humanism of his day, had "taught his people submission to divinely ordained authority." He was not just "anti-Roman," but also "anti-European, furiously nationalistic and anti-Semitic." Bismarck was "brutal and sentimental. . . a titan of unfathomable cunning. . . . To him as to Luther hatred was a joy and a passion, and although as a diplomat of aristocracy, he had European polish, he was, like Luther, anti-European."[150] Germany should turn away from Bismarck and Luther, and turn toward Goethe and Nietzsche, "intellectual [types] who [represented] the European tradition as a whole," and yet had something distinctly German about them.[151]

Nietzsche, Mann wrote in a key essay of 1947, had been much misunderstood and misinterpreted both by the Nazis and later commentators. As he wrote to Werner Schmitz in 1948, "to call Nietzsche, the European, the condemner of Bismarck and Wagner, a 'forerunner of the Third Reich,' is a crude simplification."[152] Nietzsche had not created the fascists, as the Socialists had accused him of doing; instead, the fascists had invented their own Nietzsche. Nevertheless, Mann admitted, Nietzsche offered little as an example of political responsibility. This "nonpolitical" and "innocent intellectual" who was a "delicate recording instrument" of the times, "served the Germans as a model for those traits which made them a disaster and a terror to the world, and led them ultimately to ruin themselves: romantic passion; will which is free because it has no goal and aspires to the infinite."[153]

On a cultural level, however, Nietzsche was much more valuable. His perspective was "the universal perspective, the vision of Occidental culture as a whole."[154] Thus, he had much to say to post-war Germany and Europe. He pointed toward a kind of "supradenominational religion. . . . a religiously- based and colored humanism which, out of the depths of experience, having survived many trials, includes all knowledge of other lower and daemonic elements of man's nature in its homage to the mystery of man."[155]

Mann had been working out his own ideas on a kind of "religious humanism," which vaguely resembled the religious humanism advocated by Meinecke. This new humanism would replace metaphysics and would have a pathos that was religious, albeit in a humane and secular way. In a 1947 interview, Mann stated: "The world. . . should create not only a new atmosphere, but rather also a new belief, a new religion and a new feeling for humanity and personality. That is my literary aim, and if my work has a value, then it has value on this basis."[156] Mann wanted to make perfectly clear that this new humanism was not to resemble the old overly optimistic humanism of the eighteenth century. He was thus engaging in the wider discussion of neo-humanism in Germany and at the same time distancing himself from what he perceived to be backward-looking position advocated by many, including Meinecke. Any new humanism, while it would have to look to the European tradition, had to be fully knowledgeable of the horrors of which humanity was capable. Germans, and Europeans more broadly, had to recognize that something deep within the culture had gone wrong, but culture might nevertheless offer some hope for renewal.

Mann increasingly believed that conference decisions, technical measures and legal institutions would do little to create a new order "new relationships, the recasting of society to meet the global demands of the hour." Instead, what was important was "a transformation of the spiritual climate, a new feeling for the difficulty and the nobility of being human, an all-pervasive fundamental disposition shared by everyone, and acknowledged by everyone within himself as the supreme judge." After all, claimed Mann, humanity belonged not just to the material sphere. It also occupied a higher world, "the spiritual, the moral world, the world in which there is knowledge of good and evil." In this sphere, humanity "brings to nature a conscience, becomes spirit, and spirit is the self-critique of life." In this new dispensation artists and poets would work "imperceptibly through the depth and breadth of society." They would develop new cultural foundations, strive honestly for the "idea of humanity, which is the idea of freedom and the good."[157]

Mann was satisfied that the best intellects of the epoch were preparing the way for this renewal, this new feeling of humanity, this "respect for the mystery which man is."[158] Germany also showed signs of cultural renewal. To be sure, Hitler and "the National Socialist regime [had] left behind a cultural wasteland in Germany, which [could] at first only slowly be watered and cultivated." Mann cited the examples of the journals *Die Wandlung* and *Die Gegenwart*. These journals were attempting to "raise the German spirit" and to "bring it into contact with the necessities of the time." Additionally, Mann saw the desire to read in Germany as "a good sign," of a coming cultural renewal.[159]

If Nietzsche pointed toward a religious humanism, it was Goethe, Mann argued in 1949, who could be the guide and the example for post-war Germany. After almost a year and a half of virtual silence on German issues, Mann joined with many other Germans in turning to Goethe as a helper in a time of need. Mann had written often on Goethe throughout his career. Now, reviving themes he introduced in "Germany and the Germans," Mann wanted to show that Goethe was the key source in the German tradition for both cultural and political renewal.

In "Goethe and Democracy," first presented in the United States and subsequently in England, Sweden, Denmark and Switzerland, Mann argued that Goethe had "resisted the German-Romantic cult of death, and was a friend to democracy."[160] Goethe was more than just a poet, more than just an aesthete. He was "a sage, a ruler, the last representative and spiritual captain of Europe, a great man."[161] He was bound to the best traditions of European civilization and culture. He believed himself to be a cultural Christian and was committed to the "'moral culture' of Christianity, its humanitarianism, its civilizing, anti-barbarous tendency."[162] He was always committed to European culture, "this 'priceless culture' that, for several thousand years arose, grew, spread, was suppressed, oppressed, never quite extinguished, revivified, revitalized, continues to emerge in never ending activity."[163]

Moreover, according to Mann, Goethe possessed a democratic spirit. To be sure, he had been an aristocrat and had often disparaged democracy—especially its manifestation during the French Revolution. Yet he had been, at heart, a democrat, a defender of individual freedom and equality. Finally, in Goethe "there is a foundation of unshakably great humanity and of a reliable goodness which reconciles all contradictions in a lofty, almost god-like fashion. And I think you will find even the political contradictions evident in his Weltanschauung to be dissolved in this unfailing humanity."[164]

Mann echoed these sentiments in a speech he gave in Germany during 1949, *Ansprache im Goethejahr*. He spent the first half of the speech recounting his exile and assuring the Germans that he understood their plight and empathized with them. He then turned to Goethe, who he believed could unite Germany. Goethe was a European humanist and yet he was also distinctly German. He was both "divine" and "demonic." Representing the "highest humanism," Goethe had a personality too great for any mere man, a personality "that leveled all beneath it, and that compelled admiring submission."[165] And yet, Mann did not want to oversimplify Goethe as the embodiment of the "good," the "humanitarian," the "democratic" Germany as opposed to the bad. He also recognized the alarming extent to which Germans were returning to Goethe in cult-like fashion.

Goethe, claimed Mann, was German to the core, just like Bismarck and Luther, but "in its most profoundly humanized modification; the titan molded on Olympus." Much in Goethe was "dark and demonic, superhuman, inhuman, which chill and frighten the mere humanitarian. There is in it much of that hyper-masculine and belligerent skepticism that Nietzsche described as the characteristic quality of German greatness, a hard—yes, evil—skepticism that understands everything and despises everything, that gives the mind a perilous freedom, and that is utterly remote from sentiment." Even his contemporaries saw in him a "dreadful indifference, an incredible neutrality. . . even a nihilism." Yet this "nihilism," this "nothing" was "another name for 'everything,'" because it included "everything human, for the thousandfold life of a Proteus who assumes every guise, who wants to know everything, be everything, live in every shape and form."[166]

Mann wrote that "only a eulogist could deny that Goethe was as much of an anti-ideologist as Bismarck, an aristocrat in his conception of culture, politically, as often as not, an out-and-out Tory. He was opposed to the freedom of the press, opposed to giving the masses a voice, opposed to a constitution, was convinced that 'everything sensible is in the minority'; and he sided openly with the prime minister who with deliberation carried out his plans in defiance of his king and his people." And yet, he had "a cordial affection for the individual human face, the sight of which, he confesses, could promptly heal him from melancholy; but he had little of the humanitarian faith in man, in humanity, in its capacity to be purified by revolution, in a better future." However, in Goethe one could find "a union of the urbane and the daemonic whose captivating greatness was not twice achieved in the history of civilization. A completely unconstrained and manifest synthesis of what is German and what is Mediterranean, European."[167]

The immediate context for Mann's new defense of Goethe was his first return to Germany since 1933 to accept the Frankfurt Goethe Prize. This prestigious prize, which had been given since 1927 to intellectuals in Germany who best exemplified the spirit of Goethe, had gone in the post-war period to figures such as Max Planck (1945), Hermann Hesse (1946), Karl Jaspers (1947) and Fritz von Unruh (1948). Now in an attempt to reunite the German people with their most famous living writer, the Goethe Prize committee offered the prize to Mann, who was still living in California.[168] Mann eventually accepted the prize and agreed to return to his homeland for the celebration, but with much trepidation. As he told his friend Hans Reisinger, "I cannot help feeling that this return after sixteen years of my life must stand symbolically for all Germany. For so very long, 'being taken to Germany,' 'falling into the hands of the Germans,' was a nightmare. And what am I to say? The awareness of how much we and they have drifted apart in all these years prevents me from finding the right tone. . . . I might simply restrict myself to the (very doubtful) future and to *old Goethe*."[169]

Mann spent time in Frankfurt, where he first gave the speech in Germany, Munich, Nuremberg, *and* Weimar in the Eastern Zone. Weimar, which also laid claim to the heritage of Goethe, had offered Mann its own version of the Goethe Prize along with honorary citizenship. From Johannes R. Becher Mann received an invitation to present "the formal address" for the celebration of Goethe's birthday along with the "National Goethe Prize."[170] Mann's decision to accept Becher's invitation would prove to be fateful, for his visit to the Eastern Zone would bring his reputation in West Germany to its nadir.

Mann wrote a new introduction for his speech in East Germany. Here he stated that it would have been "disloyal" not to have visited both zones. Goethe, after all, belonged to all of Germany and he, along with Mann himself, offered something that could unite the two zones.

> Eastern and Western Germany, beyond and above all differences of their regimes, all ideological, political, and economic contrasts, have found each other on cultural grounds, and have awarded, in this particularly meaningful year, their Goethe Prizes to one and the same literary personality. This seems to me an encouraging and remarkable fact, quite apart from the individual prize winner. This agreement in the sphere of culture may be considered a symbol of the unity, endangered already more than once, of Germany, and the question is quite warranted: Who should stand for and represent this unity today if not an independent writer whose home, untouched by zonal divisions, is the German language?[171]

In Goethe one could "find a way into the open out of the profound and confusing crisis in which it finds itself. . . a new feeling of human solidarity, a new humanism." Above all what must not perish were "certain acquisitions, hard-earned by mankind and inalienable—liberty, justice, and the dignity of the individual." And then, with a nod toward the social: "They, even in such an organic context as may be required by increased social obligations, must be kept sacred and transmitted to the future."[172]

Clearly, Mann had written the speech so that it would appeal both to the East and West German understanding of democracy and humanism. He was trying to find some common ground between the Germanies and, more broadly, between the Soviet Union and the United States. Such a tactic, though it served a purpose for this speech, was not just window dressing. Mann himself had become more and more concerned about the rift between the Western Allies and the Soviet Union, and he hoped that there might be some way to ease the tension. In an interview of 1947, he had stated that the "division of Europe into East and West is very dangerous for the peace. . . . The present tension between the United States and the Soviet Union could only be solved, if America would become more socialistic and the Soviet Union more democratic, so that they meet half way."[173]

Privately Mann had become increasingly skeptical of the aims of the Western Allies—in particular the United States—for Germany and Europe, though he rarely said so in public. In addition, because he was living in California, he had seen first hand the rising anti-communism of McCarthy and his cronies. This witchhunt atmosphere looked to Mann far too much like the rise of Nazism in Germany, and led him to become more and more skeptical about the prospects for Western democracy. He wrote to Agnes Meyer that "The Roosevelt era is going to have to be demolished even more thoroughly, for it was after all just one great *un-American activity*. Dear friend, let me confess to you that I already hate the Thomas Rankin Committee and its wretched activities as much as I once hated Hitler."[174] America, was "experiencing a great lowering of morale, raw avarice, political reaction, race hatred, and all the signs of spiritual depression."[175] America was beginning to look to Mann like Germany immediately before the rise of Hitler. This suggested to Mann that the political crisis had not been resolved by the defeat of fascism in Europe, and it forced him to accept Adorno's contention that the political and cultural institutions of the West, with their origins in Enlightenment, were complicit in the overall catastrophe.

Mann's misgivings about the United States and Western democracy would continue to grow. However, publicly he continued to support the West and the United States. He was certainly no defender of Soviet Communism. It was both autocratic and totalitarian, as bad, in many ways, as Nazism had been. As he wrote to Francis Biddle: "I am neither a dupe nor a fellow-traveler and by no means an admirer of the quite malicious present phase of the Russian revolution."[176] Soviet communism was not, according to Mann, Germany's future. However, Mann could not "approve of the exaggerated antibolshevisitic propaganda, behind which are reactionary elements. We must come to a modus vivendi with Russia in order to have peace. Another war would destroy Europe."[177]

Unfortunately, Mann's attempt to use Goethe, and himself, to bridge the gap between the two Germanies proved unconvincing and ineffectual. Goethe had little to say to a defeated and divided Germany, and Mann was too far removed and disengaged from the contemporary German situation. Even less convincing was Mann's claim that Goethe, despite his many anti-democratic stances, had a democratic spirit and that he therefore could be a source for democratic renewal in Germany. Many critics pointed out that Goethe had never been a democrat. Mann himself had admitted as much and then had claimed that his humanism and his humanitarianism made him a democrat at heart.[178]

Of course, Mann knew that he would be heavily criticized for going to Weimar. Voices of discontent arose even before he arrived there. Friedrich Sieburg, of *Die Gegenwart*, attacked Mann several weeks before he gave his Frankfurt speech, when Mann's impending trip to Weimar became common knowledge. There was, Sieburg claimed, an iron curtain between the two Germanies. Mann had "become the object of this confrontation. The absolute unhappiness of his relationship to Germany reaches a new level, and whatever he may say here and there, will satisfy no one, least of all himself. . . The way from Frankfurt to Weimar is short; however, it will be a crossroads for the author of *Doctor Faustus*. . . . Thomas Mann has no luck with Germany, but who would have!"[179]

As Mann suspected, his visit to Weimar drew the ire of the German press in the Western Zone. Even more abominable for the West Germans than the visit itself was Mann's refusal to say anything at all about the fact that the Russians were now using the former concentration camp Buchenwald to intern innocent

Germans. Eugen Kogon of the *Frankfurter Neuen Presse*, and author of the first book on German death camps—*Der SS-Staat: das System der deutschen Konzentrationslager*—attacked Mann for not addressing the concentration camp inmates, these "poor, suffering people." Mann simply did not understand, claimed Kogon, "the tragic reality" that Germany was divided into zones of occupation and that they could not simply choose to live in the "zone free from occupation and division—the German language." After all, the Germans had had no true choice about their fate in the post-war years. They had been subject to the wishes and will of humanity, and not "merely to a humanity established in the abstract."[180]

Mann tried to answer his critics by saying that it would have been impossible for him, as an invited guest, to make demands of the East Germans that they could not have met anyway. Those from whom he had received the invitation had no real power. Moreover, Mann claimed somewhat disingenuously that his trip was a "completely unpolitical one." He had gone as a literary figure. Better, then, to keep quiet. On one level, of course, Mann was correct. As a United States citizen and a literary figure, he could have done little to change East German political policy. He might well have brought down the wrath of the East German government and the Russians on the political prisoners. However, as his critics pointed out, he might at least have given some comfort to the Buchenwald inmates by letting them know that the outside world was aware of their plight. Moreover, Mann might have made a clear and unambiguous statement about his own position. Instead, he remained silent and his silence again became a political statement.

Whatever Mann's reasons for refusing to denounce the East German government, this incident brought his reputation in Germany to an all time low, as his German publisher Peter Suhrkamp recognized in a private letter.[181] Mann did not help matters by publicly stating upon his return to the United States that the picture in Germany was very bleak. He told American reporters that what impressed him most about Germany was its return to nationalism. Moreover, he claimed that the Western powers sympathized more with the Nazis than with the Social Democrats or democracy.[182] He criticized denazification, which he claimed had not achieved its goal, and he said that the Western Allies showed the tendency "to support fascism and nationalism and to see them as a bulwark against Bolshevism." The Soviets were no better. As a result, claimed Mann "East Germany is totalitarian; West Germany is reactionary and fascist. . . . One does not see how both parts can come together again."[183]

Mann's 1949 trip to Germany would be his last real attempt to speak on political issues—either German or Western. Though he continued to be interested in, and troubled by, contemporary politics, he seemed to return to a belief that politics could not provide the kind cultural and social bonds he deemed necessary. Thus Mann largely withdrew from public life. From the 1920s until his speeches of 1949, Mann seemed to have believed, at least some of the time, that politics, by which he meant democracy, could meet some of the fundamental human needs. By 1949, he began to recognize that such an expectation was folly. Thus he turned his attention more fully to purely cultural concerns.

Not until the year of his death, 1955, did Mann finally begin to regain some respect in Germany. In his address on Schiller in his home city of Lübeck, he again assumed the role of some kind of teacher and leader, an effort that was not rejected entirely by Germans. Yet his position in Germany remained rather complicated and defies simple explanations. In a sense, Bark and Gress are right. Mann rejected the role of insider and chose, instead, to speak as an outsider. He never felt comfortable with Germany and the Germans and might have said with his friend Adorno: "Dwelling, in the proper sense, is now impossible. The traditional residences we grew up in have grown intolerable: each trait of comfort in them is paid for with a betrayal of knowledge, each vestige of shelter with the musty pact of family interests."[184] He saw his country with unblinking honesty, and hence was never quite at home with it. But it was precisely in this role as an outsider, with an insider's knowledge, that he spoke the truth with such force. He had a double perspective that forced him to see things and events not in isolation but in relation to each other, and thus he had a more universal idea of how to think about the catastrophe. Moreover, his standpoint of exile forced him to see things not simply as they were, but how they had come to be that way. He saw the rise of Nazism and the overall catastrophe not as inevitable, but as the result of a series of historical choices made by men and women.

Despite his troubled relationship with the Germans Mann thus played a central role. Like Meinecke, he helped Germany come to terms with its past. He sounded the death knell for an old bourgeois and nationalist culture. In contradistinction to Brecht, he modeled for Germans an ethic of responsibility, rather than an ethic of conviction. He provided the Germans with figures from their own past who could help them join with the wider European tradition. He helped recover and refurbish cultural foundations. Perhaps most importantly, Mann came closer than Meinecke, Jaspers, or Brecht to explaining the unique development of Germany within the more general cultural and political crisis of the West. Like Adorno, he sought to uncover the origins of the catastrophe in the Western cultural tradition. Yet he also understood that Germans were responding in a particular way, because of their own unique history, to the crisis that other countries also faced. He demonstrated the painful truth to a German audience unwilling to listen that Nazism was not alien, was not "so forced, so foreign to our national character that it could not take root among us." Indeed, it was "stamped upon the features of our greatest and mightiest embodiments of our essential Germanness." In short, he went a long way toward explaining why his country, the country of *kultur* and music, had capitulated to Nazism. He also articulated for Germans the truth that the world's perception of "everything German, even the German mind and spirit, German thought, the German World," would be affected by the horror of the crimes perpetrated by Nazi Germany.[185] In this sense, Mann stands out from his contemporaries in his grasp of the truths and dilemmas of his age.

Yet there were also weaknesses to Mann's post-World War II work. He was certainly not now, as an old man, the person to go back and work in the rubble. He was by nature and circumstance ambivalent, ironic, skeptical, even if he was not necessarily cynical. He was therefore unable to speak as concretely and unambiguously about issues of immediate importance as the Germans expected and needed. Especially in this period of utter confusion, anyone assuming the mantle of cultural leadership needed to be clear, unambiguous, and convincing. Mann remained unsure about Germany's future and skeptical about prospects of democracy, even in the United States. Indeed, he became ever more skeptical about the possibility of any political solution to what was at bottom, in his mind at least, a cultural crisis. He distrusted the Americans, the Russians, and the Germans.

Moreover, Mann's confrontation with the German past was problematic on some levels. As a novelist, he possessed certain advantages over the historian Meinecke. Because he made no claim to objective historical truth, for example, he was able to delve into the question of German character and cultural identity by creating composite fictional characters. In addition to specific choices made by individual Germans, there was something in the German character, as seen through the fictional characters Leverkühn, Zeitblom, and others that allowed for the rise of National Socialism. However, to post-war Germans who had heard enough about "the German character," and collective guilt, who needed unvarnished truth about the past, who needed to understand where Germany had gone wrong, Mann's portrayal of the German catastrophe in *Doctor Faustus* seemed once again to blur the lines. The same was true of his literary essays and speeches of the post-war period. In "Germany and the Germans," for example, German history looked like nothing more than the history of an entire people dominated by the romantic ideal. Though Mann had argued that the Germans were responsible for their own fate and for the overall catastrophe, he had never pointed to direct and specific causes. In the end, his work was too much in the ironic mode or trope.

Finally, Mann's portrayal of German history and cultural identity seemed to most Germans shrill and accusatory. Though he recognized that, as a German artist, he had been partially responsible for the German catastrophe, he could not understand, in the way that Jaspers and Meinecke could, the compromises that one had to make to survive in a dictatorship. Although he certainly had not lived in an ivory tower, he also had not experienced the worst aspects of the Third Reich. On the one hand, this meant that he was free from the kind of self-serving defenses of writers such as Thieß and von Molo, and it allowed him to speak a certain kind of truth to his countrymen and the world. On the other hand, and despite his best efforts, he could neither empathize nor find common ground with most Germans. His portrayal of German history in *Faustus* and "Germany and the Germans" sounded like a condemnation from abroad—a demonization of the entire German people. Thus the Germans were bound to react negatively. Yet the reaction against Mann also helped redefine German cultural self-consciousness. Here was a figure who, though unarguably the greatest living

German novelist, had so vilified the German character that the Germans could feel a sense of unity and identity in their almost total rejection of him as their representative and spokesman. Unable to effect direct and immediate change, Mann, the insider who became outsider, nevertheless developed a language that spoke truth to the Germans. And he provided future generations a point of departure, a point of contact, a point of view, triangulation in a world of disequilibrium.

NOTES

1. Cited in Thomas Mann, *Tagebücher 1944-1946*, ed. Inge Jens (Frankfurt: S. Fischer Verlag, 1986), 190, 613.

2. Thomas Mann, *Letters 1889-1955*, trans. Richard and Clara Winston (Berkeley and Los Angeles: University of California Press, 1970), 355, 369.

3. Ibid., 395.

4. Denis L. Bark and David R. Gress, *A History of West Germany: From Shadow to Substance*, vol. 1 (Cambridge, Mass: Blackwell, 1993), 162.

5. Jost Hermand, *Kultur im Wiederaufbau, Die Bundesrepublik Deutschland 1945-1965* (Frankfurt, Berlin: Ullstein, 1989), 143.

6. Gordon Craig, "The Mann Nobody Knew," *New York Review of Books*, 29 February 1996, 34.

7. Joachim Fest, *Die Unwissenden Magier* (Frankfurt: Fischer, 1993), 19.

8. Donald Prater, *Thomas Mann: A Life* (New York: Oxford University Press, 1995); Ronald Hayman, *Thomas Mann: A Biography* (New York: Scribner, 1995); Klaus Harpprecht, *Thomas Mann: Eine Biographie* (Reinbeck: Rowohlt Verlag, 1995); Anthony Heilbut, *Thomas Mann: Eros and Literature* (New York: Knopf, 1996).

9. Prater, *Thomas Mann: A Life*, 525.

10. Herbert Lehnert and Eve Wessel, *Nihilismus Der Menschenfreundlichkeit: Thomas Manns "Wandlung" Und Sein Essay "Goethe und Tolstoi"* (Frankfurt am Main: Vittorio Klostermann, 1991).

11. Hermann Kurzke, *Thomas Mann, Das Leben als Kunstwerk* (Munich: C.H. Beck, 1999).

12. One sees this in stories such as "Little Lizzie," "The Way to the Churchyard," and "The Wardrobe," as well as in novels such as *Buddenbrooks* and *Death in Venice*.

13. Mann, *Letters*, 69.

14. Mann, "Thoughts on the War," in *Essays of Three Decades*, (New York: Knopf, 1947), 33.

15. For other discussions of this theme see Robert Wohl, *The Generation of 1914*; David D. Roberts "Italian Intellectuals and the Great War," *International History Review*, Vol. III, No. 2, April 1981; Roland Stromberg, *Redemption by War: The Intellectuals and 1914* (Berkeley: University of California Press, 1981).

16. Thomas Mann, *Briefe an Paul Amann*, ed. Herbert Wegener (Lübeck: M. Schmidt-Rombild, 1959), 32-33. Among the objects of Mann's attacks was his brother, Heinrich, though Mann also fought against his own inclination to be a *Zivilisationsliterat*.

17. Thomas Mann, *Reflections of a Nonpolitical Man*, trans. Walter D. Morris (New York: Fredrick Ungar Publishing Co, 1983), 78, 187-188, 201, 188-189.

18. Mann, *Letters*, 90.

19. Lehnert and Wessel, *Nihilismus*, 11-110.

20. Thomas Mann, "Goethes Laufbahn als Schriftsteller" and "Goethe als Repräsentant des bürgerlichen Zeitalters," in Thomas Mann, *Reden und Aufsätze I, Gesammelte Werke*, 12 vols. (1960-1974) (Hereafter GW) vol. 9 (Oldenbourg: S. Fischer, 1960), 340-341.

21. Thomas Mann, *Reden und Aufsätze IV*, GW, vol. 12, 933.

22. Thomas Mann, "The German Republic," in *The Weimar Republic Sourcebook*, ed. Anton Kaes, Martin Jay and Edward Dimendberg (Berkeley: University of California Press, 1994), 105, 109. A better translation of "Deutsche Menschlichkeit" is "German humanity" rather than "German humanitarianism." Thomas Mann, *Reden und Aufsätze III*, GW, vol. 11, 810

23. Thomas Mann, "The German Republic," 106, 108, 109.

24. Mann, *Letters*, 32.

25. Thomas Mann, "An Appeal to Reason," in *The Weimar Republic Sourcebook*, 150, 153, 157, 159. First published as "Appell an die Vernunft," *Berliner Tageblatt* (18 October 1930).

26. Thomas Mann, "The Sufferings and Greatness of Richard Wagner," in *Essays by Thomas Mann*, trans. H. T. Lowe-Porter (New York: Vintage, 1957), 210-211.

27. Hans Vaget, "Im Schatten Wagners," in *Im Schatten Wagners. Thomas Mann über Richard Wagner. Texte und Zeugnisse 1895-1955* (Frankfurt am Main: Fischer Taschenbuch, 1999) 326-328.

28. Mann was actually much more ambivalent about Wagner than this speech suggests. See Hans Vaget, "Im Schatten Wagners," in ibid., and "National and Universal: Thomas Mann and the Pardox of 'German' Music," in *Music & German National Identity*, ed. Celia Appelgate and Pamela Potter (Chicago and London: University of Chicago Press, 2002), 155-177.

29. "Protest der Richard-Wagner-Stadt München," *Münchner Neuste Nachrichten*, 16/17 April 1933, no. 105, 3.

30. Thomas Mann, "Thomas Mann verteidigt sich: Mißverständnisse um Richard Wagner," *Deutsche Allgemeine Zeitung*, 22 April 1933, vol. 72, no. 187, 1.

31. Thomas Mann, *Tagebücher 1933-1934*, ed. Peter de Mendelssohn (Frankfurt: S. Fischer Verlag, 1977), 54ff.

32. Thomas Mann and Hermann Hesse, *Hermann Hesse-Thomas Mann Briefwechsel*, ed. Anni Carlsson und Volker Michels (Frankfurt am Main: Suhrkamp Verlag and S. Fischer Verlag, 1999), 89.

33. Hayman, *Thomas Mann: A Biography*, 423.

34. Klaus Schröter, *Thomas Mann im Urteil seiner Zeit* (Hamburg: C Wegener, 1969), 266f.

35. Thomas Mann, *Neue Zürcher Zeitung*, 16 January 1936, cited in Thomas Mann, *Letters of Thomas Mann, 1889-1955*, trans. Richard and Clara Winston (New York: Knopf, 1971), 209.

36. See Herbert Lehnert, "Bert Brecht und Thomas Mann im Streit über Deutschland," in *Stationen der Thomas Mann Forschung*, ed. Hermann Kurzke (Würzburg: Königsberg & Neumann, 1985).

37. Thomas Mann to Ernst Reuter, 24 June 1943, reprinted in *New York Review of Books*, 12 January 1995, 48.

38. Thomas Mann, "Thomas Mann über die deutsche Schuld," *Bayerische Landeszeitung*, 18 May 1945. This text was a special broadcast produced for and distributed by the American Office of War Information shortly before the capitulation of the German

armed forces. It is not exactly clear what station broadcast it. Thomas Mann's title was "Die Lager" or "The Camps." The title used by the *Bayerische Landeszeitung* caused many Germans to believe that Mann was raising the specter of collective guilt, rather than including himself, as the text clearly states. For the text see Thomas Mann, "Die Lager," in *An die gesittete Welt: politische Schriften und Reden im Exil* (Frankfurt am Main: S. Fischer, 1986), 698ff.

39. Jaspers to Golo Mann, 30 January 1947, NJ, DLA, 75.8782.

40. Friedrich Rasche, "Thomas Mann," *Neuer Hannoverscher Kurrier*, 13 July 1945, Vol. 1, No. 8.

41. Herbert Burgmüller, "Thomas Mann und die Deutschen," *Die Fähre*, vol. 1, no. 4, 251-2.

42. UP report, 1 September 1945, cited in Mann, *Tagebücher 1944-1946*, 693.

43. Walter von Molo, *Hessische Post*, 4 August 1945.

44. Mann, *Tagebücher 1944-1946*, 693.

45. Mann, *The Story of a Novel*, 133.

46. Mann, *Tagebücher 1944-1946*, 200.

47. Thomas Mann, "Offener Brief für Deutschland," *Augsburger Anzeiger*, of 12 November 1945. Originally published in *Aufbau* as "Brief nach Deutschland. Warum ich nicht nach Deutschland zurückkkehre." As Golo Mann reported to his mother on 6 October 1945, "We gave the best possible play to Z[auberer]s letter to Molo. I had it read twice in full by our star speaker, and it will be read a third time Sunday evening, the best listening time." Cited in Mann, *Tagebücher 1944-1946*, 723.

48. Ibid.

49. Max Barth, "Abschied von Thomas Mann: ein unfreundlicher Kommentar zu einer unfreundlichen Erklärung," *Neue Volkszeitung*, 15 September 1946.

50. Frank Thieß, "Die innere Emigration," *Münchner Zeitung*, 18 August 1945. A few months later, Mann discovered that Thieß had in fact not been an opponent of Hitler's but had welcomed the Nazi seizure of power.

51. Frank Thieß, printed in Dortmunder Druckschriften-Vertriebsdienst verbreiteten Druckschrift, 1946, 5ff. This exchange continued for several months with very little new substance.

52. Harpprecht, *Thomas Mann: Eine Biographie*, 16.

53. August Enderle, "Ein Emigrant über Thomas Mann," *Der Weserkurier*, vol. 1, no. 8, 13 October 1945.

54. Herbert Lestiboudois, "Briefe an Frank Thieß," *Neue Westfälische Zeitung*, 22 January 1946.

55. Johannes R. Becher, *Briefe* (Berlin: Aufbau Verlag, 1993), 279, 283.

56. Dolf Sternberger, "Tagebuch: *Thomas Mann und der Respekt*," *Die Wandlung*, vol. 1, no. 1, 451-59.

57. Nickolaus Benkiser, "Der Faust unserer Tage: Zu Thomas Manns letztem Werk," *Badische Zeitung*, Freiburg, vol. 3, no. 24, Easter edition 1948

58. Erich Kästner, "Betrachtungen eines Unpolitischen," *Die Neue Zeitung*, 14 January 1946.

59. For example, in an interview with Dr. Karl Wehner of *Münchner Merkur* in 1947, Mann expressed his belief that the youth of Germany needed a young, unambivalent and committed leader. He himself was far too much a part of the old bourgeois century.

60. Thomas Mann, "Die Aufgabe des Schriftstellers," Geleitwort, *Der Schriftsteller*, München, Vol. 1, No. 1, 1947, printed in *Reden und Aufsätze IV*, GW, vol. 10, 779-783.

61. Ibid., 781.

62. Thomas Mann, *Reden und Aufsätze V*, GW, vol. 12, 666.

63. Mann, "Die Aufgabe des Schriftstellers," 782. In addition to his eassaystic descriptions of the task of the artist, Mann wrote two works of fiction which treated this theme: *The Tables of the Law* and *Joseph the Provider*.

64. Thomas Mann, *Deutsche Hörer* (Frankfurt am Main: Fischer, 1987), 12.

65. The speech was then distributed by the Office for Wartime Information in Europe. It appeared in excerpted form as "Vom deutschen Wesen," in the 30 June edition of *Münchener Zeitung*. *Die Neue Rundschau* published it in complete form in October 1945.

66. Thomas Mann, "Germany and the Germans," in *Literary Lectures Presented at the Library of Congress* (Washington: Library of Congress, 1973), 33.

67. Ibid., 35-6.

68. Ibid., 36.

69. Ibid., 36-8. This was not the first time Mann had linked German national identity to music. Already in 1917 he had written that music was "Germany's national art. . . . more than literature and politics, it has the power to bind and unite." Vaget, *Im Schatten Wagners*, 63. Significantly, in "Germany and the Germans" and in *Doctor Faustus* Mann attempted to distance himself from Luther and North German Protestantism, whereas in *Reflections of a Nonpolitical Man* he had identified himself with and defended this tradition and Luther.

70. Ibid., 36-8.

71. Ibid., 38-39.

72. Ibid., 40.

73. Ibid., 41.

74. Mann, *Letters*, 349.

75. Mann, "Germany and the Germans," 44-45.

76. Ibid., 45-6.

77. Ibid., 47-48.

78. Mann, *Story of a Novel*, 111.

79. A. E. Brinckmann, "Thomas Mann über Politische Freiheit," *Neues Europa*, vol. 2, no. 13, 1947, 29-34. There is little existing evidence of such letters. Mann rarely kept letters sent him by individuals he considered to be "insignificant."

80. "Hunter and Hunted," *Time*, 7 January 1946, 27-28.

81. Mann, *Briefe an Paul Amann*, 69.

82. Mann, *Tagebücher 1944-1946*, 79-80.

83. Mann, *Letters*, 345.

84. Mann, *Story of a Novel*, 30.

85. Mann, *Tagebücher 1944-1946*, 78.

86. Steven Aschheim, *Culture and Catastrophe: German and Jewish Confrontations with National Socialism and Other Crises* (New York: New York University Press, 1996), 6.

87. Mann, *Story of a Novel*, 55.

88. Thomas Mann to Charles Jackson, 4 November 1948, cited in *Tagebücher 1944-1946*, 823.

89. Ibid., 154; *Tagebucher 1944-1946*, 295.

90. Mann, "Die Aufgabe des Schriftstellers," 780.

91. Mann, *Letters*, 377.
92. Ibid., 365.
93. Ibid., 340.
94. Ibid., 24-5.
95. Ibid., 111.
96. There is also a clear element of homo-erotic love between Zeitblom and Leverkühn, which is also a metaphor for the problematic relationship between the German middle classes and the artistic elite.
97. Ibid., 45.
98. Ibid., 81.
99. Ibid., 62.
100. Ibid., 131.
101. Mann, *Story of a Novel*, 41-42.
102. Mann, *Doctor Faustus*, 391.
103. Ibid., 309.
104. Ibid., 393.
105. Ibid., 322.
106. This is symbolized in the death of his beloved nephew Echo.
107. Ibid., 24-5.
108. Ibid., 322, 379.
109. Ibid., 368.
110. Ibid., 370.
111. Blunck, a friend of Mann's in the pre-war period, had been president of the *Reichschriftumskammer* between 1933 and 1935. He never joined the Nazi party and lived in inner migration for the remainder of the war. After the war, he was denounced by an active member of the Nazi party, accused of being "the right hand man of Goebbels," and imprisoned. Blunck's brother, Rudolf, who was living in the United States at the time, appealed to Mann for help. Mann refused, claiming that he could not help a man who had been the president of the *Schriftumskammer* for the entire twelve years of Hitler's reign. When Blunck had been cleared and released, he wrote a letter of explanation to Mann. Mann continued to be unsympathetic and wrote a "philippic" to Blunck in which he attacked all writers who had remained in Germany during the "Teufelsdreck of National Socialism." Mann later, in 1948, wrote a conciliatory letter to Blunck in which he assured Blunck that he bore him no ill will. "Everyone," he wrote, "has his fate and goes his own way." Walther Blunck, *Thomas Mann und Hans Friedrich Blunck: Briefwechsel und Aufzeichnungen* (Hamburg: Troll Verlag, 1969), 113-136. Mann, *Letters*, 368-370.
112. Mann, *Doctor Faustus*, 342.
113. Ibid., 30-31.
114. Ibid., 491.
115. Mann, *Letters*, 378.
116. Mann, *Doctor Faustus*, 175, 453.
117. Ibid., 481, 175, 453.
118. Ibid., 491. As Mann noted in his diaries and *Story of a Novel*, he intended the novel to end on an even more positive note, but was convinced by Adorno that the hope for final salvation and deliverance was incongruent with the tenor of the rest of the novel.
119. Mann, *Letters*, 378.
120. Mann, *Doctor Faustus*, 510.

121. Ibid., 365.

122. Ibid., 273.

123. Johannes R. Becher to Thomas Mann, 19 January 1948, *Stiftung der Akademie der Künste*, Abteilung Literatur, Berlin, Germany.

124. Mann, *Letters*, 350.

125. Thomas Mann, "The Tragedy of Germany," in *Treasury for the Free World*, introduction by Ernest Hemingway, ed. Ben Raeburn (New York: Arco Publishing Company, 1945). See also Mann's statements on German responsibility in *An die gesittete Welt*, 675. Mann would later say that he did not believe in collective German guilt, though perhaps collective illness. Arnold Bauer, "Wandlung eines Dichters: Ein zweites Gespräch mit Thomas Mann," *Neue Zeitung*, München, 21 June 1949.

126. Mann got most of his information about the Germans from his two sons, Golo and Klaus, both of whom were in Germany after the war as American officers, and from his daughter, Erika, who was a correspondent for *Stars and Stripes*.

127. Thomas Mann, *Frage und Antwort: Interviews mit Thomas Mann 1909-1955*, eds. Volkmar Hansen und Gert Heine (Hamburg: Albrecht Knaus Verlag, 1983).

128. Hans-Geert Falkenberg, "Gespräch mit Thomas Mann," *Göttinger Universitäts-Zeitung*, 24 October 1947, cited in Mann, *Frage und Antwort*, 284.

129. Mann, *Letters*, 385-6.

130. J. H., "Gespräch mit Thomas Mann" *Die Welt*, Hamburg, 20 May 1947, cited in Mann, *Frage und Antwort*, 270-73.

131. *Die Welt*, 31 January 1948; Hans Mayer, "Doktor Faustus," *Neue Zeitung*, 12 December 1947.

132. Peter Suhrkamp to Thomas Mann, 13 August 1948, in Thomas Mann Archiv, Zürich Switzerland. (Herafter *TMA*)

133. Hans Paeschke, "Thomas Mann und Kierkegaard: Ein Briefwechsel über den "Doktor Faustus" und seine Kritiker," *Merkur*, vol. 3, no. 9, 925. .

134. Hans-Egon Holthusen, "Die Welt ohne Transzendenz," *Merkur*, vol. 3, no. 6, 38-59.

135. Walter Boehlich, "Thomas Manns *Doktor Faustus*," *Merkur*, vol. 2, no. 3, 588-603.

136. Werner Oehlmann, "Thomas Mann und die deutsche Musik," *Der Tagespiegel*, 19 February 1948.

137. Nikolaus Sombart, "Wir können uns Thomas Mann leisten," *Der Ruf*, vol. 3, no. 17, 1 September 1948.

138. Martin Beheim-Schwarzbach, 15 March 1948, *TMA*, cited in *Tagebücher 1946-1948*, edited by Inge Jens (Frankfurt: S. Fischer, 1989), 729.

139. Caroline Newton to Mann, n.d., *TMA*, cited in *Tagebücher 1946-1948*, 690..

140. Hanns Eisler to Thomas Mann, 18 January 1948, *TMA*, cited in *Tagebücher 1946-1948*, 695.

141. Walter Viktor, "Thomas Mann's *Doktor Faustus*," in *Aufbau*, Berlin, Vol. 4, 6 June 1947, 491-6.

142. Viktor Sell, *"Doktor Faustus,"* in *Die Wandlung*, vol 3, no. 5, 403-413

143. Iring Fetscher, *Studentische Blätter*, Tübingen, vol. 5, 20 June 1948.

144. Mann, *An die gesittete Welt*, 763.

145. Thomas Mann, *Tagebücher 1946-1948*, 92.

146. Mann, "Germany and the Germans"; "Schicksal und Aufgabe," 647.

147. Arnold Bauer, "Wandlung eines Dichters: Ein zweites Gespräch mit Thomas Mann," *Neue Zeitung*, 21 June 1949, Mann, *Frage und Antwort*, 297.

148. DPD/Reuter und DENA/Reuter, *Nachrichtenagenturen*, interview with Thomas Mann, 16 May 1947, cited in Mann, *Frage und Antwort*, 266.

149. Mann, *An die gesittete Welt*, 665.

150. Thomas Mann, "Goethe, the German Miracle," *The Listener*, 9 February 1950, vol. 43, no. 1098, 251.

151. Mann, "Die Aufgabe des Schriftstellers," 782.

152. Mann, *Letters*, 403.

153. Thomas Mann, "Nietzsche's Philosophy in the Light of Recent History," in *Last Essays* trans. Richard and Clara Winston and Tania and James Stern (New York: Knopf, 1959), 175.

154. Mann, "Nietzsche's Philosophy," 153.

155. Ibid., 176.

156. Interview mit einem Reutervertreter, *DPD/Reuter und DENA/Reuter, Nachrichtenagenturen*, 16 May 1947, cited in Mann, *Frage und Antwort*, 267.

157. Mann, *An die gesittete Welt*, 765.

158. Thomas Mann, "Nietzsche's Philosophy in the Light of Recent History," 177. Interestingly, Mann called this essay/speech an "essayistic epilogue" to *Faustus*.

159. J.H. "Gespräch mit Thomas Mann," *Die Welt*, Hamburg, 20 May 1947, in Mann, *Frage und Antwort*, 27-3.

160. The speech was later published in Germany in the Summer 1949 edition of *Die Neue Rundschau* and the August 1949 edition of *Die Wandlung*. Thomas Mann, "Goethe and Democracy," in *Literary Lectures Presented at the Library of Congress* (Library of Congress: Washington, 1973).

161. Ibid., 94.

162. Ibid., 99.

163. Ibid., 103.

164. Ibid., 91-92.

165. Thomas Mann, *Ansprache im Goethejahr*, held on 25 July 1949 in the Paulskirche in Frankfurt am Main, (Frankfurt am Main: Suhrkamp, 1949), 18-19.

166. Ibid, 19.

167. Ibid, 19.

168. For a full discussion of the prize and its history see Willi Wemrich, *Die Träger des Goethe Preises der Stadt Frankfurt 1927-1961* (Frankfurt am Main: Verlag August Osterrieth, 1963).

169. Mann, *Letters*, 410.

170. Johannes R. Becher to Mann, 29 October 1948, *TMA*, cited in Mann, *Tagebücher 1946-1948*, 855.

171. Mann, *Ansprache in Weimar*, 20.

172. Ibid., 22.

173. Mann, *Frage und Antwort*, 266-267.

174. Mann, *Letters*, 405.

175. Ibid., 373.

176. Ibid., 412.

177. Arnold Bauer, "Wandlung eines Dicthers," *Neue* Zeitung, 22 June 1949, in Mann, *Frage und Antwort*, 298.

178. Ibid., 298.

179. Friedrich Sieburg, "Frieden mit Thomas Mann," *Die Gegenwart*, vol. 4, no. 14. 14-16.

180. Eugon Kogon, in *Frankfurtur Neuen Presse*, 7 July 1949. Kogon, who was a former prisoner, was also commissioned to draft an official report on the "extermination factory" at Buchenwald. "Buchenwald," Editorial, *New York Times*, 19 April 1945; "Atrocity Report Issued by Army," *NYT*, 29 April 1945.

181. Peter Suhrkamp to Thomas Mann, 6 September 1949, in *TMA*.

182. "Der Unbelehrbare," *Schwarzwälder Post*, Oberndorf, 12 October 1949.

183. "Thomas Mann sieht schwarz," *Der Kurier*, Berlin, 4 May 1950, in Mann, *Frage und Antwort*, 316-17.

184. Theodor Adorno, *Minima Moralia: Reflections from a Damaged Life*, trans. E.F.N. Jephcott (London: Verso, 1974), 38.

185. Mann, *Doctor Faustus*, 481-2.

Chapter Four

Hero or Villain? Bertolt Brecht in the GDR

Bertolt Brecht's career in the German Democratic Republic has been much debated in the years since his death in 1956. For many it was during this period that Brecht abandoned the role of independent intellectual to become a party functionary. Hannah Arendt argued that he "ceased to be a poet" during his GDR years. He suffered "the only meaningful punishment that a poet can suffer . . . the sudden loss of what throughout human history has appeared as a divine gift." This loss he suffered not when he became a communist, or when he refused to break with communism during the Moscow Trials, or even when he failed to speak out about the Hitler-Stalin Pact, but only when he "had settled down in East Berlin, where he could see, day after day, what it meant to the people to live under a Communist regime."[1] Theodor Adorno called Brecht a "eulogist for complicity" who "championed" not an "imperfect socialism but a tyranny."[2] Many critics have focused on Brecht's stance during the workers' uprising of June 1953. Especially after this event, during which Brecht publicly supported the crackdown of the regime, Brecht's critics in the West, most notably Günter Grass, portrayed him as an intellectual traitor who had abandoned the very workers for whom he claimed to speak.[3] Some recent biographers, including Ronald Hayman and John Fuegi, have been equally critical of Brecht's actions during this crisis. At the one chance to overthrow the communist dictatorship and reclaim freedom, Brecht, either through cowardice or opportunism—or both—chose to support the Stalinist regime of Walter Ulbricht. Other biographers have been more sympathetic. Werner Mittenzwei, for example, has portrayed Brecht as an almost heroic figure. He did everything he could, given the strictures of life in the early GDR—including sending critical letters to key officials such as Prime Minister Otto Grotewohl and President Walter Ulbricht and spearheading direct actions against the regime. Rather than opportunism or cowardice, moreover, it was, according to Mittenzwei, Brecht's concern for the fledgling communist state that motivated him in the summer of 1953.[4]

Too often informed by cold-war assumptions and by an ex post conception of what was possible in the context, these interpretations do not present the clearest picture of Brecht's career in the GDR, or his actions at this moment of crisis. This chapter focuses on Brecht's responses to the challenges within the political crucible of the early GDR. It examines Brecht as a specific type of German intellectual, one positioned between his exile experience in Scandinavia and the United States on the one hand and his conviction, on the other, that the future of Germany lay in a socialist society that could only be guaranteed by the Soviet Union after the collapse of the Third Reich. By the time he returned to Germany, Brecht understood his creative and intellectual contribution as a commodity, in the revolutionizing sense of the term he had developed in "The Threepenny Lawsuit." He clearly recognized that his reputation as a playwright could be instrumentalized for specific ends. As he adjusted to the changing realities of life in the fledgling Communist state, he learned how to estimate and exercise his commodity value. He worked to build a new socialist culture on the ruins of the old high culture and to secure a permanent residence for his Berliner Ensemble. Along the way, he helped initiate a critical reappraisal of the German cultural tradition.

Long before his career in East Germany began, Brecht was a well-known dramatist and a controversial intellectual. He had gained recognition as a playwright during the Weimar period, when it became possible for intellectuals outside the traditional circles to gain a measure of influence.[5] Hostile to the old high culture and its values, Brecht sought to create an aesthetic—and a theater—more suitable to the modern industrial world. By the mid-1920s his ideas were developing into what he, along with Erwin Piscator, called "epic" theater, although that term was not yet explicit. By 1927 Brecht was demanding "the *radical transformation of the theater*" which would "correspond to the whole radical transformation of the mentality of our time."[6] He envisioned a theater different from "dramatic" or "Aristotelian" theater, one that did not depend on empathy and mimesis. Whereas the premise for dramatic theater was that human nature could not be changed, "epic" theater assumed that it both could change and was already changing.[7] A new theater was now possible, Brecht wrote, because technical advances permitted "the stage to incorporate an element of narrative in its dramatic productions. The possibility of projections, the greater adaptability of the stage due to mechanization, the film, all completed the theatre's equipment, and did so at a point where the most important transactions between people could no longer be shown simply by personifying the motive forces or subjecting the characters to invisible metaphysical powers."[8]

In "epic" theater, actors and spectators would experience plays differently. Actors would no longer go "wholly into their role" but would remain "detached from the character they were playing and clearly inviting criticism of him." "Epic" theater was supposed to provoke decisions from the spectator and to stimulate his/her capacity for action. Spectators were no longer "to submit to an experience uncritically (and without practical consequences) by means of simple empathy with the characters in a play. The production took the subject-matter and the incidents shown and put them through a process of alienation: the alienation that is necessary to all understanding." Whereas the dramatic theater's spectator said, "Yes, I have felt like that too—Just like me—It's only natural—It'll never change—The sufferings of this man appall me, because they are inescapable—That's great art; it all seems the most obvious thing in the world—I weep when they weep, I laugh when they laugh," the spectator of the "epic" theater responded differently. He said to himself: "I'd never have thought it—That's not the way—That's extraordinary, hardly believable—It's got to stop—The sufferings of this man appall me, because they are unnecessary—That's great art: nothing obvious in it—I laugh when they weep, I weep when they laugh."[9]

The radicalization of Brecht's theater theory coincided with his conversion to Marxism. Indeed, the idea that the spectator should learn to consider the world to be changeable helped him adapt his literary technique to his new beliefs. With the help of friends such as Carl Zuckmayer, Fritz Sternberger, Erwin Piscator, and his second wife Helene Weigel, Brecht began to move slowly toward Marxist political commitment. Zuckmayer gave him books by the Marxist theorists Georg Lukacs and Ernst Bloch.[10] From the sociologist Sternberger, who was an independent Marxist, he learned that European Drama since Shakespeare had shown the lonely individual in tension with his social environment. In the world of capitalism and large industry, however, this was no longer the case. Hence, it was necessary to liquidate the traditional aesthetic.[11] Piscator, for whom the destruction of the "theater of illusion" meant a direct attack on the bourgeoisie itself, showed Brecht the possibilities of an explicitly political theater and helped convince him to study Marx.[12] Already critical of bourgeois individualism and traditional middle-class culture, he now added some order to his leftist leanings. Yet only in the 1930s did Brecht's work show the full impact of his Marxism.

Brecht broke through with a popular success in 1928: *The Threepenny Opera*. The opera, based on John Gay's *Beggars' Opera* (with Elisabeth Hauptmann and Kurt Weill), was a critique of bourgeois society and, to a lesser extent, capitalism, but it did not even allude to the contemporary political situation and did not suggest any prescription for change. Not until he wrote a screenplay version for the opera—*Die Beule*—in 1930, when he had become a much more convinced Marxist, did Brecht put political teeth into *The Threepenny Opera*. If this opera had not been the political statement that Brecht's later works would be, it was nevertheless a rousing critical and financial success for him. *The Threepenny Opera* thus made Brecht a well-known and financially independent playwright.

As Brecht's star rose, he became more committed to Marxism and his attention turned more explicitly to politics and political art. During 1929-1930 he read heavily in Marx, Engels, Lenin, and Hegel.[13] According to his later collaborator Hanns Eisler, his political ideas were hardening into Leninism, as opposed to social democratic reform, at this time.[14] He came to accept the necessity of class struggle, a concept that became a central component of his political and aesthetic thought. But in the early 1930s he was also greatly influenced by two unorthodox Marxists: Walter Benjamin and Karl Korsch. Korsch, originally a practical politician in the Thuringian KPD (German Communist Party), was expelled from the party in 1926 for rejecting the Bolshevization of the KPD and the Comintern. He helped Brecht understand the interrelatedness of art and society. He also strengthened in the young playwright the hope that his writing could contribute to productive societal change, and this hope was central to the development of Brecht's dramatic technique. Brecht came to see that reality should be represented in such a way that the spectator did not feel at home, but rather stood critically over against it, in order to be able to change it.[15] Benjamin's influence was less direct, but no less important. The two men shared the belief that modernism in the arts was compatible with Marxism. As Stanley Mitchell has pointed out, they were also linked by "a similar historical imagination and a similar humanism."[16]

In the early 1930s Brecht not only reinterpreted his earlier plays through a Marxist lens, but also wrote a series of *Lehrstücke* or didactic plays, which were meant to be models of political commitment for children. These plays, in some ways overly simplistic in their Marxism, made Brecht a clear target of the National Socialists, as well as the police in Germany. Already under suspicion by right-wing groups in the mid-1920s, Brecht became the object of official investigation with *Die Maßnahme* (*The Measures Taken*), the most radical of the *Lehrstücke*.[17] The Brecht file in Berlin reported that he was a "communist playwright and speaker," though not officially a "party member."[18] As a result, Brecht was placed on the Nazi blacklist and had to leave Germany on the day after the Reichstag fire when over 4000 Communists and leftist intellectuals were rounded up.

Unlike many of his communist colleagues, Brecht did not settle in Moscow. On his way to America in 1941, Brecht traveled through the Soviet Union, but he did not stay partly because he feared that he, like his friends Carola Neher and Sergei Tretiakov, might disappear into the Gulag.[19] Brecht was at best ambivalent about Soviet Communism under Stalin, and this would later be significant for how he positioned himself in the German Democratic Republic. He told Benjamin during the 1930s that "In Russia a dictatorship is in power *over* the proletariat," though he was quick to add that "we must avoid disowning it for as long as this dictatorship still does practical work for the proletariat—that is, as long as it contributes to a balance between the proletariat and peasantry with a preponderant regard for proletarian interests."[20] He had also been sharply critical of Stalin in his poem "The Farmer to his Oxen," even if he had recognized Stalin's "immense merits." Yet he never broke with the Soviet Union and he never openly criticized it. Even in private, he was equivocal in his criticism of Stalinism.[21] Throughout his life Brecht recognized many of the faults of the socialist system under Stalin, but, as David Pike has shown, he believed that "the residual vices plaguing the system were outweighed by its historically guaranteed virtues and would eventually be overridden by them."[22] Moreover, if there were problems within the Communist community, Brecht believed they were best dealt with internally, not in full view of the capitalist West. Nevertheless, because of his unwillingness to join the party or accept party discipline, and because Georg Lukacs later branded him a "formalist," Brecht developed a reputation as an unorthodox and undisciplined Communist. On the one hand, his reputation as an independent voice made him an object of suspicion especially amongst hard-line Stalinists. On the other, it also made him more acceptable to many left-wing intellectuals who did not toe the party line, and it gave him a degree of independence in the post-war period.

After his emigration, Brecht continued to be political, actively fighting against fascism and Nazism. If in the 1920s Brecht, like many Communists, had underestimated the Nazis, he now understood the danger they represented. For Brecht, fascism emerged from, and was in league with, late-capitalism. Given the fluidity of international relations prior to the war and the crisis of international capitalism, this was an understandable position. Nevertheless, he recognized that fascism must be combated.[23] Temperamentally unsuited to actual combat, Brecht used the only weapon at his disposal: his pen. He published works of poetry and prose in which he openly attacked the Nazi regime. He also wrote plays that he hoped would combat National Socialism including *Furcht und Elend des Dritten Reiches* (*Fear and Misery in the Third Reich*) and *Der aufhaltsame Aufstieg des Arturo Uis* (*The Resistible Rise of Arturo Ui*).[24]

It was during his exile that Brecht wrote most of his great plays, including *Galileo, Mutter Courage* (*Mother Courage*), and *Der Gute Mensch von Szechuan* (*The Good Person of Szechwan*). Also during the 1930s, first in Berlin and then in political exile, Brecht began to codify his Marxist aesthetics and his ideas about a new theater. Brecht wanted, as he wrote to Jean Renoir, to create "a new, social and antimetaphysical art," one that departed significantly from the nineteenth-century bourgeois tradition.[25] This meant that the old high culture, with its idealism and elitism, would have to be replaced with a specifically modern culture, one that would serve the proletariat. For Brecht art was not privileged; it was not above the mundane affairs of the workaday world but was only another "productive force." The old bourgeois notion that art was "an independent phenomenon of a social nature, which can impose itself against society, which can and must manifest itself everywhere and under all circumstances, making use of the entire external world only as a medium" was no longer tenable.[26]

The most significant characteristic of art in the modern industrialized world was its commodification. As Brecht pointed out in his essay "Die Dreigroßchen Prozess" ("The Threepenny Lawsuit: A Sociological Experiment"), "the whole of art without exception is placed in this new situation." There was no "untouchable art" that was free "from every process and influence of our time." A work of art "immediately assumes commodity form, that is, it appears separately from the inventor in a form determined by the commercial possibilities in the market." According to Brecht, the commodification of art was not to be lamented but rather embraced: "The conversion of intellectual values into commodities (art-works, contracts, processes are commodities) is a progressive process, and it can be affirmed on the condition that the progress is conceived as the act of advancing and not as the result of being advanced, in other words, the commodity phase must also be seen as surmountable in its turn by the ongoing advance." Brecht continued to maintain, however, that art, though not privileged in the traditional sense, had to remain autonomous. Art itself had the power to transform a particular reality by developing dialectical thinking, demystifying social reality, and "anticipating" an alternative socio-economic system.[27]

Brecht defined his own Marxist aesthetics partly in opposition to other socialist thinkers, in particular Georg Lukacs. He could not be as restrictive in his ideas about "acceptable art" as was Lukacs. At issue between Lukacs and Brecht were both the proper treatment of the cultural tradition and dramatic theory— themes that would later haunt Brecht during his GDR years. Whereas Lukacs had attacked modernism and argued for the necessity of "realism," narrowly defined, Brecht insisted on a more open-ended definition. Lukacs focused his attention on the realism of nineteenth-century novelists such as Dickens, Stendhal, Tolstoy, and Scott. He defined realism "as a literary mode in which the lives of individual characters were portrayed as a part of a narrative which situated them within the entire historical dynamics of their society." Nineteenth-century realist novels thus contained "an epic hierarchy of events and objects, and reveal what is essential and significant in the historically conditioned transformation of individual character."[28] Lukacs rejected modernism because it lacked a sense of totality and perspective; thus, it did little more than reflect the chaos and alienation of capitalism.[29] Lukacs also believed that because modernism was the expression of avant-garde artists it could not reach the masses. Especially during the 1930s Lukacs attacked Brecht for being a "formalist," for using modernist techniques such as montage. He was particularly critical of Brecht's *Lehrstücke* which, he claimed, fell short of realism. The characters in *The Measures Taken,* for example, represented little more than abstract functions in the class struggle. Here "the strategic and tactical problems of the party are narrowed down to 'ethical problems.' From the starting-point of this world outlook, it is impossible to really recognize and portray the driving forces."[30]

Brecht responded to Lukacs in a series of essays written for the journal *Das Wort,* but not published until after his death in 1956. Lukacs, argued Brecht, had been too restrictive in his definition of realism and he had based his conception on a very limited range of examples from the nineteenth century. Hence, he had neglected the realist possibilities within modern art. Brecht did not deny that "a realist way of writing" was necessary. Literature needed to give the "broad working masses . . . truthful representations of life; and truthful representations of life are in fact only of use to the broad working masses, the people." Literature must also be "popular" in the sense that it should be "intelligible to the broad masses." Realism meant, according to Brecht, "laying bare society's causal network/ showing up the dominant viewpoint as the viewpoint of the dominators/ writing from the standpoint of the class which has prepared the broadest solutions for the most pressing problems afflicting human society/ emphasizing the dynamics of development/ concrete and so as to encourage abstraction."[31] Yet Brecht defended artistic experimentation by arguing that social reality, which was constantly changing, could be revealed or unmasked by using new formal artistic and literary techniques. These techniques were no more tied to class than were other "forces of production." Modernist techniques such as montage and alienation could be used for progressive ends. They could, for example, discredit the decadent bourgeois worldview of writers who used them such as Döblin, Kafka, or Joyce.[32]

Turning the tables on Lukacs, Brecht argued that "formalism" was the attempt to "cling to conventional forms," even when an "altered social environment" made "new demands upon art."[33] Truth was still concrete, as Brecht reminded himself daily, and it had to be understandable, but artists who had a sense of the problems of audience response could decide for themselves what forms to use at particular moments.[34] It was necessary to "make a lively use of all means, old and new, tried and untried, deriving from art and deriving from other sources, in order to put living reality in the hands of living people in such a way that it can be mastered." Brecht rejected Lukacs' charge that the proletariat could not understand artistic innovations. In his own and Piscator's experimental theater "the workers judged everything by the amount of truth contained in it; they welcomed any innovation which helped the representation of truth, of the real mechanism of society; they rejected whatever seemed like playing, like machinery working for its own sake, i.e., no longer or not yet, fulfilling a purpose." There would always be "educated persons, connoisseurs of the arts, who will step in with a 'The people won't understand that.' But the people impatiently shoves them aside and comes to terms directly with the artist."[35]

As Brecht refined his aesthetic, he also developed a clearer conception about the role of artists and intellectuals in society. He had long been opposed to traditional assumptions about the role of intellectuals—that they were the arbiters of universal values, of culture, and humanity, that they somehow stood above the fray. As his friend and sometimes advisor Carl Zuckmayer wrote, "He loathed the stereotype of the wandering poet, conscious of his mission as seer and prophet"[36] These were outdated, elitist, even oppressive notions. Now his critique sharpened as he began to see that intellectuals had been complicit in the Nazi rise to power. In the early 1930s he noted that World War I had placed German intellectuals "in a difficult position." Because they had supported the war, which turned out to be "a hopeless cause," they understandably drew the criticism and mistrust of the German people, in particular the working classes. Nevertheless, the war had shown the "true character of the intellect." It proved, in particular, that "ideas are in no way superfluous." Indeed, "ideas are very useful if they are able to provide a basis for action." For Brecht there had been only one type of intellectual in the past: the "reactionary" or bourgeois intellectual "who blended into the ruling class." Bourgeois intellectuals had been too far removed from sociopolitical reality, committed only to art for art's sake, and had served only the interests of their class. Moreover, they had either directly or indirectly supported the semi-autocratic regime of the Kaiserreich.[37]

It was during the 1930s, as he was working on the problem of intellectuals and their role in society, that Brecht began to develop his critique of German intellectuals. He envisioned at this time a novel in which the foibles and weaknesses of the mandarin intellectuals would be outlined. The novel was to focus especially on the treason committed by German intellectuals during Weimar. In Brecht's opinion, intellectuals—at least those who had corrupted and misused the intellect—bore the lion's share of responsibility for the decline of the Weimar Republic and for the victory of the Nazis: "The golden age of the Tuis (Tellekt-uell-in) is the liberal Republic, however, Tuismus reaches its summit during the Third Reich. Idealism, at its basest level, celebrates its greatest triumph." It was during this time that "the people," fell under the influence of the "most corrupt Tuis."[38] Brecht would not complete this project until 1953, in the form of a play—*Turandot*—and under very different circumstances. But elements of his critique are to be found in other places, including *Galileo, Der Hofmeister*, and the short story *Das Experiment*.

For Brecht, the present situation demanded a different kind of intellectual, a "revolutionary intellectual" who would freely choose to embrace "the struggle of classes." He was distinguished from the bourgeois intellectual in that his intellect was "dynamic, political, and liquidating." [39] Although the revolutionary intellectual represented the interests of the working classes, he did not mix with them but rather had a specifically "intellectual role" to play. The proletariat needed intellectuals, Brecht argued, "to puncture bourgeois ideology," and thus "intensify the class struggle;" it needed them for the "study of the powers that move the world;" and it needed them "further to develop pure theory."[40] They also had an educational role to play. They were to prepare the way for revolution by instructing the masses in Marxist doctrine and truth.

Brecht also came to understand his own role in a specific way. He was, like other intellectuals of bourgeois origin, working in the interests of the proletariat. Here there is a striking similarity to Antonio Gramsci's notion that, for a time, "traditional intellectuals" must take up the interests of the proletariat until "organic intellectuals" of working class origin can supplant them.[41] In an especially poignant journal entry of 1940 Brecht wrote:

One hesitates to call poets such as Hasek, Silone, [O'Casey] and me bourgeois, but this is wrong. We may make the concerns of the proletariat our own; for a certain span of time we may even be the poets of the proletariat. Then the proletariat has during this time bourgeois poets who champion its causes. . . . Nevertheless, we bear the limitations and weaknesses of our class, which make us too critical to be observing fellow soldiers. . . . In certain phases of development, when the proletariat has won but is still proletarian, the function of the bourgeois champion . . . will be formalistic. Overtaken by actual development, they create only forms. After that it is time that the new poets and soldiers appear on the scene. They find in the works of their predecessors—our works— not only the most highly developed means of expression, but rather also elements of the new culture, which always come through most sharply in struggle. Dreams always fly ahead of actions; their vagueness allows the new field to appear unrestricted; in this way they stimulate. Also important in our work is the technique of the new beginning, developed by those who have mastered the tradition, because the new beginning that does not master the tradition, easily falls back under [its] domination. One proceeds most safely if one brings us forward and uses us as dialecticians among the bourgeois poets. Thereby we stand in the forefront with bourgeois politicians, who have made the interests of the proletariat their own.[42]

Brecht further understood his own intellectual role as a commodity. The same mechanisms that gave art its commodity form also commodified the artist. The new technologies of capitalism had radically altered artistic production and thus had disposed of the old conceptions of "art" and the "artistic genius." The author was "pulled into the technical process, viewed as commodity production. The old notions of art and the artistic genius were outmoded. The protection of the author's incorporeal rights is eliminated because the producer is under too great an economic pressure."[43] Although Brecht was always aware and deeply proud of his own creativity, he also recognized that his own work and reputation had a market value, and he thought a great deal about how to exploit and position himself vis-a-vis the market. He understood that, as a playwright, he had a specific role to play. In his 1935 poem "The Playwright's Song" Brecht wrote "I am a playwright. I show/ What I have seen. In the man markets I have seen how men are traded. That/ I show, I, the playwright."[44] This part of his understanding of intellectual leadership remained with Brecht, even after he returned to Germany.

When Brecht returned to the Soviet Zone of Occupation, soon to become the German Democratic Republic, he found himself in a unique position. He had waited long enough after the end of the war, first in the United States and then in Zurich, to get a sense of the possibilities in the Western and Eastern Zones. His experience at the House Unamerican Activities Council had closed off all possibilities of the American Zone of Occupation. Brecht was called to answer the charge of communism. Though Brecht was not a Communist party member—and said so at the HUAC proceeding—he had clear communist sympathies and had written a number of Marxist plays. At the hearing he was interrogated about *Mother Courage* and *The Measures Taken*, and was asked whether or not his writings had been influenced by Marx and Lenin. Brecht obfuscated and was dismissed, with thanks, by the committee. The FBI, however, was not satisfied and intended to pursue Brecht at a later date. Before they could do so, he left the USA for Switzerland, where he lived until he returned to East Berlin. This trial was also detrimental to his position within the communist orbit, because Brecht admitted that he was not a Party member, whereas the general line from those accused was to refuse to answer the question.[45]

East Germany, and East Berlin in particular, was attractive for many reasons, primary among them the offer of his own theater and the presence of many émigré friends whom he trusted. Clearly leaning toward the Soviet Zone of Occupation by the fall of 1948, he nevertheless remained ambivalent about Soviet-style Communism. That he would confront dogmatic Marxists and Stalinists was certainly clear to him and probably created some uneasiness. Yet Brecht also recognized that there would be a large enough group of like-minded people that he could resist the dogmatists, and he knew his reputation was great enough to protect him.

Johannes R. Becher, the leading cultural official in East Berlin and Brecht's friend since Weimar, personally invited Brecht to return to Germany on 5 February 1948: "it would be highly desirable, from our perspective, if you could come here."[46] The playwright Herbert Ihering also tried to convince Brecht to return. "Berlin," he wrote in 1947, "still has the potential to be a true theater town. Precisely because so much has been destroyed and so much of the old carried away."[47] During an extended trip to Berlin's Soviet sector at the end of 1948, Brecht had discussions with many of the most important cultural and political figures in the Soviet Zone: Becher, Ihering, Arnold Zweig, Wolfgang Langhoff, head of the *Deutsches Theater*, and the Soviet cultural officer Alexander Dymschitz. He spoke little and concentrated instead on "orienting" himself.[48]

Brecht became more and more certain during his visit that only the Soviet Union could guarantee the better, socialist Germany he had always desired. Not that he was naïve about Stalin or the Soviet Union. Although he was not fully aware of the atrocities of the 1930s, Brecht remained suspicious of the Soviet Union under Stalin. Nevertheless, he believed that in the wake of utter catastrophe, the Soviet Union represented Germany's best and brightest hope. He found during his visit to Berlin, however, that few Germans in the Soviet Zone shared this view. He noted that there was a "new German misery." Everything was provisional; nothing was settled. The Germans rebelled "against the orders to rebel against Nazism." It was not only that the German workers rarely admitted that their own dictatorship came from "within," but also that they were unprepared to "overcome it." Only a few recognized that "an imposed socialism is better than none at all."[49] Brecht was also disappointed by some of the officials he met. On 6 January he was taken to the Mayor of Berlin, Fiedrich Ebert (son of the first president of the Weimar Republic), who "said neither hello nor adieu, spoke not a word to me and only uttered one skeptical sentence about uncertain projects, which would destroy what already existed." During his visit Brecht also received word from SED officials that he would not immediately receive a permanent residence for his ensemble. He could feel "for the first time the stinking breath of the provinces here."[50] East Germany nevertheless appeared to be the best place for him to spend his post-World War II career. It was certainly better than the alternative—a capitalist West Germany that was rehabilitating old Nazis to an alarming extent—from Brecht's perspective. Despite the problems and challenges, and perhaps because of them, this was a "great time for art."[51] New professional opportunities along with the chance to shape an entire culture were powerful enticements.

From the beginning of the occupation, the Soviets and the party leaders had recognized the importance of the cultural sphere and of intellectuals. Stalin himself had said that intellectuals were to be "engineers of the human soul."[52] If Germans were to make the transition from Nazism to socialism, intellectuals would need to play a key role, especially in the process of reeducation. For officials such as Becher it was necessary to root out the intellectual and cultural infrastructure of National Socialism and rebuild the culture on a democratic basis.[53] This process, according to Becher, included coming to terms with the immediate past and building a new socialist identity on the basis of the more progressive aspects of the German tradition. Becher thus spearheaded the effort to create the *Kulturbund zur demokratischen Erneuerung*, the aim of which was "active production in the area of literature, science, and art toward the intellectual and moral destruction of Nazism, participation in the intellectual rebirth of the German people toward democracy and progress, encouragement of free scientific research and of all cultural life, popularization of the classical inheritance of German intellectual life."[54] Through their work in film, theater, the arts, and literature, intellectuals could help create a "radical break with the reactionary past."[55] In addition to their educational role, they would lend credibility to the GDR and might also be able to convince their left-leaning comrades still in exile to return to the East and be a part of the new society.

When Brecht returned to Germany there was still some openness and flexibility in the cultural life of the GDR. Although David Pike has argued that the die was cast for a Stalinist-style dictatorship, and its attendant cultural politics, even before Germany's partition, Gerd Dietrich has plausibly argued that some room for maneuver continued to exist in cultural politics even into the mid-1950s, when the political situation became much more restrictive.[56] There would be windows of opportunity, especially in 1953 during the disequilibrium that followed Stalin's death.

The challenges for intellectuals, and the opportunities available, were significantly different than they had been during Brecht's Weimar and exile years. Accordingly, Brecht began to rethink his own role as an intellectual. He never produced any theoretical pieces on this question, but he further refined his conception of intellectual responsibility and his own view of himself as he responded to the post-war challenges. He knew that he was breaking new ground and he was convinced that intellectuals needed to play a leading role in transforming the culture during this moment of crisis and opportunity. East Germany had not been transformed by a Marxist revolution. Instead, the Soviets had had to liberate the Germans, and they were imposing socialism from above. But the process of creating a new socialist Germany required more than making a state; it also required creating a community, and culture was essential to this process. To be sure, Brecht did not desire a return to the old high culture, of which he was deeply critical. Instead, a new socialist culture had to be created. Although there is no evidence that Brecht ever read Antonio Gramsci, his ideas about forming a new socialist culture are similar to those outlined by Gramsci in *Prison Notebooks*. In particular, Gramsci, like Brecht, believed that for a "complete" revolution to occur, a common culture, "a common intellectual and moral awareness," an alternative cultural "hegemony" had to develop.[57] For this to happen in the GDR, however, Brecht believed there had to be a certain amount of freedom, especially for artists and intellectuals. They—he—could not simply be the propaganda mouthpiece of the party. As he told Wolfgang Harich in 1951 the function of art in a time of struggle was to serve as propaganda for the party. Yet "the requirement of art works for us is higher: content and form."[58] This view put him at odds with the party officials of the SED (Socialist Unity

Party).[59] Hence it became necessary for him to use his international prestige as he moved into a central position in the GDR.

Brecht still believed his most important contribution was artistic, through his plays and his theater ensemble, but he also came to recognize that he could, and must, exercise a more direct kind of political influence through his position as a cultural official. Indeed, it was during the post-1948 period that he began to build his second career as a skilled and influential political intellectual. Although he gradually came to understand the need to work within the political system, however, he never wanted to cross the line to become a professional politician or to subordinate himself to the party apparatus—a position that he recognized would have denied him his commodity value.

Brecht was never one to shy away from conflict or criticism. Although he would accept party discipline when necessary, he was also prepared to fight the party elite on issues he deemed essential. Effective criticism, he believed, was part and parcel of building a new socialist culture, through which the values and aspirations of the working class could be expressed. Naturally, it took some time for him to get the lay of the land, but gradually, as he gained political experience, he discovered how best to influence cultural policy to get what he wanted, and what he believed best for the GDR. This usually meant working behind the scenes, in his capacity as a member of the Academy of the Arts, of which he became a founding member in 1949.[60] Brecht would continue to exercise a leading role in the Academy and indeed would eventually use it as a way to effect policy change. He believed it was crucial that the Academy control artistic production *and* cultural policy. It needed to have autonomy and guarantee a certain amount of limited freedom within the cultural sphere.[61] He wanted his own theater, to be sure, but he recognized that it would mean nothing if he did not have some autonomy. Although Brecht was usually unwilling to criticize the party openly in a public forum—and he was never willing to criticize policies of the GDR to the West—he was prepared to stand his ground on crucial issues, especially behind the scenes. But he chose his battles carefully. As Manfred Jaeger pointed out in 1973, "He [Brecht] knew that he was in the midst of a societal revolution, into which he wanted to introduce certain changes—that which was difficult but not futile, risky, but not impossible."[62]

Like Becher, Brecht believed that in order to transform itself, the new Germany would have to distance itself from its older, unhealthy traditions. In particular, Brecht thought it necessary to initiate a critical reappraisal of the German intellectual tradition, which he believed was largely responsible for the "German misery." In works such as *Der Hofmeister*, *Turandot*, and his production of Goethe's *Urfaust* he attacked the mandarin tradition of German culture.[63] Brecht also believed that the new German state had to be built around a commitment to peace. Accordingly, he worked toward such positive ends as nuclear disarmament through his position in PEN.[64] In the crucial events of 1951 and 1953 Brecht's treatment of both of these themes would land him in trouble with the party elite.

Throughout the post-war period, Brecht's main priority was the theater. It was here, as a playwright and director, that he believed he could best contribute to a new socialist society and help create a new socialist identity. Indeed, Peter Huchel later recalled that for Brecht "the theater was the most important thing; for it he made compromises."[65] Brecht considered the theater to be so important because through it he could help create a kind of socialist public sphere, a place where people could come together and think critically about their current situation and the Germany they hoped to create. His first objective was thus to assemble a first-rate ensemble of actors and directors and to find a permanent home for it. Upon his return he began to build up his ensemble, many of whom he brought back from war-time exile. He emphasized to earlier collaborators such as Caspar Neher that "theater people" were accorded "many privileges." To Bertolt Viertel he noted that "the audience is magnificent" and that theater people were "getting a lot of money to bring first-rate people here." In an (ultimately unsuccessful) effort to woo Erwin Piscator, he wrote that in Berlin there was "unrestricted freedom of movement and it's perfectly peaceful. . . . The time is right, you shouldn't wait too long, now everything is fluid, and the direction of the flow will be determined by the talents at work. You'd be welcomed with open arms."[66]

That Brecht was given state support for his theater troupe almost immediately upon his return illustrates just how important the Soviets and the SED believed him to be. He did not disappoint. The Berliner Ensemble quickly became a drawing card and showpiece—indeed was one of the very few important cultural achievements of the entire German Democratic Republic. Largely because of his reputation and the early success of his theater, of which the 1949 Berlin premiere of *Mother Courage* is only the most prominent example, Brecht also enjoyed privileges not available even to most intellectuals in East Germany, including, eventually, a car, two houses and freedom to travel outside the GDR. He also hedged his bets, and maintained his commodity status, by securing an Austrian passport, a Swiss bank account, and a West German publisher. Hence he had a degree of independence that few others possessed. This independence, along with his international reputation, gave Brecht advantages that allowed him to challenge the regime.

Neither these advantages nor his membership in the Academy of the Arts, however, gave Brecht carte blanche in the GDR. Communist officials were never prepared to give him everything he wanted. For example, he did not receive a permanent residence for his ensemble, *Schiffbauerdamm*, until 1954. Between 1949 and 1954, Brecht had to share the *Deutsches Theater* with Wolfgang Langhoff, an arrangement that he considered unacceptable in the long term, but tolerable in the short term. Moreover, Brecht was always at the mercy of the party elite for state funding, for ticket distribution and for reviews of his plays in the party papers. Many in the party were deeply suspicious of him, as they were of all émigré intellectuals who had not spent wartime exile in Moscow. In addition, Brecht had a reputation as a renegade Marxist and a formalist, thanks in no small part to the attacks leveled against him by Georg Lukacs. Among his most important critics was Walter Ulbricht, who distrusted him and even assigned intellectuals such as Wilhelm Girnus, an editor of the party mouthpiece *Neues Deutschland*, to keep an eye on him. But Ulbricht also understood that Brecht lent credibility to the regime and more or less tolerated him. Brecht recognized this and emphasized his international reputation at every opportunity in order to secure and maintain his position. Another important foe was Fritz Erpenbeck, editor of *Theater der Zeit, Vorwärts* and *Volkszeitung* and later director of the Central Program Committee of the Ministry for National Culture. Erpenbeck showed his hand already in 1949 by accusing Brecht of relapsing into formalism with *Mother Courage*, which premiered in East Berlin to great acclaim in January 1949.[67] However, Brecht always had important friends and allies in the party as well, including Otto Grotewohl, Wilhelm Pieck, and, most significantly, Becher. These important figures, along with a number of intellectuals such as Wolfgang Harich, helped promote his career and his causes. Indeed, they were sometimes willing to risk their own careers in order to protect Brecht. Over time, Brecht became a master at using their support to promote his goals.

In addition to the early success of *Mother Courage*, Brecht also had other successes as a playwright and director, including his adaptation of Jacob Michael Reinhold Lenz's play *Der Hofmeister*—his first post-war attempt to assess the German intellectual tradition. Set in Prussia and Saxony after the Seven Years' War, the play examines the life and disastrous career of a private tutor, Läuffer. Läuffer, an aspiring intellectual, is hired and exploited by a member of the Prussian gentry to tutor his son Fritz and to teach his daughter some religion for her first communion. The daughter falls in love with her tutor, and when it is discovered she is pregnant, he takes refuge with his former mentor, Wenzeslaus. Läuffer then begins to fear that the same disaster will repeat itself with the teacher's ward. He castrates himself, and thus becomes acceptable to society. For Brecht, this act of castration represented the impotence of German intellectuals in the face of their country's greatest challenges. More specifically, *Der Hofmeister (The Tutor)* was a satire "of the period during which the German bourgeoisie built its system of education."[68] The story was "not purely symbolic; indeed, the self-emasculation of the intellectuals, virtually all of whom, as a caste so to speak, were driven into the teaching profession at about that time, is presented quite realistically through a flesh and blood example. In other words, the physical castration not only *signifies* intellectual self-emasculation, but is represented as a grotesque way out of Läuffer's social situation."[69] In addition to its historical significance, the play aimed to show why German intellectuals had been unable to withstand the Nazi threat.

The play premiered on 15 April 1950 and was received positively in both East and West. Paul Rilla noted that the play was not Lenz's *Hofmeister* but rather "a Brechtian interpretation," but it was nevertheless an "extraordinary and exemplary production."[70] Even Erpenbeck, one of Brecht's harshest critics, was favorably impressed. This was indeed a high point of "realistic theater," though Erpenbeck noted that despite Brecht's theories, he had not been "distanced" from the emotions of the actors but rather had been "spellbound" and "bewitched" and thus raised to catharsis.[71] Only a few criticisms were raised against the play, and those focused on the negative portrayal of the German cultural heritage.

If Brecht had some successes, he also faced setbacks during his first three years in East Germany. Perhaps the most notable came with the production of the opera *Das Verhör des Lukullus* (*The Trial of Lukullus*). The opera is set in classical Rome and revolves around the judgment of the Roman general Lucullus in the underworld by a peasant, a slave, a fishwife, a baker, and a courtesan. Although they acknowledge his great victories, they ultimately condemn him for having sacrificed 80,000 men and sentence him to be thrown into the abyss.[72] The controversy surrounding the opera revolved around two central charges: pacifism and formalism. The condemnation of Lukullus was perceived by the SED officials to be a condemnation of war in general. It made no clear distinction between defensive wars and wars of aggression. In the context of 1951, when the Korean Conflict was becoming the next battlefield in the Cold War, pacifism was not an acceptable stance in the Eastern Block. The more serious charge, formalism, was aimed at Paul Dessau, Brecht's musical collaborator. His music was attacked because, among other things, of its atonality and instrumentation. Even before its first performance, Ernst Meyer was sharply critical of the opera. In an official report to the Secretariat of the Central Committee Meyer reported that the opera contained "all the elements of formalism, shown through a predominance of destructive, corrosive dissonances and mechanical mysticism . . . the classical traditions are not developed further." Instead, it "represents only a negation of the classical tradition and national art."[73]

Dessau, who was much less secure than Brecht, wanted to pull back after the initial reactions against the opera, but Brecht was opposed to giving in so quickly. He told Dessau, as he recalled in his *Arbeitsjournal*, that the material was important at this moment, especially when "the American threats are so hysterical." Dessau feared attacks on the form of the opera, but Brecht assured him, and Dessau agreed, that "the form of the opera is the form of its content." In addition, he told Dessau that "criticism is never to be feared; one either counters it or accepts it, that is all."[74] Brecht thrived on conflict and believed that the only way to effect change was to heighten conflict. Even at great personal risk, Dessau accepted Brecht's advice and pushed forward.

The formalism debate, which had raged in the Soviet Union during the 1930s, came to East Germany in 1948 but really heated up in late 1950 and early 1951. In 1948 Alexander Dymschitz, the chief cultural officer of the Soviet military administration, renewed the debate in an article for *Tägliche Rundschau*. Here he maintained that in German painting formalism had predominated and had been a characteristic sign of bourgeois decadence.[75] At the third party congress of the SED in 1950 the debate about realism and formalism in art was officially taken up again in an effort to define acceptable national art. The debate continued, but after the Formalism Campaign of 1951 began, there seemed to be only two possibilities: either art was rooted in the national soil or it was foreign and therefore decadent. In a November 1951 article N. Orlow condemned all formalism as decadent. It was empty of positive content and therefore had a deleterious influence on the people of the GDR. What the German people needed, argued Orlow, was "a culture which made the historical struggle of the German people and the whole world for freedom from slavery and exploitation clearly understandable."[76] Orlow followed this article up with a series of articles in January 1951 entitled "Wege und Irrwege der Moderne," in which he demanded that "all influence of Western decadence and the cult of ugliness in art" was to be fought.[77]

In the GDR the charge of formalism was closely connected to that of cosmopolitanism. According to Ernst Hoffmann, an SED Central Committee member, cosmopolitanism was the "ideal of the 'money man,' a man without a country." A cosmopolitan was completely indifferent to the destiny of his own country and was cynically contemptuous of all moral bonds and national duties. He was "out to kill the working men of all peoples and transform them into abstract, schematic objects of exploitation, tear them out of the connection with their own people and class, and rob them of their national characteristics."[78] The fight against both formalism and cosmopolitanism became part of the communist nationalism of the post-1949 era in East Germany. The SED needed to consolidate power in the fledgling GDR, and everything had to be subordinated to this goal. As Jeffrey Herf has noted, communist nationalism, with its focus on the future, also "went hand in hand with the task of unburdening the Germans of their difficult past."[79] For intellectuals, this meant forgetting the recent past and returning, in hagiographic fashion, to the classics of the German cultural tradition including Goethe, Bach, and Heine.

Connected in inextricable ways with the attempt of the SED to consolidate power was the gradual narrowing of possibilities in the cultural sphere. Culture needed to prop up the state, to serve as a propaganda mouthpiece for party policy. As a way to control culture in a more thoroughgoing way, the party created new institutions, *das Amt für Literatur* and *die Staatliche Kommission für Kunst*, in 1951. These institutions were designed to lead the attack against formalism and to make sure that artists toed the party line. Any art seen to be in conflict with the hardening line was considered formalistic, cosmopolitan, even inimical to the national interest. And to be branded a formalist or a cosmopolitan meant to be connected to the West—an especially dangerous charge in this context. As the key official Hans Lauter pointed out in 1951, formalism, "under the pretext of developing something 'completely new,' without being connected to the previous traditions . . . leads to the uprooting of national culture which leads to the destruction of national consciousness, promotes cosmopolitanism and thus signifies a direct support of the politics of war of American imperialism."[80]

The charges against *Lukullus* were thus serious and Brecht and Dessau were in a precarious position. The opera was nevertheless allowed to premiere, but only for a tightly controlled audience. A formal discussion took place on the same day about the opera and the general problems of formalist art. During this discussion, Brecht refused to back down. He defended not only the opera itself but also, and more importantly, the necessity for artistic freedom. A few days later Wilhelm Pieck "invited" both Brecht and Dessau to a "personal discussion" at his apartment. Also present were Grotewohl, Paul Wandel, Anton Ackermann, and Hans Lauter.[81] Unfortunately, no record of this meeting survives, but the opera was shelved until the proper changes could be made.

Although he privately disagreed with the demands, and although he continued to defend himself, the opera, and Dessau in official meetings and in private letters, Brecht was willing to bow to the wishes of the party elite at this time. As he wrote to Anton Ackermann "I've spent Easter morning studying the objections that have been raised to the opera *Lucullus*, and have begun at once to rework the text in such a way as to render even a *mistaken* opinion that the work embodies pacifist tendencies impossible. Indeed, I owe you thanks for insisting that *activity* must be mobilized against wars of conquest."[82] He understood that he was still, in some ways, negotiating from a position of weakness. In the event, Brecht and Dessau made several important changes, which the party accepted.[83] Among other things, Brecht changed the title to *Die Verurteilung des Lukullus (The Condemnation of Lukullus)*;" Dessau added three arias; and in section nine the frieze was changed to show that the king was to be preferred to Lukullus because he was fighting a defensive war, not one of conquest.

Brecht's private notes and correspondences indicate that he understood the debate about formalism and cosmopolitanism was part of the process of consolidating power in the new GDR. The very term "formalism" was being used in such a vague way that it could mean anything and nothing at the same time. Brecht commented to Käthe Rülicke that the Orlow article "had caused much discussion, most of it stupid." According to Brecht, Orlow and others never even offered a definition for the term "formalism." They said only that it should be "fought against."[84] Surely tired of the battle he had already waged with Lukacs in the 1930s, Brecht agreed that there was reason enough to fight formalism, but "the struggle against formalism must be directed as much against the liquidation of forms as against their predominance." Proper socialist art should not oppose all new forms, but only "those forms that distort reality" and it should favor "impulses that promote socialism."[85]

Brecht also believed that the GDR was still in a transitional stage. As Peter Huchel recalled years later, Brecht "saw the GDR as a great construction site which still needed a great deal of work."[86] One problem was that it had not yet ridded itself of the vestiges of traditional patterns of thinking. "It is a great misfortune of our history," Brecht wrote in 1951, "that we must achieve the construction of the new without having achieved the demolition of the old. Probably for that reason we look at the construction [of the new] undialectically. That we see it in such a way has the disadvantage that we cannot sufficiently express the daily struggle against the old that we still have to achieve. We seek continually to produce the 'harmonic,' and the 'An-und-für-sich-Schöne' instead of realistically the struggle for harmony and beauty."[87] For Brecht, the new needed to be built not by returning to the old classical culture. Indeed, classical German culture had been indicted in the overall catastrophe.

Moreover, Brecht objected to the party's meddling in cultural affairs. He always believed that the Academy of the Arts should have control over artistic production and cultural politics. As Brecht's assistant Rülicke recounted "Brecht does not wish to learn from Ulbricht how one poetizes, but rather the politicians should learn from the poets, who represent the entire society. . . . The politicians can say nothing about artistic forms!"[88] He would later say that the cultural policy of the party had produced "disastrously bad results," and he would look for his opportunity to make important changes.[89]

The battle over *Lukullus* taught Brecht some important lessons—lessons that would prepare him for his next showdown with the party. It had shown him just what was at issue and what the stakes were. Moreover, it had helped him determine who his enemies and allies were. Steeled by this experience, Brecht was determined to continue pursuing his primary goals: securing a permanent home for his theater troupe and regaining a measure of autonomy in the arts. He now understood that the best way to affect change was through politics, by making policy changes.

In 1953 a confluence of political and cultural events provided a window of opportunity for Brecht to achieve the goals he sought. Beginning in the summer of 1952 Ulbricht's regime had attempted to speed up the transformation of the GDR toward socialism, and it expected the cultural elite to step in line. No longer would there be even the limited amount of artistic freedom that had been allowed to exist since 1945. In February and March 1953 Hanns Eisler and Brecht came under attack for their treatment of the Faust theme. This theme had been much under discussion in both East and West Germany, especially after the celebration of Goethe's two hundredth birthday in 1949, and was directly connected with the attempt to find a usable cultural tradition. The Faust figure thus gave Brecht the opportunity to deal with two of his most important themes during the post-war period: the bourgeois cultural tradition and the relationship of intellectuals to "the people."

Although the Berliner Ensemble's production of Goethe's *Urfaust* was a minor one, Brecht participated in and directed the dramaturgical discussions at the Berliner Ensemble. Here he stated his views of the Faust figure, who, like Läuffer in *Der Hofmeister*, was a symbol of the traditional intellectual in Germany. Brecht's Faust was no longer a great hero, superior to the devil. Instead, he represented bourgeois decadence, and was an intellectual traitor who betrayed the people. Rülicke recalled that Brecht had said during discussions in January 1953 that Faust was "a parasite; he spunges off of books and knowledge until he is glutted. He lives on that which they offer him, but he never pays." Men like him "produce nothing; they only take." Faust

> makes a pact with a devil . . . according to which he will receive a life of luxury. . . . A scholar has risen to too great a height. He wants to get his feet back on the ground. It is accomplished through this pact. . . . The idea is simply that the man has lost the ground from under his feet and needs the devil in order to regain it. At bottom, it is the love story of an intellectual with a girl from the petit bourgeoisie—and it must be brought about with the help of the devil.[90]

At the same time, Eisler was composing an opera, *Johann Faustus*. He developed his own conception of the Faust figure in collaboration with Brecht, who reworked the text for the opera.[91] These two pieces and the Faust theme in general were discussed in the Academy of the Arts in early 1953. Eisler, in particular, came under heavy fire. As with *Lukullus*, the charges were formalism, cosmopolitanism, and, now, denigration of a "national hero." Alexander

Abusch, a key member of the Academy of Arts presidium and himself a recent victim of the Ulbricht regime, was especially critical, as was Johanna Rudolph, who wrote that Brecht and Eisler "should keep in mind the situation in which the German people finds itself and the tasks that stand before it. *Faust* represents the best in the German people. The defense of this great creation of our national culture, the struggle against the adulteration of the classical should be the desire of every humanistic writer."[92]

By 1953 any criticism of the classical German tradition was regarded by the party elite as an attack on the GDR, which was trying to forge an identity as a "people's democracy," one that was in line with preceding progressive cultural and political developments. The regime thus censured not just Eisler and Brecht, but other dissident intellectuals who deviated from the norm, including the editor of *Sinn und Form*, Peter Huchel. *Sinn und Form*, the brainchild of Becher, had been first the official journal for the *Kulturbund* and then the literary mouthpiece for the Academy of the Arts.[93] Huchel, who was not a member of the party, always maintained a high degree of independence and often came into conflict with the SED. He continued to publish works by "Western" Marxists— essays by Benjamin, Adorno, Horkheimer, and Marcuse—even after this became dangerous. He was also attacked for printing a piece by Brecht on Emil Barlach. At that time, Huchel later recalled "whoever was for Barlach, supported American imperialism."[94] In addition, Huchel printed both the libretto of *Johann Faustus* and a *Faustus* essay by Ernst Fischer during 1952. In the political crucible of the early GDR, this kind of independence could no longer be tolerated. Hence, there was an attempt to oust Huchel and dissolve the journal. In the presidium meeting of the Academy on 13 May the decision was made "to prepare for the liquidation of the journal *Sinn und Form* and the dismissal of the editor-in-chief Peter Huchel."[95] Huchel was informed on 2 June, upon his return from a trip to Moscow, that he was being removed. Under extreme pressure, he agreed to step down on 10 June. Furious, Brecht demanded of Huchel that he "protect" his "position, just as I protect mine." In a statement that clearly shows how well Brecht understood his own role and his instrumentalization, he pointed out that *Sinn und Form* and the Berliner Ensemble, were "the best calling cards of the GDR."[96]

Brecht admitted at several meetings of the Academy that there were some problems with the journal, but this was not sufficient cause to liquidate it. Such an action would be typical of past behavior. His effort to protect Huchel brought Brecht into conflict with Abusch, who had been behind the attempt to force Huchel out. Huchel claimed that he had "never before seen Brecht so excited."[97] Especially after 17 July, when the regime was in some disarray, Brecht insisted to Abusch that Huchel should both continue as editor and be allowed to handpick the members of a commission to advise him on the content. In the event, Brecht was able to save Huchel and the journal for the time being and in July Huchel rescinded his resignation.

It was also during these few months that Eisler's opera came under heaviest fire. Wilhelm Girnus, along with cultural functionaries Heinz Kamnitzer and Hans Rodenberg, were especially critical. Brecht and Arnold Zweig defended

the opera. Following their discussions in closed meetings of the Academy, Girnus published a highly critical article in *Neues Deutschland* in which he attacked
Eisler's Johann Faustus for formalism.[98] Abusch also published an essay in
which he attacked the opera *and* distanced himself from his earlier work *Irrweg
einer Nation.* He attacked *Faustus* for its portrayal of the intelligentsia as "traitors" to the progressive forces in German history. Whereas Goethe's Faust was
"a great positive hero of German drama," and a direct predecessor of Socialist
Realism, Eisler's Faustus had "betrayed" his peasant roots.[99] Even Walter Ulbricht on 27 May openly criticized Brecht and Eisler for their formalism that
made Goethe's Faust "into a caricature."[100]

Eisler, a party member, faced not only censure but also, possibly, impris-
onment or exile. During the months of May and June members of the Academy
continued to discuss the proper response to this piece. In these meetings Brecht
defended both Eisler and, more generally, the need for artistic freedom.[101] He
also went on the attack himself, criticizing the cultural politics of the GDR. Already on 22 February he had defended Eisler, and by implication himself, to
Hans Mayer: "Another word about the 'negativism' that certain people—I don't
know if you are one of them—attribute to Eisler's Faust. Surely a justified desire
for positive heroes (models) mustn't lead us to reject the portrayal of great figures like Faust, whose influence can be just as positive in the social sense. Literature shows that tragedy can perform some of the functions of comedy, a certain social clarification, I mean."[102] Eisler's opera, claimed Brecht, was "an
important literary work because of its great national theme, because of the conceptual nexus, because of its language, because of the richness of its ideas." In
the meeting of 27 May 1953 Brecht agreed with Eisler's critics that German
history "cannot and must not be represented negatively." He also agreed that
German poetry, of which Goethe's Faust was the preeminent example, could not
be sacrificed, but rather had to be made into the property of the people. But,
according to Brecht, Eisler agreed with his critics on this matter. In Brecht's
opinion Eisler had "made a positive contribution to the great Faust-Problem, of
which German literature need not be ashamed."[103]

Eisler understood how important Brecht's support was at this moment. As
he wrote to his wife on 28 May, "There was again an intense evening with much
declamation. *Brecht* brought forth brilliant theses about and for the *Faustus.*"
Nevertheless, he noted, Brecht's words had had "no effect."[104] Ultimately, the
opposition toward Eisler was too strong. In mid-June under heavy pressure he
left East Berlin for Vienna, where he went into a deep depression. There he remained until late in the year, when he, with Brecht's help, penned a letter of
apology to the Central Committee of the SED. He would eventually return to the
GDR and resume his career, though much sobered by this event.

Brecht was extremely frustrated, especially with cultural policy and the direction of change. In a much-cited journal entry of 4 March he wrote: "Our productions in Berlin have almost no echo any more. In the press critiques appear
months after the first production, and there is nothing in them, outside of some
miserable sociological analyses. The public is the petit-bourgeois public of the
Volksbühne. Workers make up hardly 7 percent."[105] Changes had to be made.

While formalism was still at issue, the political context was different in 1953 than it had been in 1951. Important changes were occurring in the leadership of the SED during the spring and early summer of 1953, all culminating in the workers' uprising of 16 and 17 June. The leadership had tried to speed up transformations of East German social and political life in the spring and summer of 1952 with a number of reforms. One of the most important was the attempt to get the industrial workers to produce more for their wages. The part of this policy that became most controversial during 1953 was the proposal to increase work norms by 10 percent. Not surprisingly, this generated discontent among the workers, which made the job of enforcing the norms more difficult. The job was made still more difficult when Moscow informed Ulbricht that it disapproved of the SED line. Beria, head of the secret police in the USSR and seemingly Stalin's heir apparent, was sharply critical. Moscow itself was experiencing rapid change after Stalin's death in March 1953. The Soviet leadership initiated a "New Course," which included a measure of political decentralization and a focus on the production of consumer goods. In East Germany, there was naturally a good deal of political uncertainty and factionalism. In early June, Ulbricht, Grotewohl and Oelßner were summoned to Moscow to be informed about the new party line.

On 9 June the East German Politburo issued a communiqué admitting its mistakes and accepting a soviet-imposed change of course. Not mentioned at all, however, were the raised work norms. The communiqué was published on 11 June in the SED party organ *Neues Deutschland*. Incensed by the retention of the raised norms, workers confronted party officials and instituted slow-downs and protests beginning on 12 June. The tension continued to escalate and on 16 June construction workers at "Stalin Allee Block 40" and workers from a hospital building site in Friedrichshain marched to the trade union headquarters to demonstrate. They then went to the House of Ministries demanding to meet with Ulbricht and Grotewohl, but instead got Heavy Industry Minister Fritz Selbmann and Robert Havemann, president of the GDR Peace Council. The workers demanded the withdrawal of the new norms and, unsatisfied with the responses, called for a general strike. In the early morning of 17 June tensions escalated still further. The workers demanded not only the retraction of work norms, but also the dropping of prices, free elections, and the resignation of the government. These demands got little or no response from the authorities and led to further frustration and eventually violence.[106] By the evening of 17 June Soviet tanks and troops rolled in and restored order.[107]

Although some policy changes were implemented in the wake of this uprising, including the withdrawal of the raised work norms, Ulbricht, who was for a time in danger of losing power, responded with a crackdown. The party leadership arrested over 6000 people involved in the uprising, including not only strikers and leaders of the uprising, but also thousands of SED members who had not taken the party line. Moreover, there was a purge of dissident factions at the top of the SED including Minister of State Security Wilhelm Zaisser, Justice Minister Max Fechner, and Rudolf Herrnstadt, editor of the SED party newspaper *Neues Deutschland*.

Brecht, whose response to the government crackdown has been the subject of heated controversy, understood that this was a crucial moment, and he seized the opportunity to initiate some important changes in cultural policy. He was troubled by this event, as documents in his archive suggest. Käthe Rülicke, who was at his side almost constantly during this crisis, recalled that Brecht was "deeply disturbed that in Germany of all places the workers (and it *was* workers) would set themselves against the first workers' government." He was "deeply depressed that even in Germany, which had experienced fascism and which had every reason to be thankful that this rabble was gone, set itself against a workers government." Rülicke suggested that Brecht was sympathetic to the workers but believed that "everything must be done so that it does not come to another catastrophe."[108]

Publicly, Brecht said nothing about the uprising, but he did write to both Ulbricht and Grotewohl, as well as to the Soviet officer Vladimir Semyonov, in support of the regime. To Ulbricht he wrote: "History will pay its respects to the revolutionary impatience of the Socialist Unity Party of Germany. The great discussion [exchange] with the masses about the speed of socialist construction will lead to a viewing [in the sense of probing, checking] and safeguarding of the socialist achievements. At this moment I feel I must assure you of my allegiance to the Socialist Unity Party of Germany."[109] This sentence contained Brecht's suggestion that a discussion of mistakes by the party leadership should take place, rather than further oppression. It also indicates how far Brecht would go in protesting oppression privately, even if he had to clothe his protest in assurances of loyalty. Since Brecht was personally extremely cautious, the sentence to Ulbricht is remarkable. In the same vein, he asked Grotewohl what "the Academy of Arts and the Berliner Ensemble" could do to help. To Semyonov he declared his "unswerving friendship to the Soviet Union."[110] At the same time, Helene Weigel sent a letter to the Central Committee of the SED in which she stated the "solidarity of the Berliner Ensemble with the goals of the German Democratic government." She then offered to help clarify the situation "over the radio or in other performances."[111]

Although willing to give his private support to the regime, Brecht was less willing to support it publicly at this moment. On 17 June at a special meeting of the Presidium of the Academy of the Arts, Abusch and Rudolf Engel suggested that the Academy issue a "manifesto" that would serve as a "declaration of support" for the regime. Brecht demurred. It was impossible, he said, because those present could not speak for the entire Academy. It was also necessary for the regime to take an official position first. The Academy could not possibly respond to a non-response. According to the protocol, Brecht argued "that a simple declaration of support in the current situation would be wrong." Instead, a project of longer-term significance should be initiated, a project, that would involve "the active participation of the Academy and the reformation of cultural life."[112]

A few days later, on 21 June, only the last line of Brecht's letter to Ulbricht was published in *Neues Deutschland*. Naturally upset that the letter had been published at all, especially in this form, he was furious that his suggestion of a debate about mistakes had been omitted. He understood that this could damage his reputation abroad, especially in West Germany, and he could not afford to lose his commodity value at this moment. He learned from Peter Suhrkamp that since his "declaration of loyalty" appeared in *Neue Zeitung*, theaters in the West were refusing to put on his plays.[113] He protested to Gustav Just, the editor of *Sonntag*, who subsequently reported to Ulbricht, that he believed this action was "tactless because no one had discussed with him publication in this form." In his view, it would be "detrimental" to his work, intended for the entire German nation.[114]

Almost immediately, Brecht began trying to repair the damage and to provide a clearer picture of his position. On 23 June he issued a statement, along with Slatan Dudow and Wolfgang Langhoff, and others, in which he expressed his hope "that the workers, who demonstrated out of justified dissatisfaction, are not placed on the same level with the provocateurs, so that the urgent and necessary discussion about the mistakes made on all sides isn't made impossible before it even begins."[115]

Meanwhile, behind the scenes in meetings at the German Academy of the Arts and the Berliner Ensemble, he began to push for reform of cultural policy. Ultimately, he believed that mistakes made by the regime, especially in cultural policy, had led to this crisis. While he could not agree with the actions of the workers, he could certainly understand their laments. The point was to create a classless society. It was thus necessary to recognize the gap between the facts of life as it currently was and the desired goal. This gap could not simply be denied or overlooked without abandoning the principles of Marxism itself. In meetings of the Academy and the Berliner Ensemble during the weeks following 17 June, Brecht participated in numerous discussions about the current situation and the necessity of changing cultural policy. At a meeting of the Berliner Ensemble on 24 and 25 June he discussed his view of the crisis. He had the impression that "in the early stages it was a serious and shocking matter that even workers were demonstrating here." He granted that they were "fully justified" in doing so. He recognized that they had been kept from "venting their embitterment." But he also pointed out that Nazi elements were at work. Berlin was in "a spiritual condition" like that of the "Nazi period." It was, in Brecht's opinion, "one of the key mistakes of the SED and the regime that these Nazi elements . . . have not been destroyed." Moreover, it was "a mistake . . . that it was a taboo, it was forbidden, to speak of the Nazi era." Only "the magnificent culture of the German people, only the positive" was spoken about. This was one of the main points in the "superfluous discussion about the Faustus text." It was also one of the complaints against *Der Hofmeister*. Yet from Brecht's point of view, "the entire Nazi gang is still present; it no longer rules, but spiritually is still very much alive." But no one was supposed to talk about it; it was supposed to be "hushed up."[116] It stood to reason, then, that much of the crisis had been precipitated by the cultural politics of the SED. "Cultural politics," he wrote, "has had disastrously bad results."[117]

If Brecht recognized that the regime had made mistakes, he also believed that the excesses of 16 and 17 June were partly the result of provocation by fas-

cist elements within East Germany, as well as by West German provocateurs. As
he wrote to Suhrkamp,

> The Socialist Unity Party has made mistakes which were extremely serious for
> a socialist party and which antagonized some workers, including old socialists.
> I am not a party member. But I respect many of its historical achievements, and
> I felt at one with it—not because of its mistakes but because of its good quali-
> ties—when it was attacked by fascist, warmongering rabble. In the struggle
> against war and fascism I have always supported it and still support it. You ask
> about my attitude towards the events of 16 and 17 June. Was it a popular upris-
> ing, an attempt "to win freedom," as the overwhelming majority of the West
> German press claims? Was I indifferent, not to say hostile, to a popular upris-
> ing, was I against freedom, when on 17 June in a letter to the Socialist Unity
> Party, the last sentence of which was published, I expressed my readiness to
> contribute in my own way (in artistic form) to the absolutely indispensable de-
> bate between the workers and the government? For three decades I have tried in
> my writings to champion the cause of the workers. But in the night of 16 June
> and the morning of 17 June, I saw the stirring of demonstrations of the workers
> degenerate into something very far from an attempt to win freedom. The work-
> ers had reason to be embittered. The unfortunate, unintelligent measures taken
> by the government in an attempt to precipitate the development of heavy indus-
> try in the GDR outraged peasants, artisans, tradesmen, workers and intellectu-
> als alike. . . . Such measures as . . . the general stepping up of norms at a time
> when the cost of living remained unchanged or had actually gone up, drove the
> workers . . . into the streets and caused them to forget the undoubtedly great
> advantages that the expulsion of the Junkers, the socialization of Hitler's war
> industry, planned production and the smashing of the bourgeois monopoly of
> education had won them. Yet even in the early hours of 17 June the streets dis-
> played a grotesque mixture of workers not only with all sorts of déclassé youth,
> who poured through the Brandenburg Gate, across the Potsdamer Platz, and in
> columns across the Warschauer Brücke, but also with gross, brutish figures
> from the Nazi era, the local product, who hadn't been seen gathered into bands
> for years, *but who had been here the whole time.* The slogans changed quickly.
> "Down with the government" was followed by "Hang them"; the gutter took
> over. . . . In the provinces "liberation" went on. But when the prisons were
> stormed, strange prisoners emerged from the "Bastilles"; in Halle the onetime
> commandant of Ravensbrück concentration camp, Erna Dorn. She made incen-
> diary speeches in the marketplace. In some places there were assaults on Jews,
> not many, as there aren't many Jews left. And all day long RIAS suspended its
> regular programs, broadcast incendiary speeches, with refined voices mouthing
> the word "freedom". Everywhere those elements were at work, who think day
> and night of the welfare of the workers and the "common people" and who
> promise those high living standards which in the end turn out to be dying stan-
> dards. There seemed to be ringleaders who were ready to lead the workers di-
> rectly to the freedom of the munitions factories. For several hours, until the oc-
> cupation forces stepped in, Berlin was on the brink of a third World War.[118]

Although Brecht undoubtedly overemphasized the role of Western provocateurs, this was not *mere* window dressing. Brecht genuinely believed that the
new socialist society he hoped to help build had been endangered from without
and within. The crisis was in part due to mistakes made by the SED leadership,

including its failure to deal sufficiently with its recent past, to root out all traces of Nazism, but it also resulted, in Brecht's opinion, from fascist elements in Germany. It is unclear if Brecht ever recognized how much his position in this regard was informed by Soviet and East German propaganda. He did have access to Western newspapers and magazines, and he recognized that RIAS, the chief news agency, was poorly informing the citizenry of the GDR about world events.[119] It is clear, however, that Brecht's decision to support the regime was motivated partially by his desire to improve the new socialist society that was being constructed in the GDR—which included purging it of fascist elements. Also crucial, however, was the return of autonomy in the arts. Brecht did not argue for absolute artistic freedom. As he pointed out, "One cannot create a republic of artists, where each can produce whatever he wants. Especially not in a Germany that has gone through two decades of Nazi rule."[120] Nevertheless, as he wrote in his poem "Not what was Meant," there needed to be "freedom of artistic expression from narrow-minded bureaucrats."[121] Furthermore, Brecht maintained that artists and intellectuals, not politicians, needed to control overall cultural policy.[122]

Personal professional motivations were also significant for Brecht's thinking at this moment. These different concerns and interests were always present in the post-war Brecht, but in changing proportions and configurations. This was indeed a moment of opportunity and crisis for Brecht, a moment in which his personal, professional, and ideological interests converged. He recognized that he might finally be able to gain a permanent residence for his theater, but he also knew that the theater would be of little value unless he had some artistic control. Brecht thus began to use a number of tactics to force change and, at the same time, get the *Theater am Schiffbauerdamm*. He continually emphasized his international prestige and his domestic reputation. Perhaps most importantly, he utilized his relationships with important intellectuals and party officials. As Meredith Heiser-Duron has pointed out, he "worked successfully with an unlikely combination of four people" including Johannes Becher, Otto Grotewohl, Paul Wandel, and Wilhelm Girnus.[123] Behind the scenes he pushed for changes in cultural policies and convinced these and other cultural figures to back his plans, though with a few exceptions he refused to "go public" with his criticisms of cultural policies.

In closed meetings, he pushed the Academy of the Arts to issue suggestions for changing cultural policies in the wake of 17 June. On 12 July the Academy, after facing much resistance from Grotewohl and others, succeeded in publishing a list of ten suggestions, most of which were designed to return a degree of autonomy to artists. Among the most important suggestions was that artists had to be responsible for the publication and production of their works of art. In addition, it was necessary for the Academy to have a say in the choice of "the leading individuals who are responsible for artistic questions," so that "professional qualifications" could be established. Finally, the Academy stated that "the events of 17 June" had proven that "the struggle against fascism in all its forms must be taken up again with renewed vigor—even by artists."[124] All of these suggestions clearly bear Brecht's stamp, and a close examination of the proto-

cols suggests that he was very influential in their development. No one in the
Academy possessed the combination of intellectual and political gifts that
Brecht did. For this reason, he was its natural leader at this moment. In addition,
his colleagues tolerated his leadership, even when they disliked him personally,
because he was prepared to defend the autonomy they so desperately wanted.

Brecht also continued to press his own case for the *Theater am Schiffbauerdamm*. Again and again he emphasized his importance as an internationally famous playwright to the party. On 15 June, even before the uprising, he had written to Grotewohl: "You have probably heard that the wildest rumors have been
circulating in West Germany about friction between the government of the
German Democratic Republic and myself. If the Berliner Ensemble, which is
known far beyond the borders of Germany, were to take over the *Theater am
Schiffbauerdamm*, my solidarity with our republic would be evident to all."[125]

To Girnus at a private meeting in August, he again stressed his international
reputation and that of the Berliner Ensemble. At this same meeting, Brecht gave
Girnus an article to be published in *Neues Deutschland*, "Kulturpolitik und die
Akademie der Künste," in which he reaffirmed the right of the Academy "to
exercise criticism." He pointed out that the Academy itself had made mistakes
and hence had undermined the confidence of many artists in the new state, without which "no new state can be built." But art had to be autonomous; it had to be
allowed to follow "its own rules." One of the most significant mistakes in cultural politics, he claimed, was that the GDR had "all too quickly" turned away
from the "immediate past" in order to embrace its future; yet the future depended upon "release from the past." The groundwork for a new culture had
been laid. However, if the GDR were to reach its full potential, to create a "general productivity of the entire nation," art would have "to create a new impulse."[126]

Although Brecht generally refused to criticize the regime in public, he also
published at this time two poems that were critical of the regime. His twofold
aim with these poems was to destroy *Das Amt für Literatur* and *Die staatliche
Kommission für Kunst* and to replace them with a ministry of culture, headed by
his friend Becher. In a private conversation with Wolfgang Harich, an influential
philosopher and journalist—and also one of his closest allies during this period—Brecht revealed much about his plans. When he asked how they should
proceed, Harich suggested that they should follow Tito's example in Yugosla-
via. Brecht replied, "You are insane. You will end up on the gallows. That is
dangerous! Anyway, I want nothing to do with the strife between Titoists and
Stalinists. . . . My plays should be played in Moscow and in Belgrade. For this
reason, I will not join a party. I am for communism in general, but not for these
individual forms: Stalin-Tito, it's all the same to me. And you must be careful.
We want to make something real. We want to get rid of the bureaucrats in cultural politics. You write an article against the one article and I will add a few
poems and then we will have Johannes R. Becher as minister of culture."[127]

Harich's article, which appeared on 14 July, criticized not only the art commission in general, but also specific individuals, including Girnus and Helmut
Holtzhauer, one of the key members of the *Kunstkommission*. On 15 July Brecht

published *Das Amt für Literatur* in the *Berliner Zeitung*. In this poem he directly criticized the control office for publishing only works "with ideas familiar to the Office for Literature from the newspapers."[128] In "Unidentifiable Errors of the Arts Commission" he was sharply critical of the *Kunstkommission*. Here he claimed that "the highest officials of the Arts Commission/ Paid their tribute to the noble custom of/ Accusing oneself of certain errors, and/ Muttered that they too accused themselves of certain errors. Asked/ What errors, however, they found it wholly impossible to/ recall/ Any specific errors. Everything that/ The Academy held against them had been/ Precisely no error, for the Arts Commission/ Had not suppressed it exactly, had just not pushed it./ Despite the most earnest ruminations/ They could recall no specific errors, nonetheless/ They were most insistent that they had/ Committed errors—as is the custom."[129]

Privately, Brecht hammered away at officials including Grotewohl and Minister of Public Education Paul Wandel.[130] To Wandel he wrote that "the Arts Commission should be ruthlessly and sweepingly dissolved." It had made enemies of all the artists and it had "managed to bring the most progressive principles into something close to disrepute." It could no longer function appropriately because it had been "publicly discredited." Brecht pointed out that its administrative tasks could better be performed by the "Ministry of Culture, and the Cultural Section of the Socialist Unity Party," which "could exert a far more authoritative influence in artistic matters." What could be the point in "prolonging a creeping malaise, a feeling, ruinous to all creativity, of being at the mercy of an all-powerful institution that is unable to make its demands understood? What we need now is simply to leave artists free to produce; they can do so much if left alone (and intelligently guided)."[131]

In a few short, but decisive, months Brecht managed to achieve most of his goals. He not only succeeded in saving Huchel and blunting the attack on Eisler and himself, but he was also instrumental in replacing *Das Amt für Literatur* and *Die staatliche Kommission für Kunst*—the two institutions created to direct the anti-formalist campaign—with a new Ministry of Culture, headed by his friend and ally Becher. This Ministry of Culture was established in early 1954 and shortly thereafter Brecht was appointed to a council whose responsibility it was to "advise" Becher on cultural policy. Such a position was ideal for Brecht, who always preferred to work behind the scenes.[132] As a result, he was able, in the short term, to effect cultural policy in a direct way. Finally, Brecht obtained a permanent residence for his theater, the *Schiffbauerdamm*, in the wake of this controversy.

Despite these achievements Brecht has been criticized for refusing to support the actions of the workers. The picture that has emerged of Brecht during this crucial period is one marked by cowardice and a self-serving ethic. John Fuegi has argued that Brecht was exposed as "a loyal henchman of the executioners" and that "his independent position, the platform of "inner opposition," was suddenly revealed as a grotesque illusion." Ronald Hayman has drawn a similar picture of Brecht at this moment, though he is less certain of Brecht's motivations. He notes that Brecht rushed "to express blind support for the dogmas of orthodoxy," but he is unsure whether he did so out of cynicism, "wanting the Party leaders to reward him with a theatre, or committedly."[133]

There is merit to these criticisms, but Fuegi and Hayman have missed the mix of idealism and opportunism that informed Brecht's thinking at this moment. His actions in 1953 were based on a number of often contradictory considerations. Self-interest, opportunism, and an idealistic belief that the GDR represented the best opportunity for Germany's future played a complex and interrelated role. Brecht did not see this crisis as the end of the line. He saw it as a "Blütezeit," a precious moment of opportunity when the new socialist state could begin to bloom. As he noted on 20 August, he could not evaluate "the terrible events of 17 June as simply negative." In the proletariat, he still saw the only power that could bring capitalism to an end.[134] For Brecht, reality was always changeable. Moreover, he often seemed to believe that change could only come through crisis. One sees this, for example, in his understanding of criticism of a work of art: "When I criticize a work . . . I bring the work into a crisis, that is I criticize it. It has to prove under the worst circumstances that it can function as a work of art."[135] The new GDR was for Brecht like a work of art. The events surrounding 17 June had brought it into a crisis, had illustrated that it was not functioning properly and thus had to be improved. Brecht believed that he could help, that he could work actively toward a new direction.[136]

Fuegi, Hayman, and others who attack Brecht for his stance in 1953 have also lost sight of the context. They have assumed that public deviation from, and criticism of, the party line on the workers was a viable option in 1953, and that such a stance would have accomplished a change in the regime. Yet the evidence clearly shows that those who publicly deviated from the party line suffered severe reprisals. Brecht understood the political realities—especially after his experience with *Lukullus* in 1951—and although he was committed to certain long-term goals, he had to improvise and, often, make compromises as he went along. He knew, for example, that showing no support for the regime would have accomplished nothing. Indeed, it would surely have stripped him of any influence as a cultural functionary and would likely have killed his chance to get the *Theater am Schiffbauerdamm*. Brecht also understood that a permanent home for his theater was crucial, but it would have meant nothing if he had not had some degree of control over artistic production. The way to effect policy change *and* obtain a permanent residence for his theater was thus to support the regime in public and work behind the scenes.

This did not mean that Brecht was not conflicted about his actions, especially as he began to recognize that a new course had not really been initiated after all. Indeed, there is significant anecdotal and literary evidence—the *Bukow Elegies* and *Turandot*—that Brecht knew he had compromised himself in this instance, that he had not maintained a critical distance from the regime. He wrote both the poems and the play, neither of which was published in his lifetime, while at his vacation home in Buckow reflecting upon the events of 17 June. In "Changing the Wheel" he wrote "I sit by the roadside/ The driver changes the wheel./ I do not like the place I have come from./ I do not like the place I am going to./ Why with impatience do I/ Watch him changing the

wheel." In "Great Times, Wasted" he showed his disappointment with the outcome of the June days: "I knew that cities were being built/ I haven't been to
any./ A matter for statistics, I thought/ Not history.// What's the point of cities,
built/ Without the people's wisdom." Perhaps most telling is "Nasty Morning."
Here he wrote: "The silver poplar, a celebrated local beauty/ Today an old harri-
dan. The lake/ A puddle of dish-water, don't touch!/ The fuchsias amongst the
snapdragon cheap and vain./ Why?/ Last night in a dream I saw fingers pointing
at me/ As a leper. They were worn with toil and/ They were broken.// You don't
know! I shrieked/ Conscience-stricken."[137]

Brecht's final play, *Turandot*, is equally illuminating for his position in
1953. This play, which was not performed during his lifetime, has not aroused
much curiosity among historians. But it is crucial both because it brings final
form to Brecht's critique of intellectuals, begun in the 1930s, and because it illustrates that Brecht recognized the oppression in the GDR as well as his own
role in that oppression. As *Turandot* begins, there is no cotton to be had in China
because the Emperor and his brother Jau Jel have a monopoly. They are waiting
for the price to rise so that they can make a larger profit. The clothes makers
(Kleidermacher) and those without clothes (Kleiderlosen) begin to unite in protest. Kai Ho, an ex-Tui who is the incarnation of communism, leads an insurrec-
tion. Jau Jel calls in the Tuis to invent elaborate excuses for the shortage of cotton. Essentially, the greatest minds of the kingdom are engaged in a competition
of lies. The most successful liar, the "greatest whitewasher," will save the regime and receive the Emperor's daughter, Turandot, in marriage. The undertak-
ing is hopeless because everyone already knows the truth. The different com-
petitors, who range from Ka Müh, a figure who resembles Albert Camus, to
Munka Du, reminiscent of Adorno, all fail to offer viable explanations and are
executed. Gogher Gogh, a Hitler-like figure who wants to become a Tui but has
failed the entrance exam, burns half of the imperial cotton stock under the nose
of the remaining Tuis. Thus the remainder can be sold on a rising market. He
then uses brutal force to eliminate the Tuis and marry Turandot. But Turandot
refuses to marry him, and before he can force her, Kai Ho's supporters break
in.[138]

On one level, the play is a critique of the mandarin tradition of intellectual
leadership in Germany in which intellectuals sold themselves, and their intellects, to the state. Gogher Gogh is the armed monster, who has sprung from the
head of the Tuis, the truth of their lies. On another level, however, Brecht was
also pointing out that intellectuals in a capitalist society—and the GDR although
not capitalist, also was not fully socialist—can only sell their opinions. They are
commodified. He was also criticizing the continuation of a type of knowledge
and intellectual leadership in the GDR and suggesting that the consequences had
been disastrous. In order to bind the people to the new state, there was a privi-
leging of bourgeois intellectuals, like himself. This was in some measure necessary, but also had disastrous consequences. *Turandot* was thus also a criticism of
the situation in East Germany and a self criticism. Brecht surely recognized that
he, too, had become a Tui, that he, too, had whitewashed the actions of Ulbricht's regime.

The only positive figures in the play are Kai Ho, who represents the useful and engaged intellectual and who is, for that reason, excluded from the Tuis (Tellektuellin), and the old peasant Sen, who is the embodiment of Kai Ho's practical thinking. It is Sen who points out that all is not right: "Injustice reigns in the land, and in the Tui school one learns only why it must be so. It is true that stone bridges are built over the widest rivers, but they lead the powerful into idleness, and the poor wander over them into slavery. It is true, there is a medicine, but through it one is healed to do injustice, and the other to be enslaved. One buys opinions like fish, and thus thinking is brought into disrepute." The engaged intellectual must, like Sen, show reality for what it is.

No doubt Brecht wished to see himself in this role, but he also knew he had compromised himself to achieve his goals. Still, he had survived. He had bent and not broken, a tack he alluded to in his poem "Iron," also part of the *Bukow Elegies*: "In a dream last night/ I saw a storm./ It seized the scaffolding/ It tore the cross-clasps/ The iron ones, down./ But what was made of wood/ Swayed and remained."[139]

Although it is certainly true that Brecht did nothing to improve the immediate situation of the workers, as Fuegi and Hayman point out, this criticism does not really get at the heart of the matter. The short-term economic goals of the workers were not Brecht's priorities, even if he regretted the poor conditions. Long-term cultural transformation was paramount. In the context of the early GDR the way to achieve this transformation, Brecht believed in 1953, was to secure autonomy in the cultural sphere by working behind the scenes and to force the regime to admit and then correct its mistakes. For a time, at least, he seems to have thought that a sea change could be effected. According to Käthe Rülicke he genuinely wanted to "make socialism a reality." He knew, of course, that in "a formerly Nazi country this is difficult to bring about." But he imagined, he dreamed, of a "new city" with "new people," the "best theater," and the "best politicians" where socialism could be built. After 17 June Brecht hoped, and often still believed, that his dream would "in fact be realized." The "foundation" had been laid on which socialism could be built. His was an ethic of conviction. For this reason, he even considered joining the party in the months that followed. But Brecht was ultimately disappointed by the lack of change.[140]

If Brecht cannot necessarily be seen as a villain during this period, he also cannot properly be called a hero, as Werner Mittenzwei has portrayed him. Brecht did have choices, and he did make compromises. He did not have to write letters of support to East German and Soviet officials. He could have defended the workers in a more public way. He might well have chosen to leave the GDR and work toward socialism in another context. But to such a one the idea of switching sides at this particular moment seemed almost unthinkable, because at precisely this time the West German state was rehabilitating old Nazis to an alarming extent, making the GDR in contrast look very much like the anti-fascist state that its self-serving state religion proclaimed it to be. Brecht remained in East Berlin because he was committed to the GDR and thought he could accomplish something there in spite of a party apparatus that was Stalinist and basically unsympathetic, often even hostile, to his ideas about political art.

He was in general agreement with Soviet and East German policies, and he made concessions that he believed were justified by the need to combat the continuing influence of fascism. Hence, he devoted his talents and energies to creating a truly socialist Germany that he consigned to the future, even as he knew better than most the problems that East Germany faced in the present. Ultimately, this led him to put his name and talents at the service of a political state that was narrow-minded and often oppressive. If Brecht had lived through 1956 and into the later 1950s, he too might have become as disenchanted—and disenfranchised—as other antifascists who returned from exile to the GDR and later left it, such as Ernst Bloch. But in 1953 Brecht read the situation differently, and a careful look at the evidence shows us that this can be interpreted not simply as opportunism on his part, even if it was clearly a miscalculation.

The other charge leveled against Brecht is irrelevance. Critics such as David Pike, Peter Davies, and Stephen Parker have claimed that despite the changes he was able to bring about in 1953, he had no long-term influence on the GDR.[141] And, of course, there is some validity to this charge when one considers only cultural policy. Very soon after his death there was a final crackdown on dissident intellectuals. In the wake of the Hungarian Revolution, Wolfgang Harich, Walter Janka, Gustav Just and other dissident intellectuals were imprisoned, often for long terms. But Brecht's inability to achieve long-term policy change was not necessarily the result of the approach he took in 1953. Nor does it discredit what he was able to accomplish in this context. For a few short years he was able to regain a measure of autonomy in the arts. Moreover, he represented a type of intellectual that many future East German intellectuals would aspire to become: committed to artistic freedom, willing to be critical, willing to take some risks, but not to jeopardize his position.[142] Contemporaries have confirmed that precisely Brecht's instrumentalization in the fifties was for many a welcome or even indispensable counter balance to the GDR's conservative stuffiness of the projected socialist culture of the German nation. Not surprisingly, his commodity value lost its power over time for reasons that are more or less evident, and that were not necessarily his fault. But the critique of intellectuals he developed during this time around the notion of "Tuismus" engages a model of the public intellectual in which the self-image of the artist and thinker as a socially and politically engaged person corresponded to the expectations of the public. Partisan without being bound to a party, independent of official institutions yet experienced at surviving within institutions, prepared to entertain risks and undertake unconventional experiments: this was how Brecht accommodated a world which he envisioned as changeable. His antagonistic worldview fed on crisis and found its most productive, creative impulse in the escalation of contradictions. For this he found plenty of material in the early years of the GDR and introduced some innovative poetic and aesthetic strategies to give it form.

NOTES

1. Hannah Arendt, *Men in Dark Times* (New York: Harcourt, Brace & World, 1968), 213-215.
2. Theodor Adorno, "Commitment," in *Notes to Literature III*, trans. Shierry Weber Nicholsen (Columbia: Columbia University Press, 1992), 86.
3. Günter Grass, *Die Plebejer proben den Aufstand: Ein deutsches Trauerspiel* (Darmstadt and Neuwied: Hermann Luchterhand Verlag, 1966).
4. Werner Mittenzwei, *Das Leben des Bertolt Brecht oder Der Umgang mit den Welträtseln*, vol II (Berlin and Weimar: Aufbau Verlag, 1986), 482-541.
5. Gay, *Weimar Culture*, 7.
6. Bertolt Brecht, "The Epic Theater and its Difficulties," in *Brecht on Theatre: The Development of an Aesthetic*, ed. John Willett (New York: Hill and Wang, 1964), 23.
7. Bertolt Brecht, *Versuche*, vol. 2, (Berlin: Suhrkamp, 1957), 104.
8. Bertolt Brecht, "The Epic Theatre," 70.
9. Brecht, "The Epic Theater," 70-71.
10. Carl Zuckmayer, *Als wär's ein Stück von mir. Hören der Freundschaft* (Frankfurt am Main: Fischer, 1966), 381.
11. Bertolt Brecht, *Schriften I, 1914-1933* (1992), vol. 1, *Werke, Große kommentierte Berliner und Frankfurter Ausgabe*, (hereafter GKBF) ed. Werner Hecht, Jan Knopf, Werner Mittenzwei, Klaus-Detlef Müller (Berlin and Weimar: Aufbau and Suhrkamp, 1980-2000), 202-204; 674-676.
12. Bertolt Brecht, *Schriften zur Politik und Gesellschaft I*, (Berlin and Weimar: Aufbau Verlag, 1968), 79.
13. Ronald Hayman, *Brecht: A Biography* (New York: Oxford University Press, 1983), 142.
14. Hans Bunge, *Fragen Sie mehr über Brecht. Hanns Eisler im Gespräch* (Munich: Rogner und Bernhard, 1970), 96-7.
15. Bertolt Brecht, *Schriften V, Theatermodelle "Katzgraben" Notate 1953* (1994), vol. 25, GKBF, 9.
16. Stanley Mitchell, introduction to Walter Benjamin, *Understanding Brecht* (Frankfurt am Main: Suhrkamp, 1973), ix.
17. Bertolt Brecht, *Die Maßnahme*, in *Stücke III*, vol. 3, GKBF.
18. Werner Mittenzwei, *Das Leben des Bertolt Brecht*, 357.
19. Brecht later wrote poems about these two friends. See the poem "Ist das Volk unfehlbar?" (1939), *Gedichte IV* (1993), vol. 14, GKBF, 435.
20. Walter Benjamin, *Reflections: Essays, Aphorisms, Autobiographical Writings*, trans. Edmund Jephcott, ed. Peter Demetz (New York: Schocken, 1986), 218-219.
21. Eugene Lunn, *Marxism and Modernism* (Berkeley: University of California Press, 1982), 77.
22. David Pike, *Lukacs and Brecht* (Chapel Hill: University of North Carolina Press, 1985), 232.
23. Benjamin, *Reflections*, 218.
24. Bertolt Brecht, *Stücke IV, VII*, vols. 4, 7, GKBF.
25. Bertolt Brecht to Jean Renoir, 17 March 1937, in *Bertolt Brecht Letters 1913-1956*, trans. Ralph Manheim, ed. John Willett (New York: Routledge, 1981), 249.
26. Bertolt Brecht, "The Threepenny Lawsuit: A Sociological Experiment," in *Bertolt Brecht on Film and Radio*, trans. and intro. Marc Silberman (London: Methuen, 2000), 50, 27, 51.

27. Brecht, "The Threepenny Lawsuit," 163, 179-180, 195. See also Brecht, *Schriften zur Politik und Gesellschaft*, vol. I, 1919-1941, (Berlin and Weimar: Aufbau-Verlag, 1968), 121-123.

28. The clearest and most complete discussion of Brecht's complicated relationship to Lukacs is Eugene Lunn, *Marxism and Modernism*, 75-128. See also David Pike, *Lukács and Brecht* (Chapel Hill: University of North Carolina, 1985).

29. Georg Lukacs, "Reportage or Portrayal?" in *Essays on Realism* (Cambridge, Massachusetts: MIT Press, 1981), 45-75.

30. Lukacs, "Reportage or Portrayal?" 70-71; see also Georg Lukacs, "Aus der Not eine Tugend," in *Marxismus und Literatur*, vol. 2 (Reinbek bei Hamburg: Rowohlt, 1969), 166-177.

31. Bertolt Brecht, "The Popular and the Realistic," in *Brecht on Theater: The Development of an Aesthetic* (New York: Hill and Wang, 1964), 107-109.

32. Brecht, "Notizen über realistische Schreibweise," *Schriften II*, vol. 22.2, GBFA, 628-30.

33. Brecht, "Die Expressionismus Debatte," *Schriften II*, vol. 22.1, GBKA, 418.

34. Walter Benjamin noted in 1934 that on the ceiling of Brecht's study in Svendborg, Sweden, were "painted the words 'Truth is concrete.' On a window sill stands a little wooden donkey that can nod its head. Brecht has hung a little notice around its neck saying, 'I, too, must understand it.'" Benjamin, *Reflections*, 206.

35. Brecht, *Brecht on Theater*, 109-111. See also "Weite und Vielfalt der realitischen Schreibweise," and "Praktisches zur Expressionismusdebatte," *Schriften II*, 424-432, 419-422; *Arbeitsjournal*, 12-14, 28-29.

36. Zuckmayer, *Als wär's ein Stück von mir*, 379.

37. Brecht, *Schriften zur Politik und Gesellschaft*, 86, 88, 90.

38. Bertolt Brecht, *Stücke XIV* (Berlin and Weimar: Aufbau-Verlag, 1968), 360. "Tui," or "Tellekt-uell-in" was Brecht's shorthand for "intellectual."

39. Brecht, "Schwierige Lage der deutschen Intellektuellen," in *Schriften zur Politik und Gesellschaft*, 86-90.

40. Brecht, "Wozu braucht das Proletariat die Intellektuellen?" in *Schriften zur Politik und Gesellschaft*, 90-91.

41. Antonio Gramsci, *Prison Notebooks* (New York: International Publishers, 1971), 6-22.

42. Brecht, *Arbeitsjournal*, 143.

43. Brecht, "Threepenny Lawsuit," 182.

44. Bertolt Brecht, *Poems 1913-1956*, ed. and trans. John Willett and Ralph Mannheim (New York: Methuen, 1976), 258.

45. John Fuegi, *Brecht & Co*, 478-486.

46. Becher to Brecht, Bertolt Brecht Archiv, Chausseestraße, Berlin, Germany, (Hereafter BBA) 1340/55.

47. Ihering to Brecht, 21 April 1947, *Deutsche Akademie der Künste*, (Hereafter DAK) rep. 09 II ia, no. 214. For a general discussion of cultural life in Berlin after World War II, please see Wolfgang Schivelbusch, *In a Cold Crater: Cultural and Intellectual Life in Berlin, 1945-1948* (Berkeley and Los Angeles: University of California Press, 1998).

48. Brecht, *Arbeitsjournal*, 849.

49. Ibid., 864.

50. Ibid., 889.

51. Bertolt Brecht, *Schriften III*, vol. 23, GKBF, 129.

52. Cited in Wolfgang Emmerich, *Kleine Literaturgeschichte der DDR. Erweiterte Neuausgabe* (Leipzig: Gustav Kiepenheuer, 1996), 43.

53. Johannes R. Becher, "Bemerkungen zu unseren Kulturaufgaben," in *Publizistik*, vol. 2. (Berlin: Aufbau, 1978), 362-63.

54. Johannes R. Becher, "Schaffung eines 'Kulturbunds für die demokratische Erneuerung,'" a note of Pieck's from 6 June 1945, *Archiv des Instituts für die Geschichte der Arbeiterbewegung*, NL 36/734, cited in Schivelbusch, *In a Cold Crater*, 75.

55. Johannes R. Becher, "Vortrag von J.R. Becher," Spring 1945, SAPMO-BA, ZPA, IV 2/11/199, 19, cited in Norman M. Naimark, *The Russians in Germany* (Cambridge: Harvard University Press, 1995), 398.

56. David Pike, *The Politics of Culture in Soviet-Occupied Germany*, (Stanford: Stanford University Press, 1995); Gerd Dietrich, *Politik und Kultur in der SBZ* (Bern: Peter Lang Press, 1993).

57. Gramsci, *Prison Notebooks*, 57-8; Walter Adamson, *Hegemony and Revolution: A Study of Antonio Gramsci's Political and Cultural Theory* (Berkeley: University of California Press, 1980), 170-171.

58. BBA, 1340/55.

59. The Socialist Unity Party was formed out of the Communist party (KPD) and the Socialist Party (SPD) in April 1946.

60. On 29 June 1949 Paul Wandel, the president of the German administration for National Culture in the Soviet Zone of Occupation, informed Brecht that he had been named to a committee which had as its aim the creation of "a German Academy of the Arts in Berlin as a successor to the former Prussian Academy. . . . I invite you to membership in this preparatory committee and ask you to attend the first organizational meeting on Monday, 4 July 1949." BBA, 211/66, 795/01.

61. Brecht, *Schriften III*, 126.

62. Manfred Jaeger, *Sozialliteraten: Funktion und Selbstverständnis der Schriftsteller in der DDR* (Düsseldorf: Bertelsman Universitätsverlag, 1973), 169.

63. According to Peter Davies and Stephen, "the deutshce Misere" theory was developed by Alexander Abusch in *Irrweg einer Nation* (1945). It "held that the development of the German nation and state had, for various reasons, not been able to follow the course laid down in orthodox historical materialism, and that, therefore, the reactionary forces in German history had been stronger than the progressive forces. One symptom of this had been the failure of the 'intelligentsia' to cooperate with the 'revolutionary peasantry proletariat', producing a disastrous separation of 'Geist' and 'Macht' which led intellectuals either to collaborate with repressive regimes or to retreat into aestheticism." Peter Davies and Stephen Parker, "Brecht, SED Cultural Policy and the Issue of Authority in the Arts: the Struggle for Control of the German Academy of the Arts," in *Bertolt Brecht: Centenary Essays*, ed. Steve Giles and Rodney Livingstone (Amsterdam, Atlanta: Rodopi, 1998), 181.

64. PEN, an international writers' organization, was formed in 1921 and dedicated to advancing literature, extending free expression, and fostering international cooperation. It seeks to dissolve national, ethnic, and racial hatreds.

65. Peter Huchel, *Werke II* (Frankfurt: Suhrkamp Verlag, 1984), 375.

66. Brecht, *Letters*, 454, 464, 466.

67. Fritz Erpenbeck, *Die Weltbühne*, 18 January 1949.

68. Bertolt Brecht, *Schriften IV*, vol. 24, GKBF, 392.

69. Brecht, *Letters*, 491-492.

70. Paul Rilla, *Berliner Zeitung*, 18 April 1950.

71. Fritz Erpenbeck, *Neues Deutschland*, 16 April 1950.

72. Bertolt Brecht, *Das Verhör des Lukullus, Stücke VI*, vol. 6, GKBF.

73. Ernst Hermann Meyer, "Das Verhör des Lukullus" (Brecht/Dessau), 12 March 1951, DAK, Ernst-Hermann-Meyer-Archiv, Sign.-Nr. 565.

74. Brecht, *Arbeitsjournal*, 943.

75. Alexander Dymschitz, "Über die formalistische Richtung in der deutschen Malerei. Bemerkungen eines Außenstehenden," *Tägliche Rundschau*, 14, 19 November, 1948.

76. N. Orlow, "Das Reich der Schatten auf der Bühne," *Tägliche Rundschau*, Sunday, 19 November 1950.

77. N. Orlow, "Wege und Irrwege der Moderne" *Tägliche Rundschau*, 21-23 January 1951.

78. Ernst Hoffmann, "Die Bedeutung der ideologischen Offensive in der Sowjetunion für Deutschland," 793-794, cited in Jeffrey Herf, *Divided Memory* (Cambridge: Harvard University Press, 1997), 111-112.

79. Herf, *Divided Memory*, 110.

80. Tagung des ZK der SED, 15-17 March 1951, IfGA, ZPA IV, Blatt 2, cited in Joachim Lucchesi, *Das Verhör in der Oper: Die Debatte um Brecht/Dessaus "Lukullus" 1951* (Berlin: BasisDruck, 1993), 103.

81. Pieck to Brecht, 20 March 1951, BBA, 135/12

82. Brecht, *Letters*, 500.

83. Otto Grotewohl to Brecht, 30 April 1951, BBA, 135/19.

84. BBA, 1340/45.

85. BBA, 1340/89.

86. Peter Huchel, *Werke II*, 375.

87. Bertolt Brecht, "Konstructive Kritik," *Prosa II, Romanfragmente und Romanentwürfe* (1989), vol. 17, GKBF, 103.

88. Käthe Rülicke, "Notiz zu Gesprächen mit Bertolt Brecht," 13 March 1951, BBA 1340, 49, 48.

89. BBA, 1447/119.

90. BBA, 1340/27.

91. Bertolt Brecht, *Journale II*, 333.

92. Johanna Rudolph, *Neues Deutschland*, 28 May 1953; Alexander Abusch, "Faust—Held oder Renegat in der deutschen Nationalliteratur?" *Sontag*, 17 May 1953. See also "Das 'Faust'-Proben und die deutsche Geschichte: Bemerkungen aus Anlaß des Erscheinens des Operntextes 'Johann Faustus' von Hanns Eisler," *Neues Deutschland*, 14, 16 May 1953.

93. BBA, 795/24

94. Huchel, *Werke II*, 374.

95. Werner Hecht, *Brecht Chronik* (Berlin: Suhrkamp, 1997), 1057.

96. Peter Huchel, *Europäische Ideen*, cited in Hecht, *Brecht Chronik*, 1061.

97. Huchel, *Werke II*, 375.

98. Wilhelm Girnus, "Das Faust Problem und die deutsche Geschichte. Bemerkungen aus Anlaß des Erscheinens des Operntextes 'Johann Faustus' von Hanns Eisler," *Neues Deustchland*, 27 May 1953.

99. Alexander Abusch, *Sinn und Form*, 4 (1953), 3/4, 179-94.

100. Walter Ulbricht, *Neues Deutschland*, 28 May 1953, cited in Hecht, *Chronik*, 1059.

101. This episode is most clearly discussed in Meredith Heiser-Duron, "Brecht's Political and Cultural Dilemma in the Summer of 1953," *Communications*, vol. 30, Ns 1 & 2, 50-52.

102. Brecht, *Letters*, 514.

103. Bertolt Brecht, "Thesen zur Faustus-Diskussion," *Mittwochgesellschaft*, Deutsche Akademie der Künste, 27 May 1953, in Hans Bunge, *Die Debatte um Hanns Eislers 'Johann Faustus' Eine Dokumentation* (Berlin: BasisDruck, 1991), 161.

104. Hanns Eisler, *Musik und Politik*, 2 vols., ed. Günter Mayer (Leipzig: Deutscher Verlag für Musik, 1985), 278.

105. Brecht, *Arbeitsjournal*, 1008.

106. Ostermann, *Uprising in East Germany, 1953*, 160ff.

107. The police force of the GDR had been ineffective at stopping the demonstrations.

108. BBA, 2164/05-06.

109. Bertolt Brecht, *Briefe* (Frankfurt am Main: Suhrkamp, 1981), 1793.

110. Ibid., 1795.

111. BBA, 7/07

112. DAK, 18/35-6.

113. Suhrkamp to Brecht, 19 June 1953, BBA, 787/58.

114. Stiftung Archiv der Parteien und Massenorganisationen der DDR im Bundesarchiv, Berlin, cited in Brecht, *Schriften III*, GKBF, vol. 23, 548.

115. "Dringlichkeit einer grossen Aussprache," 23 June 1953, *Neues Deutschland*, cited in Brecht, *Schriften III*, 250

116. BBA, 1447/102.

117. BBA, 1447/119.

118. Bertolt Brecht to Suhrkamp, 1 July 1953, in *Letters*, 516-518.

119. A letter from Gerhard Eisler to the Berliner Pressenvertrieb states that Brecht was to be allowed to obtain copies of *Die Welt, Die Neue Zeitung, Der Spiegel, Revue, Quick, Münchener Illus, Newsweek, Time*, and *Life*, BBA, 838/71.

120. BBA, 1447/121.

121. Bertolt Brecht, *Poems 1913-1956*, 437-438.

122. DAK, 118/435.

123. Heiser-Duron, "Brecht's Political and Cultural Dilemma," 52.

124. "Erklärung der Deutschen Akademie der Künste: Vorschläge an die Regierung übergeben," *Neues Deutschland*, 12 July 1953.

125. Brecht, *Letters*, 515.

126. Bertolt Brecht, *Kulturpolitik und die Akademie der Künste, Neues Deutschland*, 13 August 1953, cited in Brecht, *Schriften III*, GKBF, vol. 23, 256-260.

127. Wolfgang Harich, Hoover Institution's East German Oral History Project, Interview with Wolfgang Harich, 1 December 1990, cited in Heiser-Duron, "Brecht's Political and Cultural Dilemma," 53.

128. Brecht, *Poems*, 436-7; *Gedichte V* (1993), vol. 15, GKBF, 267, 471.

129. Ibid., 436; also in *Gedichte V*, 268, 471.

130. Wandel was appointed "deputy prime minister in charge of coordination of issues relating to sciences, public education and arts" in 1952. See "Record of Conversation of Leaders of the Socialist Unity Party of Germany, W. Pieck, W. Ulbricht, and O. Grotewohl with J.V. Stalin," 28.

131. Brecht, *Briefe*, 520-521.

132. Becher to Brecht, February 24, 1954, BBA, 832/04.

133. Hayman, *Brecht: A Biography*, 370.

134. Bertolt Brecht, *Journal II* (1998), vol. 27, GKBF, 346f; see also *Arbeitsjournal*, 520.

135. BBA, 1340/61.

136. BBA, 2164/24

137. Brecht, *Poems*, 439-440.

138. Bertolt Brecht, *Stücke*, vol. XIV (Aufbau-Verlag: Berlin und Weimar, 1968).

139. Brecht, *Poems*, 442.

140. BBA, 2164/24-25.

141. Pike, *The Politics of Culture in Soviet-Occupied Germany*; Davies and Parker, "Brecht," 181.

142. Renate Rechtien, 'Relations of Production? Christ Wolf's Extended Engagement with the Legacy of Bertolt Brecht', in Davies and Parker, 196ff.

Conclusion

By 1955 Jaspers, Mann, Meinecke, and Brecht seemed irrelevant to many in divided Germany. Incapable of understanding or dealing effectively with the post-war challenges, they had done little to promote thoroughgoing cultural and political change in East and West Germany. Mann and Jaspers, now citizens elsewhere, seemed to have abandoned Germany and therefore abdicated their positions as cultural leaders. Meinecke, who died the previous year at 92, had seemed during the last years of his long life to be little more than a figurehead used to prop up the fledgling Free University of Berlin. Brecht, in the East, appeared to be a prophet of complicity, one who sacrificed individual judgment and initiative to a political allegiance that helped to undermine the very notion of a distinctively *moral* responsibility. There was a sense, moreover, that they all belonged to a tainted generation of intellectuals. What one commentator wrote of Thomas Mann and Hermann Hesse in 1951 might easily have been written of the others as well:

> What can intellectuals like Mann and Hesse still mean for Germans today? The German youth needs someone who can live and feel with it. It needs someone to direct its action. . . . The task which today's German writer has is much more than just spiritual analysis. He must live in the rubble and think about rebuilding. . . . This cannot come from the masters of yesterday. We need leaders, and perhaps we will have to wait on them, who will not speak ironically or out of self-torment, but who have the courage to call bad bad and good good and who are free enough not to get caught up in the nets of a new dogmatism. Then we can begin again."[1]

Whether or not this judgment was fair, it represented the sentiments of many in the post-war period, especially the so-called "skeptical generation"— those who were too young to be complicit with the Nazi regime, but who were old enough to develop their political consciousness in the 1950s. In the West many found the leadership efforts of younger intellectuals such as the recently formed *Gruppe 47* more convincing. These men and women—Heinrich Böll, Günther Eich, Hans Werner Richter and others—claimed to be realists. Un-

167

bound by ideology, they lived and worked in the rubble rather than speaking from the imperial heights. They spoke clearly, criticized the policies of the allies, and taught young Germans to understand the hard realities of the period. Also appealing were the efforts of the Frankfurt School theorists, who were sharply critical of the escapist, apolitical culture of the new Federal Republic. Theodor Adorno pointed out in 1950 that despite the appearance of "political interests," West German culture tended toward "spiritualization," which made people content with the "comfort and safety of the provincial."[2] Among intellectuals in the GDR, dissidents such as Walter Janka, Gustav Just, and Wolfgang Harich, who went to prison in the 1956 for their criticism of the Ulbricht regime, sometimes seemed more attractive, if no more effective, than Brecht.

If in the 1950s and beyond, the leadership efforts of Mann, Brecht, Jaspers, and Meinecke were deemed irrelevant, sometimes even counterproductive, these men had seemed to many in the very different circumstances of 1945 the ideal leaders. Untainted with the stain of Nazism, they understood that the challenges facing Germany were myriad and that meeting those challenges would require economic, political, social, and cultural readjustment. They were prepared to move beyond traditional roles, to use their influence and moral authority to break from the old mandarin and *Dichter* traditions.

The experiences of these four intellectuals from 1945-1955 illustrate how dramatically the circumstances and priorities had changed in this brief period. During the first three years of the occupation the Soviet Union and the Western allies had demanded that the Germans be re-educated, and had supported and supervised German efforts at cultural renewal. Moreover, the educated German public on both sides of the ideological divide had often embraced the leadership efforts of an older generation of intellectuals that represented the most positive aspects of the earlier culture. There was thus a brief window of opportunity both to address the cultural and political crisis in a new way and to offer a different kind of leadership.

After 1948, however, the former allies increasingly devoted their attention to economic and political reconstruction, and the emerging Cold War context closed off possibilities for cultural renewal. Similarly the Germans themselves came to believe that the priority was adjustment to the political and economic realities of occupation, not cultural reconstruction. By 1949, the western powers were concerned above all with making West Germany an ally against the Soviet Union and its eastern European satellites—including East Germany. With the blessings of the Americans, British, and French, West Germans turned away from any thoroughgoing reexamination of their cultural traditions and institutions. They looked instead to the material advantages that the economic miracle brought. Insofar as they were concerned about culture, it was in the escapist, backward-looking, and uncritical way noted by Adorno and others. On the whole, West Germans were not prepared to engage in a critical dialogue about their troubled past that Meinecke, Mann, and Jaspers all demanded.[3]

In East Germany, too, the Cold War context changed the priorities and limited the scope for intellectual leadership. In the immediate post-war period, the German communists demanded the "moral rebirth of the German people."[4] This included "a reevaluation of the entire historical development of the German people" and an examination of "the positive and negative forces influential in German intellectual life."[5] Especially after 1948, however, when the formalism/socialist realism debate reemerged, the SED demanded that all discussion of the German cultural tradition be used to lend credibility to the new socialist state. In particular, the "progressive" elements of German history and culture needed to be integrated into the new constitutive narrative of the GDR. Thus a critical reassessment of the recent (and more distant) past—including great cultural figures such as Schiller and Goethe, Bach and Beethoven—became virtually impossible. Although there remained some opportunities for significant cultural leadership until 1956, especially in the immediate aftermath of Stalin's death in 1953, room for maneuver quickly closed down. Moreover, such involvement brought with it the dangers of complicity, as Brecht himself came to understand in all too personal a way.

In retrospect, then, it is clear that as the political circumstances and priorities changed, so too did the scope for leadership. Meinecke, Mann, and Jaspers were most effective during the early phase of reconstruction, between 1945 and 1948, when the situation in western Germany seemed most open and fluid. Even during this period, however, we have seen that none of their efforts was a clear-cut success. Brecht, living in different circumstances and under different pressures, was most effective between 1949 and 1953. He, too, faced many obstacles and setbacks that limited his effectiveness. Yet during the post-war period each of these men took risks, explored new and untried forms. Transported into a new cultural and political context that challenged their own values and ideas, they sacrificed many of their old assumptions and habits that seemed to prevent an unhampered view of the new reality. In the process, they not only helped transcend their own earlier tradition of intellectual leadership, but also pointed beyond the narrow overreaction of the subsequent generation that demanded "only" socio-political engagement from intellectuals. They proffered a different, more nuanced understanding of intellectual responsibility, one that renounced strict apoliticism, but also recognized that "engagement" could come in different forms.

A crucial part of this new understanding was that the proper role for intellectuals is to articulate a message, an attitude, an opinion to and for the public. Although they may not be the purveyors of universal truths and values, they do speak from a considered and thoughtful position about what concerns a large number of people. In short, they create a new set of ideas that inform and guide public opinion. Along the way, intellectuals often must raise troubling questions, confront orthodoxy and dogma, and make people uncomfortable. Also crucial to the new conception is a willingness to lead in practical, symbolic, and theoretical ways.

In tentatively groping toward a new understanding of intellectual responsibility, these men contributed to long-term cultural development in divided Germany. In particular, they helped to organize public discourse about the War and its attendant atrocities. Thus they established lasting categories and patterns for

depicting the mid-century catastrophe, including the question of responsibility
and guilt. They took for granted that there was a general cultural crisis that had
contributed to the triumph of National Socialism, World War II, and the destruction of European Jewry. Both German and Western culture had broken down in
the face of catastrophe. Not only had culture failed to avert ultimate horror, but,
as Jean Amery pointed out, it "led straight into a tragic dialectic of self-
destruction."[6] Dan Diner has made a similar point, arguing that the Holocaust
constituted a "far reaching, fundamental rupture," which touched "the very
foundations of certainty about civilization" itself, therefore undermining the
fundamental premises of human co-existence.[7] On one level, then, these four
intellectuals saw that any diagnosis had to be found on the level of cultural
foundations. They recognized that things like the "death of God," the crisis of
values, and the eclipse of authority—the traditional categories employed by
Ringer's mandarins and Craig's *Dichter* to address the cultural crisis—were
important. But they saw that specific causes were more amenable to improvement than these grand ideas. Hence, they tried not to be prophets of despair, or
to offer *only* general prescriptions for change, but rather to offer more specific
prescriptions to more specific aspects of the cultural and political crisis.

Although they did not agree on the exact nature of the catastrophe, they
agreed that it emerged, at least partially, from the Western cultural tradition.
Here they were not alone. As Anson Rabinbach and Steven Aschheim have illustrated, there were many others who indicted Western culture—most famously
Theodor Adorno, Max Horkheimer, and Martin Heidegger. In *Dialectic of
Enlightenment*, Adorno and Horkheimer argued that the catastrophe had
emerged from the chief cultural agent of Western Europe—Enlightenment. According to Aschheim, this work became "perhaps the most definitive contemporary statement of the intimate nexus between culture, barbarism and catastrophe."[8] Heidegger traced the cataclysm of World War II back through the history
of Being to the emergence of metaphysical thinking. Brecht, in typical Marxist
fashion, saw Germany as subject to the overall crisis of late capitalism, along
with its bourgeois cultural manifestations, that affected Europe generally. For
Mann, Nazism, as a variant of European fascism, was one response to a general
cultural and political crisis—a crisis to which Germany was particularly vulnerable.[9] Meinecke, too, saw Germany as responding to more general trends affecting the entire West, including industrialization, modernization, and the rise of
mass politics. Likewise, Jaspers pointed to broader European and worldwide
developments: "what has happened today has its causes in general human events
and conditions, and only secondarily in the special intra-national relations and
the decisions of single groups of men. What is taking place is a crisis of mankind. The contributions, fatal or salutary, of single peoples and states can only
be seen in the framework of the whole, as can the connections which brought on
this war, and its phenomena which manifested in new, horrible fashion what
man can be."[10] Unlike Heidegger, Adorno, and Horkheimer, however, these men were not
merely side-stepping the German dimension as they dealt in more general terms
with the crisis. They recognized that the catastrophe had emerged from within

the specifically *German* cultural tradition. Indeed, it was crucial that the crisis had manifested itself in this particular form in Germany, and these four figures sought to explain why and how that had happened. Thus, especially in the immediate post-war period, they believed it was on the level of German distinctiveness that the most plausible diagnosis could be found. For Mann, it was precisely that aspect of high culture that was most German—its musicality and subjectivity—that accounted for its unique path toward catastrophe. Mann also agreed with Jaspers that the old political Germany, which tended toward illiberalism and authoritarianism, had so far been a disastrous experiment. As Jaspers put it "the political aspect of [Germany] is only one dimension, and an unhappy one at that, a history that proceeds from one catastrophe to another."[11] Meinecke tended to be more sanguine; he emphasized the strengths and the weaknesses of the first German state, along with the greatness of German cultural development. For Meinecke, it was the mistaken paths taken in the nineteenth century—above all by Bismarck and his successors who brought about the triumph of power over culture—that were so problematic. Meinecke, Mann and Jaspers all agreed, however, that the political sphere was only a reflection of the cultural sphere, the political crisis only one aspect of the cultural one. For Brecht, too, the political crisis was bound up with the cultural one in Germany. It was the individualist bourgeois culture embodied in the German intellectual tradition that had played the most significant role in bringing about the culture that led into Nazism.

Yet none of these figures was as pessimistic about the possibility of renewal as Adorno and Horkheimer, on the one hand, and Heidegger on the other, for whom the catastrophe represented "a permanent sign of unredeemed history."[12] For intellectuals such as Adorno, Horkheimer, and Heidegger, redemption could no longer be found in culture, and intellectuals could do little more than critique Enlightenment or wait for a new dispensation. For Mann, Meinecke, Jaspers, and Brecht, however, it still seemed possible to find some measure of redemption in the ruins of the German and Western cultural traditions. Although none now hoped for total redemption, all were motivated by hope, not desperation. To some extent, Nazism had emerged from German culture, but all recognized that the evils of Nazism were not fully coincident with the German tradition. Nor was the broader European tradition hopelessly tainted. Thus, Germany needed to reconnect to its best cultural and intellectual traditions—in particular those it shared with other European nations.

If they recognized that German high culture and the intellectuals who promoted it were partially responsible for bringing about the catastrophe, they responded by leading in ways that went beyond the traditional patterns of earlier generations. To be sure, none of the three "western" intellectuals sought to play an active political role or tried to determine public policy in a direct way. Indeed, they were concerned deliberately not to do so. The Germans, as Meinecke, Mann, and Jaspers all correctly recognized between 1945 and 1948, had no direct control over the political sphere and little influence over allied policy during the occupation. In any case, these three figures, like so many others of their generation, believed that direct participation in the political process led to disappointment and possibly even disaster, as in the case of Martin Heidegger and

Carl Schmitt during the Third Reich. To speak about politics in a general conceptual way, to reground German political thought in Western traditions of liberty and democracy, was an acceptable, even a necessary role for intellectuals to play. Sometimes, as with Meinecke and Heuss, it was even possible for the ideas of intellectuals to influence the thinking of elected officials. However, this influence was usually indirect and always incidental.

Meinecke and Jaspers became "engaged" in other ways as well. Jaspers played a significant role in recreating the foundation for the German university system in general, and in rebuilding Heidelberg University specifically. He co-wrote the new constitution for Heidelberg University, became co-editor for *Die Wandlung*, and reestablished his own philosophical seminar. Meinecke helped revive the *Historische Zeitschrift*, reestablished his historical seminar, tried to integrate former students who had emigrated back into German cultural life, and became the first rector of the Free University of Berlin. Mann, less directly involved, nevertheless also continued his earlier more "political" direction by discussing key political and cultural themes such as democracy, responsibility, and the emerging Cold War. He again assumed the mantle of guide and educator, even if his refusal to return to Germany limited his effectiveness in this regard.

In the East, Brecht went beyond the Mandarin and *Dichter* tradition to become directly and intentionally political. Although never predisposed to be a statesman himself, he understood that the way to bring about cultural change was through politics. As a founding member of the German Academy of the Arts, he had direct contact with and influence over political figures such as Johannes Becher. In the crucial months after Stalin's death, he helped shape the direction of cultural policy in East Germany—at least for a time. Thus, he offered, on one level, direct engagement. But he, like Meinecke, Mann, and Jaspers, also recognized that the solutions to the cultural crisis could not be found simply at the level of socio-political engagement. There were deeper cultural problems that demanded cultural solutions.

Even at the level of cultural foundations, however, there was something deeply political about what these men were trying to do. To rediscover a nation, to recreate its values, to infuse that nation with its culture, properly restored, while at the same time distancing it from its troubled past—all of this was highly political, explosively so. The Germans needed to be brought to an awareness of what united them in order to regain a sense of national identity and collective purpose, even if events conspired to thwart these efforts in both East and West Germany. They needed, as Günter Grass has his Oscar say, "a point of vantage, a point of departure, a point of contact, a point of view."[13]

Each of these men recognized that Germany lacked both an accepted historical tradition and a common body of cultural and political experience that could supply it with clear direction in the immediate post-war period. Its language, its images, its categories, its way of conceiving the world seemed unable to explain or encompass all that had happened. But these intellectuals, even Brecht, emphasized the need to work through the past, to find what had gone wrong, and then connect with the healthier traditions that would allow a stabilizing, productive relationship with the past.

The most important first step was to initiate a public discussion of the collective German past—including especially the issues of guilt and responsibility. As Meinecke put it, the chief cultural task was to purify and intensify Germany's "moral" or "inner existence." Germans needed to work through their past because, as Jaspers stated, "how we remember will be significant for what we become," and they sought to promote a national dialogue in both traditional and new fora for public discussion.[14] Mann, for example, demanded that Germans accept responsibility they bore "for their own misery and not some democracy and the occupation troops. They must accept the consequences therefore, that they led themselves into the darkness and that they served this regime for twelve years. They have squandered their national power, the German intelligence, their spirit of inventiveness, courage and efficiency in the service of a mad regime."[15] Meinecke recognized, in his better moments, the need for individual contrition. Although he pointed blame primarily toward Hitler and his henchmen, he also recognized that all Germans bore guilt for Nazism, World War II, and the destruction of European Jewry. Brecht, too, believed that Germans had to accept responsibility for Hitler and the Nazis in order to move forward. Indeed, this was part of what was at issue for him in the crucial years between 1951 and 1953. But Brecht stopped short of demanding individual contrition, emphasizing instead the culpability of all "classes," even the workers, in Germany. Jaspers, on the other hand, insisted that individuals confront Germany's Nazi past, as both an act of personal purification and a civic obligation. A moral stand of this kind was more than simply bearing witness to one's own personal conviction; it was at the same time a potentially influential symbolic act, one that reverberated outward among the expectations and values of others. This action might provoke other individuals to participate in similar expiations, which might in turn produce still more encouraging results to convince still broader numbers of people. As more people joined in, a gradual erosion of old habits and expectations would occur, and a collective expiation could be brought about.

Sometimes the categories these men employed in attempting to create a thoroughgoing reappraisal of the past were problematic. As we have seen, Jaspers' concept of metaphysical guilt obscured more than it enlightened. Mann's emphasis on the German character lacked specificity and met with fierce resistance. Meinecke employed categories such as fate and chance, which suggested that he was eschewing individual responsibility. Brecht too often relied on traditional Marxist categories that presented Nazism as a variant of fascism, and fascism as little more than the end stage of monopoly capitalism.

There is also little doubt but that these men, despite their best efforts, failed to create a collective expiation in the immediate post-war period. But it was never possible to achieve final catharsis, to work through the past once and for all, as controversies from the 1960s until the present indicate. These men saw themselves as initiating a much longer process. They helped begin the process of *Vergangenheitsbewältigung* by posing difficult questions and offering new categories for understanding—questions and categories that continue to inform contemporary discussion. Their arguments differed, sometimes dramatically, on one level. On a deeper level, however, their positions complemented each other and, taken together, helped a generation of Germans get at the heart of the dilemma. It would be up to subsequent generations to build on the work they had done.

Meinecke, Mann, Jaspers, and Brecht also understood that mastering the past required more than a critical dialogue, more than sweeping away the remains of National Socialism. When all of German history stood under a cloud, Germans needed to have confidence in the positive side of their tradition; they needed to reconstruct a healthy national identity. Thus, they sought some kind of usable past—a cultural bedrock—on which to build a new Germany. As Meinecke wrote, the "high mission of German historical writing for the future" was "to give evidence of both love and severity for our past and to proceed to the task of maintaining what was truly good in it, recognizing what was valueless, and taking warning from it when one has to take action."[16]

The attempt to reconnect to the positive aspects of the German tradition was fraught with difficulty because so much of German history—and culture—seemed tainted. All of these figures nevertheless believed it was necessary. They understood that national communities are, in an important sense, constituted by their past. It is possible to speak of a national community as a community of memory, one that does not forget its past. In order not to forget that past, a community is involved in retelling its story, its constitutive narrative, and in so doing, it offers examples of men and women who have embodied and exemplified the meaning of the community. These stories of collective history, of exemplary individuals and traditions, are an important part of the narrative that is so central to a community of memory. The communities of memory that tie us to the past also turn us toward the future as communities of hope.

For Meinecke, the cultural bedrock was Goethe. In Goethe and his era, Meinecke found what he took to be the best and most spiritually pure elements in the German tradition. By emulating Goethe and his age, Germans could "win back a spiritual contact with the other Occidental countries." Also important was Burckhardt, who emphasized the importance of culture over politics. Thus, Meinecke was arguing that the answer to the current crisis could be found within the German tradition—before the industrial revolution, the rise of the masses and political unification.[17]

Mann, too, found something uniquely German and European about Goethe. Goethe understood and generally accepted the European notions of liberty and equality. Unlike Meinecke, however, Mann found even Goethe to be suspect. After all, Goethe himself had been elitist, provincial and inegalitarian at times. On the whole, Mann was more skeptical than Meinecke that the answer to the current situation lay within the German tradition. If Germany were to rebuild its culture on a solid footing, it would need to look to the broader European intellectual and political traditions. Specifically, he wished to posit the idea of a new religious humanism based on the best aspects of German and European culture.

Jaspers, like Mann, recognized the importance of rebuilding Germany on the basis of both the German and the European traditions. He, too, understood that the Germans needed to have confidence in their culture, and Goethe had been an important part of the best German tradition.[18] However, he was not the proper model for post-World War II Germans. Goethe, like other great intellectual lights of the past including Burckhardt, Kant, Kierkegaard and others, needed to be seen not as a guide but as a "signpost." More important for Germany's immediate future was the European tradition. In particular, Germans needed to reconnect to three concepts which built "the characteristic structure of Europe—freedom, history, science."[19] For Jaspers, however, the answer to the current crisis lay not just in the European tradition, but also in the broader history of humanity. Germans needed to look back to the Axial period, between 800-200 BC, the first age of fundamental cultural transformation, when the three great civilizations of the world had arisen: India, China, and Europe. Here Germans and Europeans, facing a new axial period, would find the cultural bedrock.

Brecht, too, despite his more radical position, wanted the Germans to reconnect to the positive aspects of the German and Western tradition—the radical "progressive" tradition. To be sure, Brecht, unlike many in the GDR, insisted that this be done in a thoughtful, critical way. Thus he did not spare even Goethe and Schiller from criticism. Yet Brecht pointed toward healthier aspects of the tradition. In particular, he defended the Marxist tradition of engaged intellectual leadership.

The attempts of these four to reconnect Germany with its own and broader Western traditions were sometimes troubling for contemporaries. Most problematic was a tendency to cast what purported to be a usable past in terms that made the past seem irrelevant to younger contemporaries. For example, as many critics at the time recognized, Meinecke's emphasis on Goethe and Goethe societies illustrated a fundamental lack of understanding of the post-war challenges. Meinecke could not see that Goethe had little to offer a Germany in its transition toward twentieth-century Western political culture. The Germans of 1945 could no more return to an eighteenth-century mindset than Henry Morgenthau could return Germany to the status of a land "largely pastoral and agricultural in nature." Similarly, the attempts of Mann and Jaspers to make of Germany a *Kulturnation* were perhaps short-sighted. The model of the future clearly lay with a mass democracy and a mass consumer society, much like the society that virtually all of the other Europeans were longing for after World War II, not in the distant European past or the culture of some ancient Axial period.

Brecht's attempt to find a usable past was also problematic. Although he was sharply critical of the Weimar Republic, which he called the "golden age of the Tuis," he also found there the most progressive elements of German culture and sought to restore the Marxist tradition of critical, engaged intellectual leadership in an East Germany that, ironically, increasingly tried to distance itself from this model.

These men were thus, to a certain extent, caught in an older world, unable fully to break out of the old molds, the old traditions. Yet working out of the tradition did not mean simple conservatism, defense of the status quo, or even escapism. These four figures did not simply reinforce existing patterns of behavior, replicate the inheritance of the past unaltered, or diminish possibilities for new patterns to emerge. Instead their post-war work led to the belief that what had been experienced and consecrated in the past could open onto something new and positive; it could be projected dynamically toward the future. It implied that human endeavors possess a cumulative quality, so that each individual's efforts, and each generation's achievements, might contribute to the building of something partially new. The pieces of the culture had to be assembled slowly, one by one. What shape this collective creation would take was unclear. Only succeeding generations could answer this question, but this older generation began the process of moving beyond older categories of understanding. They thus helped to reconcile rupture with continuity by creating new trajectories for German cultural development.

NOTES

1. Heinz Thurm, "Thomas Mann, Hermann Hesse und wir Jungen," *Die Umschau*, vol. 2, no. 5, 612-15.
2. Theodor Adorno, "Auferstehung der Kultur in Deutschland?" *Frankfurter Hefte*, vol. 5 (May 1950), 470f.
3. Jan-Werner Müller, et al., have recently argued that under the placid surface of the economic miracle, there was a great deal of intellectual ferment in the FRG. Even in the 1950s West German intellectuals were wrestling with the recent past and thus providing a cornerstone for the development of democratic political culture. Jan-Werner Müller ed., *German Ideologies Since 1945: Studies in the Political Thought and Culture of the Bonn Republic* (New York: Palgrave, 2003).
4. Johannes R. Becher, "Rede an München," *Deutsche Bekenntnis*, 71, cited in Pike, *The Politics of Culture*, 74.
5. "Leitsätze des Kulturbundes [3 July 1945]," *Um die Erneuerung der deutschen Kultur*, 69, cited in Pike, *The Politics of Culture*, 160.
6. Jean Amery, *The Mind's Limits: Contemplations by a Survivor in Auschwitz and its Realities*, trans. Sidney Rosenfeld and Stella P. Rosenfeld (Bloomington, Indiana: Indiana University Press, 1980), 8, cited in Steven Aschheim, *Culture and Catastrophe: German and Jewish Confrontations with National Socialism and Other Crises* (New York: New York University Press, 1996), 2. See also Zygmunt Bauman, *Dialektik der Ordnung: Die Moderne und der Holocaust* (Hamburg: Europäische Verlagsanstalt, 1992).
7. Dan Diner, "Vorwort des Herausgebers," in Dan Diner, ed., *Zivilisationsbruch: Denken nach Auschwitz* (Frankfurt: Fischer, 1988), 7-13. See also Dan Diner, "Zivilisationsbruch, Gegenrationalität, Gestaute Zeit." Drei interpretationsleitende Begriffe zum Thema Holocaust," in Hans Erler, Ernst Ehrlich, Ludger Heid eds., *Meinetwegen ist die Welt erschaffen: Das intellektuelle Verdächtnis des deutschsprachigen Judentums* (Frankfurt: Campus Fachbuch, 1997)
8. Steven Aschheim, *Culture and Catastrophe: German and Jewish Confrontations with Nationalism Socialism and Other Crises* (New York: New York University Press, 1996), 7.
9. Mann, *Story of a Novel*, 55.
10. Karl Jaspers, *The Question of German Guilt*, 24-5.
11. Jaspers, *Philosophical Autobiography*, 64.
12. Rabinbach, *In the Shadow of Catastrophe*, 34.

13. Günter Grass, *The Tin Drum*, trans. Ralph Manheim (New York: Knopf, 1993), 41.

14. Karl Jaspers, "Geleitwort," 3.

15. Mann, *Frage und Antwort*, 271.

16. Meinecke, *The German Catastrophe*, 108.

17. Ibid., 115f.

18. Jaspers, *Philosophical Autobiography*, 64. See also Jaspers, *The European Spirit*, 134.

19. Ibid., 34.

Bibliography

ARCHIVES

Bertolt Brecht Archiv (BBA), Berlin, Germany
Deutsches Literaturarchiv (DLA), Nachlaß Karl Jaspers (NJ), Marbach, Germany
Geheimnis Preußischer Staatsarchiv Kulturbesitz (GSA), Nachlaß Friedrich Meinecke (NM), Berlin.
Marshall Research Library (MRL), Smith-Crum Papers, Lexington, Virginia
Deutsche Akademie der Künste (DAK), Berlin, Germany
Thomas Mann Archiv (TMA), Zurich, Switzerland
Universitätsarchiv Freie Universität zu Berlin (UA, FuB), Berlin, Germany
Universitätsarchiv Heidelberg (UAH), Heidelberg, Germany

PRIMARY SOURCES

Abusch, Alexander. "Faust—Held oder Renegat in der deutschen Nationalliteratur?" *Sontag*. 17 May 1953.
Adorno, Theodor. "Auferstehung der Kultur in Deutschland?" *Frankfurter Hefte*. Vol. 5 (May 1950): 453-477.
———. *Jargon der Eigentlichkeit: Zur deutschen Ideologie*. Frankfurt am Main 1964.
Barth, Max. "Abschied von Thomas Mann: ein unfreundlicher Kommentar zu einer unfreundlichen Erklärung." *Neue Volkszeitung*. 15 September 1946.
Bauer, Arnold. "Wandlung eines Dichters: Ein zweites Gespräch mit Thomas Mann." *Neue Zeitung*. 21 June 1949.
Becher, Johannes R. *Briefe*. Berlin: Aufbau, 1993.
Benda, Julien. *Treason of the Intellectuals*. Translated by Richard Aldington. New York: W.W. Norton, 1969.
Brecht, Bertolt. *Arbeitsjournal*. 2 vols. Edited by Werner Hecht. Frankfurt am Main: Suhrkamp, 1973.
———. *Bertolt Brecht on Film and Radio*. Translated and edited by Marc Silberman. London: Methuen, 2000.
———. *Brecht on Theatre: The Development of an Aesthetic*. Translated and edited by John Willett. New York: Hill and Wang, 1964.
———. *Briefe*. Frankfurt am Main: Suhrkamp, 1981.

————. *Gedichte 4, 1928-1939*. Vol. 14, *Große kommentierte Berliner und Frankfurter Ausgabe* (hereafter GKBF). 31 vols. Edited by Werner Hecht, Jan Knopf, Werner Mittenzwei, Klaus-Detlef Müller. Berlin and Weimar: Aufbau and Suhrkamp, 1980-2000.

————. *Gedichte 5, 1940-1955*. Vol. 15, GKBF (1993).

————. *Journale 2*. Vol. 27, GKBF (1993).

————. *Letters 1913-1956*. Translated by Ralph Manheim. Edited by John Willett. New York: Routledge, 1981.

————. *Marxismus und Literatur*. Vol. 2. Reinbek bei Hamburg Rowohlt, 1969.

————. *Poems 1913-1956*. Edited and translated by John Willett and Ralph Mannheim. New York: Methuen, 1976.

————. *Prosa 2, Roman Fragmente und Romanentwürfe*. Vol. 17, GKBF (1989).

————. *Schriften I, 1914-1933*. Vol. 21, GKBF (1993).

————. *Schriften II, 1933-1942*. Vol. 22, GKBF (1993).

————. *Schriften III, 1942-1956*. Vol. 23, GKBF (1993).

————. *Schriften IV, Theatermodelle "Katzgraben"—Notate 1953*. Vol. 24, GKBF (1994).

————. *Schriften zur Politik und Gesellschaft I & II*. Berlin and Weimar: Aufbau, 1968.

————. *Stücke*. 15 vols. Berlin and Weimar: Aufbau, 1968.

————. *Stücke II*. Vol. 2, GKBF (1980).

————. *Stücke III*. Vol. 3, GKBF (1980).

————. *Stücke IV*. Vol. 4, GKBF (1980).

————. *Stücke VI*. Vol. 6, GKBF (1980).

————. *Stücke VII*. Vol. 7, GKBF (1980).

————. *Versuche II*. Berlin: Suhrkamp, 1957.

Brinckmann, A. E. "Thomas Mann über Politische Freiheit." *Neues Europa*. Vol. 2. No. 13: 29-34.

Boehlich, Walter. "Thomas Manns *Doktor Faustus*." *Merkur*. Vol. 2. No. 3: 588-603.

Curtius, Ernst Robert. "Goethe oder Jaspers?" *Die Zeit*. 28 April 1949.

Dahl, Wilhelm, Friedrich Meinecke, and Gustav Radbruch. *Die Deutschen Universitäten und der heutige Staat: Referate erstattet auf der Weimarer Tagung deutscher Hochschullehrer am 23. und 24. April 1926*. Tübingen: J.C.B. Mohr, 1926.

Dymschitz, Alexander. "Über die formalistische Richtung in der deutschen Malerei. Bemerkungen eines Außenstehenden." *Tägliche Rundschau*. 19 and 24 November 1948.

Erdmann, Karl. "Die Deutsche Katastrophe." *Kölner Universitäts-Zeitung*. Vol. 7.

Enderle, August. "Ein Emigrant über Thomas Mann." *Der Weserkurier*. Vol. 1. No. 8: 13.

Fetscher, Iring. *Studentische Blätter*. Tübingen. Vol. 5. 20 June 1948.

Geiss, Immanuel. "Wie es zur 'deutschen Katastrophe' kam, Die gesammelten Werke Friedrich Meinecke's abgeschlossen." *Frankfurter Rundschau*. 13 January 1971.

Girnus, Wilhelm. "Das Faust Problem und die deutsche Geschichte Bemerkungen aus Anlaß des Erscheinens des Operntextes 'Johann Faustus' von Hanns Eisler." *Neues Deustchland*. 27 May 1953.

Hofmann, Heinz. "Bücher zur Zeitgeschichte." *Aufbau*. 23 October 1946.

Holborn, Hajo and G.P. Gooch. "Irrwege in unserer Geschichte." *Der Monat*. Vol. 1: 5.

Holldack, Heinz. "Eine Selbstkritik des Bürgertums." *Hochlandredaktion*. December 1946: 176.

Holthusen, Hans-Egon. "Die Welt ohne Transzendenz." *Merkur*. Vol. 3. No. 6: 38-59.

Jaspers, Karl and Karl H. Bauer. *Briefwechsel 1945-1968*. Edited by Renato de Rosa. New York and Berlin: Springer, 1983.

Jaspers, Karl and Martin Heidegger. *Briefwechsel, 1920-1963.* Frankfurt am Main and Munich: Klostermann and Piper, 1990.

Jaspers, Karl. "Antwort an Sigrid Undset." *Neue Zeitung.* 4 November 1945.

———. "Die Erneuerung der Universität." In Karl Jaspers and Fritz Ernst. *Von lebendigen Geist der Universität und vom Studieren.* Heidelberg: L. Schneider, 1946.

———. *Die geistige Situation der Zeit.* Berlin: Walter de Gruyter, 1931.

———. *Die Idee der Universität.* Berlin: Springer, 1923.

———. *Die Idee der Universität.* Berlin: Springer, 1946; *The Idea of the University.* Edited by Karl Deutsch. Translated by H.A.T. Reiche and H.F. Vanderschmidt. Boston: Beacon Press, 1959.

———. "Ein Selbst-Portrait." In *Jaspers Today: Philosophy at the Threshold of the Future.* Edited by Edith Ehrlich. Washington D.C.: University Press of America, 1987.

———. *The European Spirit.* Translated by Ronald Gregor Smith. London: SCM Press, Ltd, 1948.

———. *Existentialism and Humanism.* New York: R. F. Moore Co., 1952.

———. *The Future of Germany.* Translated. and edited by E.B. Ashton. Chicago and London: University of Chicago Press, 1967.

———. "Geleitwort." *Die Wandlung.* Vol. 1. No. 1: 3.

———. "Hochschulreform? Das Gutachten des Hamburger Studienausschluβes für Hochschulreform." *Die Wandlung.* Vol. 4.

———. *Origin and Goal of History.* Translated by Michael Bullock. New Haven: Yale University Press, 1953.

———. *Philosophie und Welt: Reden und Aufsätze.* Munich: Piper, 1958.

———. *The Question of German Guilt.* Translated by E.B. Ashton. New York: Dial Press, 1947.

———. "Thesen zur Frage der Hochschulerneuerung." In *Karl Jaspers: Philosopher Among Philosophers/Philosoph unter Philosophen.* Edited by Richard Wisser and Leonard H. Erlich: 293-331. Wurzburg: Konigshausen & Neumann, 1993.

———. "Volk und Universität." *Die Wandlung.* Vol. 2. No. 1: 56.

———. "Warum ich Deutschland verlassen habe." In *Schicksal und Wille.* Edited by Hans Saner. Munich: Piper, 1967.

———. *Way to Wisdom.* New Haven: Yale University Press, 1951.

Kästner, Erich. "Betrachtungen eines Unpolitischen." *Die Neue Zeitung.* 14 January 1946.

Lestiboudois, Herbert. "Briefe an Frank Thieß." *Neue Westfälische Zeitung.* 22 January 1946

Lucchesi, Joachim, ed. *Das Verhör in der Oper: Die Debatte um Brecht/Dessaus "Lukullus" 1951.* Berlin: BasisDruck, 1993.

Lukács, Georg. *Essays on Realism.* Cambridge, MA: MIT Press, 1981.

Mann, Thomas. *Ansprache im Goethejahr.* Frankfurt am Main: Suhrkamp, 1949.

———. *Briefe an Paul Amann.* Edited by Herbret Wegener. Lübeck: M. Schmidt Rombild, 1959.

———. *Doctor Faustus: The Life of the German Composer Adrian Leverkühn, as Told by a Friend.* Translated by H. T. Lowe-Porter. New York: Alfred Knopf, 1948.

———. "Germany and the Germans." In *Literary Lectures Presented at The Library of Congress.* Washington: Library of Congress, 1973.

———. *Essays by Thomas Mann.* Translated by H. T. Lowe-Porter. New York: Vintage, 1957.

———. *Essays of Three Decades.* Edited by Clara Winston. New York: Knopf, 1947.

———. *Frage und Antwort: Interviews mit Thomas Mann 1909-1955.* Hamburg: Albrecht Knaus, 1983.

———. "Goethe and Democracy." In *Literary Lectures Presented at the Library of Congress*. Library of Congress: Washington, 1973.

———. *Last Essays*. Translated by Richard and Clara Winston and Tania and James Stern. New York: Knopf, 1959.

———. *Letters 1889-1955*. Translated by Richard and Clara Winston. New York: Knopf, 1971.

———.*Reden und Aufsätze 3*. Vol. 9, *Gesammelte Werke* (hereafter GW). Frankfurt am Main: S. Fischer, 1960.

———. *Reden und Aufsätze 4*. Vol. 10, GW.

———. *Reden und Aufsätze 5*. Vol. 11, GW.

———. *Reden und Aufsätze 6*. Vol. 12, GW.

———. *Reflections of a Nonpolitical Man*. Translated by Walter D. Morris. New York: Fredrick Ungar Publishing Co, 1983.

———. *The Story of a Novel: The Genesis of Doctor Faustus*. Translated by Richard and Clara Winston. New York: Knopf, 1961.

———. *Tagebücher 1933-1934*. Edited by Peter de Mendelssohn. Frankfurt: S. Fischer, 1977.

———. *Tagebücher1944-1946*. Edited by Inge Jens. Frankfurt: S. Fischer, 1986.

———. *Tagebücher 1946-1948*. Edited by Inge Jens. Frankfurt: S. Fischer, 1989.

———. "Thomas Mann verteidigt sich: Mißverständnisse um Richard Wagner." *Deutsche Allgemeine Zeitung*. April 22, 1933. Vol. 72. No. 187.

———. "The Tragedy of Germany." *Treasury for the Free World*. Introduction by Ernest Hemingway. Edited by Ben Raeburn. New York: Arco Publishing Company, 1945.

Mann, Thomas and Hermann Hesse. *Briefwechsel*. Edited by Anni Carlsson and Volker Michels. Frankfurt am Main: Suhrkamp and S. Fischer, 1999.

Meinecke, Friedrich. *Ausgewählter Briefwechsel*. Edited by Ludwig Dehio and Peter Classen. Stuttgart: K.F. Koehler, 1962. Vol. 6, *Werke*. Edited by Hans Herzfeld, Carl Hinrichs, Walter Hofer, Ebert Kessel, Georg Kotowski. Munich, Darmstadt, Stuttgart: Oldenbourg, 1957-1979.

———. *Autobiographische Schriften*. Vol. 8, *Werke*. Edited by Eberhard Kessel. Stuttgart: K. F. Koehler, 1969.

———. "Bismarcks zwiespältiges Erbe." *Der Kurier*. 2 October 1946. No. 195: 3.

———. *Das Zeitalter der deutschen Erhebung, 1795-1815*. Bielefeld and Leipzig: Velhagen & Slafing,1924.

———. *Die Entstehung des Historismus*. Vol 3, Edited by Carl Hinrichs. Munich: Oldenbourg, 1965

———. *Die Idee der Staatsraison in der neueren Geschichte*. Vol. 1, *Werke*. Edited by Walther Hofer. Munich: Oldenbourg, 1963.

———. *The German Catastrophe*. Translated by Sidney B. Fay. Cambridge, Mass: Harvard University Press, 1950.

———. "Irrwege in unserer Geschichte." *Der Monat*. Vol. 1: 3.

———. *Politische Schriften und Reden*. Vol. 2, *Werke*. Edited by Georg Kotowski. Darmstadt: Siegfried Toeche-Mittler, 1979.

———. *Ranke und Burckhardt*. Berlin: Akadamie, 1948.

———. *Zur Geschichte der Geschichtsschreibung*. Vol. 7, *Werke*. Edited by Eberhard Kessel (Munich: Oldenbourg, 1968).

———. *Zur Theorie und Philosophie der Geschichte*. Vol. 4, *Werke*. Edited by Eberhard Kessel. Munich: Oldenbourg, 1959.

———. "Zur Selbstbesinnung." *Münchener Zeitung*. No. 2. June 16, 1945.

Oehlmann, Werner. "Thomas Mann und die deutsche Musik." *Der Tagespiegel*. 19 February 1948.

Orlow, N. "Das Reich der Schatten auf der Bühne." *Tägliche Rundschau.* Sunday, 19 November 1950.

———. "Wege und Irrwege der Moderne." *Tägliche Rundschau.* 21 and 23 January 1951.

Paeschke, Hans. "Thomas Mann und Kierkegaard: Ein Briefwechsel über den 'Doktor Faustus' und seine Kritiker." *Merkur.* Vol. 3. No. 9: 925.

"Protest der Richard-Wagner-Stadt München." In *Münchner Neuste Nachrichten.* Vol. 16/17. No. 105: 3.

Sell, Viktor. "Doktor Faustus." *Die Wandlung.* Vol 3. No. 5: 403-413

Sieburg, Friedrich. "Frieden mit Thomas Mann." *Die Gegenwart.* Vol. 4. No. 14.

Sombart, Nikolaus. "Wir können uns Thomas Mann leisten." *Der Ruf.* Vol. 3. No. 17 (1 September 1948).

Sternberger, Dolf. "Tagebuch: Thomas Mann und der Respekt." *Die Wandlung.* Vol. 1. No. 1: 451-59.

Tent, James F., ed. *Academic Proconsul: Harvard Sociologist Edward Y. Hartshorne and the Reopnening of German Universities, 1945-1946. His Personal Account.* Trier Wissenschaftlicher, 1998.

Thieß, Frank. "Die innere Emigration." *Münchner Zeitung.* August 18, 1945

Thurm, Heinz. "Thomas Mann, Hermann Hesse und wir Jungen." *Die Umschau.* Vol. 2. No. 5.

Undset, Sigrid. "Die Umerziehung der Deutschen." *Neue Zeitung.* 25 October 1945.

Viktor, Walter. "Thomas Mann's *Doktor Faustus.*" *Aufbau.* Vol. 4. (June 1947): 491-6.

SECONDARY SOURCES

Abendroth, Wolfgang. "Das Unpolitische als Wesensmerkmal der deutschen Universität." *Nationalsozialismus und die deutsche Universität:* 189-208. Berlin: Walter de Gruyter & Co, 1966.

———. "Die deutschen Professoren und die Weimarer Republik." In *Hochschule und Wissenschaft im Dritten Reich.* Edited by Jörg Tröger: 11-25. Frankfurt: Campus, 1984.

Adamson, Walter. *Hegemony and Revolution: A Study of Antonio Gramsci's Political and Cultural Theory.* Berkeley: University of California Press, 1980.

Adorno, Theodor. *Minima Moralia: Reflections from a Damaged Life.* Translated by E.F.N. Jephcott. London: Verso, 1974.

———. *Notes to Literature III.* Translated by Shierry Weber Nicholsen. Columbia: Columbia University Press, 1992.

Amery, Jean. *The Minds Limits: Contemplations by a Survivor in Auschwitz and Its Realities.* Translated by Sidney Rosenfeld and Stella P. Rosenfeld. Bloomington, IN: Indiana University Press, 1980.

Arendt, Hannah. *Men in Dark Times.* New York: Harcourt, Brace & World, 1968.

Arendt, Hannah and Karl Jaspers. *Correspondence, 1926-1969.* Edited by Lotte Köhler and Hans Saner. Translated by Robert and Rita Kimber. San Diego, New York, London: Harcourt Brace & Company, 1992.

Aschheim, Steven. *Culture and Catastrophe: German and Jewish Confrontations with National Socialism and Other Crises.* New York: New York University Press, 1996.

Bark, Denis L. and David R. Gress. *A History of West Germany: From Shadow to Substance.* Vol. 1. Cambridge, Mass: Blackwell, 1993.

Bauman, Zygmunt. *Dialektik der Ordnung: Die Moderne und der Holocaust.* Hamburg: Europäische Verlagsanstalt, 1992.

Benjamin, Walter. *Reflections: Essays, Aphorisms, Autobiographical Writings.* Translated by Edmund Jephcott. Edited by Peter Demetz. New York: Schocken, 1986.
———. *Understanding Brecht.* Frankfurt am Main: Suhrkamp, 1973.
Benkiser, Nickolaus. "Der Faust unserer Tage: Zu Thomas Manns letztem Werk." *Badische Zeitung.* Vol. 3. No. 24. (Easter edition 1948).
Besson, Waldemar. "Friedrich Meinecke und die Weimarer Republik." *Vierteljahrshefte für Zeitgeschichte.* Vol. 7. No. 1. (April 1959).
Blunck, Walther, ed. *Thomas Mann und Hans Friedrich Blunck: Briefwechsel Und Aufzeichnungen.* Hamburg: Troll, 1969.
Bugenstab, Karl-Ernst. *Umerziehung zur Demokratie! Re-education-Politik im Bildungswesen der U.S. Zone 1945-1949.* Düsseldorf: Bertelsmann Universitätsverlag, 1970.
Bunge, Hans. *Die Debatte um Hanns Eislers 'Johann Faustus' Eine Dokumentation.* Berlin: BasisDruck, 1991.
———. *Fragen Sie mehr über Brecht. Hanns Eisler im Gespräch.* Munich: Rogner und Bernhard, 1970.
Cho, JoAnne. "A Cosmopolitan Faith in Karl Jaspers: Decoupling Commitment And Narrowness." *Journal of Ecumenical Studies.* Vol. 37. No. 1 (2000): 55-72.
Craig, Gordon. "Engagement and Neutrality in Weimar Germany." in *Literature and Politics in the Twentieth Century.* Edited by Walter Laqueur and George Mosse: 57-66. New York: Harper and Row, 1967.
———. *Politics of the Unpolitical: German Writers and the Problem of Power, 1770-1871.* New York: Oxford University Press, 1995.
———. "The Mann Nobody Knew." *New York Review of Books.* 29 February 1996: 34.
Clark, Mark and Craig Pepin. "Dilemmas of Education for Democracy: American occupation, university reform, and German resistance." *Educational Policy Borrowing: Historical Perspectives.* Edited by Kimberly Ochs and David Philips. Oxford, U.K.: Symposium Books, 2004.
Clark, Mark. "A Prophet Without Honour: Karl Jaspers in post-World War II Germany, 1945-1948." *Journal of Contemporary History.* Vol. 37. No. 2: 197-222.
Dietrich, Gerd. *Politik und Kultur in der SBZ.* Bern: Peter Lang Press, 1993.
Diner, Dan, ed. *Zivilisationsbruch: Denken nach Auschwitz.* Frankfurt: Fischer, 1988).
Eisler, Hans. *Musik und Politik.* 2 vols. Edited by Günter Mayer. Leipzig: Deutscher Verlag für Musik, 1985.
Emmerich, Wolfgang. *Kleine Literaturgeschichte der DDR. Erweiterte Neuausgabe.* Leipzig: Gustav Kiepenheuer, 1996.
Erbe, Michael, ed. *Friedrich Meinecke Heute: Bericht über ein Gedenk-Colloquium zu sinem 25. Todestag am 5. und 6. April 1979.* Berlin: Colloquium, 1981.
Erler, Hans, Ernst Ehrlich, Ludger Heid, eds. *Meinetwegen ist die Welt erschaffen: Das intellektuelle Vernächtnis des deutschsprachigen Judentums.* Frankfurt: Campus Fachbuch, 1997.
Fest, Joachim. *Die Unwissenden Magier.* Frankfurt: Fischer Taschenbuch, 1993.
Fuegi, John. *Brecht & Co: Sex, Politics, and the Making of the Modern Drama.* New York: Grove, 1993.
Gay, Peter. *Weimar Culture: The Insider as Outsider.* New York: Harper & Row, 1968.
Gilbert, Felix. *A European Past: Memoirs 1905-1945.* New York: W. W. Norton & Co., 1988.
Giles, Geoffrey. "Reeducation at Heidelberg University." *Paedagogica Historica.* Vol. 23. No. 1 (1997).
Giles, Steve and Rodney Livingstone, eds. *Bertolt Brecht: Centenary Essays.* Amsterdam, Atlanta: Rodopi, 1998.

Gramsci, Antonio. *Selections from the Prison Notebooks.* Translated by Quintin Hoare and Geoffrey Nowell Smith. New York: International Publishers, 1971.

Grass, Günter. *Die Plebejer proben den Aufstand: Ein deutsches Trauerspiel.* Darmstadt and Neuwied: Hermann Luchterhand, 1966.

―――. *The Tin Drum.* Translated by Ralph Manheim. New York: Knopf, 1993.

Habermas, Jürgen. *The New Conservatism: Cultural Criticism and the Historians' Debate.* Edited and translated by Shierry Weber Nicholsen. Cambridge, Mass: MIT Press, 1989.

―――. *Stichworte zur geistigen Situation der Zeit.* Frankfurt am Main: Suhrkamp, 1979.

Harpprecht, Klaus. *Thomas Mann: Eine Biographie.* Reinbeck: Rowohlt, 1995.

Hayman, Ronald. *Brecht: A Biography.* New York: Oxford University Press, 1983.

―――. *Thomas Mann: A Biography.* New York: Scribners, 1995.

Hecht, Werner. *Brecht Chronik.* Berlin: Suhrkamp, 1997.

Heiber, Helmut. *Walter Frank und sein Reichsinstitut für Geschichte des neuen Deutschlands.* Stuttgart: Institut für Zeitgeschichte, 1966.

Heiser-Duron, Meredith. "Brecht's Political and Cultural Dilemma in the Summer of 1953." *Communications.* Vol. 30. No. 1 & 2.

Herf, Jeffrey. *Divided Memory: The Nazi Past in the Two Germanys.* Cambridge, Mass. and London: Harvard University Press, 1997.

Hermand, Jost. *Kultur im Wiederaufbau. Die Bundesrepublik Deutschland 1945-1965.* Frankfurt, Berlin: Ullstein, 1989.

Heß, Jürgen C., Hartmut Lehmann, and Volker Sellin. *Heidelberg 1945.* Stuttgart: Franz Steiner, 1996.

Hofer, Walter. *Geschichte zwischen Philosophie und Politik.* Stuttgart: W. Kohlhammer, 1956.

Huchel, Peter. *Werke II.* Frankfurt: Suhrkamp , 1984.

Iggers, George. *The German Conception of History: The National Tradition of Historical Thought from Herder to the Present.* New Hampshire: Wesleyan University Press, 1988.

Jaeger, Manfred. *Sozialliteraten: Funktion und Selbsverständnis der Schriftsteller in der DDR.* Düsseldorf: Bertelsman Universitätsverlag, 1973.

Jarausch, Konrad and Michael Geyer. *Shattered Past: Reconstructing German Histories.* Princeton and Oxford: Princeton University Press, 2003.

Kaes, Anton, Martin Jay, and Edward Dimendberg, eds. *The Weimar Republic Sourcebook.* Berkeley: University of California Press, 1994.

Knudsen, Jonathan B. "Friedrich Meinecke." In *Paths of Continuity: Central European Historiography from the 1930s through the 1950s.* Edited by Lehmann, Hartmut and James van Horn Melton, 40-56. Washington, D.C.; Cambridge, England; New York: German Historical Institute; Cambridge University Press, 1994.

Koselleck, Reinhart. *Bildungsbürtum im 19. Jahrhundert. Teil II. Bildungsgüter und Bildungswissen.* Stuttgart: Klett-Cotta, 1989.

Kurzke, Hermann. *Thomas Mann, Das Leben als Kunstwerk.* Munich: C.H. Beck, 1999.

Lehnert, Herbert and Eve Wessel. *Nihilismus Der Menschenfreundlichkeit: Thomas Manns "Wandlung" Und Sein Essay "Goethe und Tolstoi."* Frankfurt am Main: Vittorio Klostermann, 1991.

Lunn, Eugene. *Marxism and Modernism.* Berkeley: University of California Press, 1982.

Mann, Golo. "The German Intellectuals." In *The Intellectuals.* Edited by George B. de Huszar, 458-469. Glencoe Illinois: The Free Press, 1960.

―――. *Erinnerungen und Gedanken Eine Jugend in Deutschland.* Frankfurt: Fischer, 1991.

Mannheim, Karl. "The Problem of Generations." In *From Karl Mannheim.* Edited by Kurt Wolff, 351-98. New Brunswick: Transaction, 1993.

Meineke, Stephan. *Friedrich Meinecke: Persönlichkeit und politisches Denken bis zum Ende des Ersten Weltkrieg.* Berlin and New York: Walter de Gruyter, 1995.

Mitscherlich, Alexander and Margarete. *Die Unfähigkeit zu trauern.* Munich: Piper, 1967.

Mittenzwei, Werner. *Das Leben des Bertolt Brecht oder Der Umgang mit den Welträtseln.* 2 Vol. Berlin and Weimar: Aufbau, 1986.

Müller, Jan-Werner, ed. *German Ideologies Since 1945: Studies in the Political Thought and Culture of the Bonn Republic.* New York: Palgrave, 2003.

Naimark, Norman M. *The Russians in Germany.* Cambridge, Mass. and London: Harvard University Press, 1995.

Natter, Wolfgang G. *Literature at War 1914-1940: Representing the "Time of Greatness" in Germany.* New Haven, CT, and London: Yale University Press, 1999

Ostermann, Christian, ed. *Uprising in East Germany, 1953.* New York and Budapest: Central European Press, 2001.

Ott, Hugo. *Martin Heidegger: A Political Life.* Translated by Allan Blunden. New York: HarperCollins, 1993.

Pepin, Craig. *The Holy Grail of Pure Wissenschaft: University Ideal and the University Reform in Post World War II Germany.* Ph.D. Dissertation. Duke University, 2001.

Pike, David. *Lukács and Brecht.* Chapel Hill: University of North Carolina Press, 1985.

———. *The Politics of Culture in Soviet-Occupied Germany.* Stanford: Stanford University Press, 1995.

Pois, Robert. *Friedrich Meinecke and German Politics in the Twentieth Century.* Berkeley, California: University of California Press, 1972.

Prater, Donald. *Thomas Mann: A Life.* New York: Oxford University Press, 1995.

Rabinbach, Anson. *In the Shadow of Catastrophe: German Intellectuals Between Apocalypse and Enlightenment.* Berkeley, California: University of California Press, 1997.

Remy, Steven. *The Heidelberg Myth: The Nazification and Denazification of a German University.* Cambridge, Mass: Harvard University Press, 2002.

Ringer, Fritz. *The Decline of the German Mandarins: The German Academic Community, 1890-1933.* Hanover and London: University Press of New England, 1969.

Roberts, David. *Benedetto Croce and the Uses of Historicism.* Berkeley, California: University of California Press, 1987.

Rorty, Richard. *Essays on Heidegger and Others: Philosophical Papers.* Vol. 2. Cambridge: Cambridge University Press, 1991.

Said, Edward. *Representations of the Intellectual.* New York: Vintage Books, 1996.

Saner, Hans. *Karl Jaspers in Selbstzeugnissen und Bilddokumenten.* Reinbek bei Hamburg: Rowohlt, 1970.

Schieder, Theodor. "Die deutsche Geschichtswissenschaft im Spiegel der Historischen Zeitschrift." *Historische Zeitschrift.* Vol. 189 (1959): 64-7.

Schilpp, Paul Arthur, ed. *The Philosophy of Karl Jaspers.* La Salle Illinois: Open Court Press, 1981.

Schröter, Klaus. *Thomas Mann im Urteil seiner Zeit.* Hamburg: C Wegener, 1969.

Schwabe, Klaus. *Wissenschaft und Kriegsmoral: Die deutschen Hochschullehrer und die Politischen Grundfragen des Ersten Weltkrieges.* Göttingen: Musterschmidt, 1969.

Sterling, Richard. *Ethics in a World of Power: The Political Ideas of Friedrich Meinecke.* Princeton, New Jersey: Princeton University Press, 1958.

Stromberg, Roland. *Redemption by War: The Intellectuals and 1914.* Berkeley: University of California Press, 1981.

Tent, James F. *The Free University of Berlin: A Political History.* Indiana University Press: Bloomington, 1988.

Vaget, Hans. *Im Schatten Wagners: Thomas Mann über Richard Wagner. Texte und Zeugnisse 1895-1955.* Frankfurt am Main: Fischer Taschenbuch, 1999.

————. "National and Universal: Thomas Mann and the Paradox of 'German' Music." In *Music & German National Identity*. Edited by Celia Appelgate and Pamela Potter, 155-177. Chicago and London: University of Chicago Press, 2002.

Vierhaus, Rudolf. "Bildung." In *Geschichtliche Grundbegriffe: historisches Lexikon zur politisch-sozialen Sprache in Deutschland*. Vol. 1. Edited by Otto Brunner, Werner Conze and Reinhart Koselleck, 508-51. Stuttgart: E. Klett, 1972.

Vossler, Otto. *Humboldt und die deutsche Nation: Humboldts Idee der Universität*. Darmstadt: Wissenschaftliche Buchgesellschaft, 1967.

Weber, Max. *Gesammelte politische Schriften*. Edited by Johannes Winckelmann. Tübingen: J. C. B. Mohr, 1988.

Wemrich, Willi. *Die Träger des Goethe Preises der Stadt Frankfurt 1927-1961*. Frankfurt am Main: August Osterrieth, 1963.

Wohl, Robert. *The Generation of 1914*. Cambridge, Mass: Harvard University Press, 1979.

Wolin, Richard. *The Heidegger Controversy: A Critical Reader*. Cambridge, Mass.: MIT

Zuckmayer, Karl. *Als wär's ein Stück von mir. Hören der Freundschaft*. Frankfurt: Fischer, 1966.

Index

About the Author

Mark Clark is Associate Professor and Chair of the Department of History and Philosophy at the University of Virginia's College at Wise. He teaches modern European and modern European intellectual history and is author of several articles on German intellectual and cultural life after World War II.